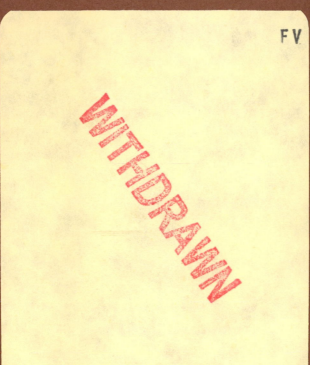

A Guide to
Intelligence
and
Personality Testing

A Guide to Intelligence and Personality Testing

– including actual tests and answers

by
Victor Serebriakoff

The Parthenon Publishing Group
International Publishers in Science & Technology

Casterton Hall, Carnforth,
Lancs, LA6 2LA, U.K.

120 Mill Road, Park Ridge
New Jersey, U.S.A.

Published in the UK and Europe by
The Parthenon Publishing Group Limited,
Casterton Hall, Carnforth,
Lancs. LA6 2LA, England   ISBN 1 85070 185 7

Published in the USA by
The Parthenon Publishing Group Inc.,
120 Mill Road,
Park Ridge,
New Jersey 07656   ISBN 0 940813 29 7

Printed in Great Britain by A. Wheaton & Co. Ltd, Exeter

Contents

Foreword

All of us are fascinated by intelligence and personality, especially our own. We compare ourselves constantly, even though it may be on a subconscious level, to others, and we evaluate our own personalities constantly, in the same way. There is no more fascinating conversation to most people than a discussion of 'the smarts' and who has them and who doesn't. We discuss intelligence constantly, although we often do not realize we are doing it. Every time we make a value judgement on someone's behaviour, we are evaluating that person's intelligence, and rating him (or her) as smart or not so smart.

It is for this reason that Victor Serebriakoff, the Honorary International President of Mensa, an organization composed only of those individuals who have scored in the top 2% on a properly supervised intelligence test, has written this book for the non-professional. Here, in one place, and easily available, are an interesting series of tests for adults and children, to give a rough estimate of an individual's intelligence and personality traits, as defined in the text. Quizzes and tests, as long as one's future is not riding on them are a great deal of fun, and most people like to take them. Here's the chance for the interested reader to acquire a measuring scale that will serve as a preliminary estimation in these areas. With luck, the tests may help some individual realize that he is not living up to his potential; and do something about it.

The average reader will learn much here that I have not previously seen in a popular book. The section detailing how an intelligence test is made up is excellent. It is the perfect answer to individuals who ask why Mensa does not make up its own intelligence test — it simply isn't possible. Read that section and you'll see why.

Of course, since this book is about human ability and its measurement, it is bound to be controversial. Anything about intelligence is controversial. Mr

Serebriakoff has made his point of view clear, but has backed it up with citations from eminent researchers in the field. Even if we don't agree with a point of view, we owe it to ourselves to obtain as much information on the subject as possible. Nothing is gained by shutting eyes and ears to another point of view.

Victor Serebriakoff will not be disturbed by any swirls of controversy. In the nearly 30 years that I have had the pleasure of knowing this dynamo of irrepressible spirit and energy, he has never shrunk from controversy. He has welcomed it and enjoyed the opportunity to engage in intellectual sparring bouts with his opponents.

It is his qualities of intellectual ability, irrepressible energy, and a forceful manner, that have helped turned Mensa from a small, unknown group into a household word. He has soared around the world, spreading the concept of Mensa, and in less than 40 years has seen it grow from scarcely a dozen, all British members to nearly 80,000 world wide, speaking a variety of languages, and united only by their intelligence and their membership in Mensa. This book represents Victor Serebriakoff at his most typical, witty, enthusiastic, and capable of conveying that enthusiasm to others.

Abbie F. Salny
Supervisory Psychologist of American and International Mensa

Preface

> *'Know then, thyself, presume not God to scan.*
> *The proper study of mankind is man.'*
>
> Alexander Pope

'Know thyself,' may be the most difficult advice of all. Psychology, man's self-exploring discipline, is accepted as a science in the anglophone world, but in the francophone world it is still classed as a branch of philosophy. Many philosophers of science feel that to earn its status as a science a subject must come down out of the philosophical clouds to the earth of solidity, rigour and number.

If any branch of psychology has enough rigour to claim scientific status it is psychometrics, the science of mental measurement. The pioneer work of Galton, Terman, Burt, Spearman, Binet, Guilford and Cattell has been consolidated and validated for half a century. There are few serious students of the subject who are prepared to reject the practical value of intelligence tests however much argument there may be about their theoretical basis.

Industry makes increasing use of them, the educationalist is often helpless without them, psychiatrists need them for a proper understanding of their patients, and faith in them and the demand for them by the general public is ever growing.

This is an expert layman's book for laymen. The professional code of psychologists does not allow them to publish IQ and personality tests for the general public. I break the traditional reticence on the subject for a good reason. I want to explain the art and correct the erroneous denigration of these

5

useful tests by those with ulterior motives. I also think that as the demand for mental ability grows the general public needs to be much better informed on the subject. They ought to have the chance to make a preliminary assessment, of themselves, their children and of those they may want to work with or employ.

The tests will provide perhaps the best first approximate check-up that unqualified laymen are likely to get hold of. They are closely modelled on and parallel with well established but confidential tests. They have been standardized and keyed to the unobtainable tests using samples of Mensa members and candidates whose true scores were known. These tests will give an estimate which will be 'near enough' for many purposes.

ACKNOWLEDGEMENTS

I must acknowledge the enormous help I have had over 35 years from the members of Mensa in many lands who have guided my thoughts and study in this field. Among professional psychologists I must mention my friend, the late Professor Sir Cyril Burt, and other friends, the Professors Philip Vernon, Ray Cattell, Hans Eysenck and Robert Green. Drs Conrad Graham and Abbie Salny, Mensa's psychological adviser, have helped my comprehension.

I must especially acknowledge Dr Steven Langer, my collaborator and friend, also Dr E. Butler of the Adam Smith Institute who helped very much with the cross-standardizations and my friends, Kenneth and Barbara Russell, who equally helped much with detailed work on the tests. Mr Harold Gale, the Executive Director of British Mensa, my wife Win, John McNulty and Kenneth Hegerty pitched in also. Further, many Mensans, Mensa candidates and the Mensans attending successive Mensa At Cambridge Conferences have acted as willing guinea pigs for cross-standardizations.

The virtues, if any, of the book must be shared with these kind folk. Any errors and mistakes are down to me.

Victor Serebriakoff

Mensa

Mensa is a unique society. It is basically a social club – but a club with a difference. Members have to qualify at the level of the top 2% on an intelligence test. Mensa is proud of its diversity; its members come from all walks of life and have an astonishingly wide variety of interests and occupations. It is this protean aspect that enables Mensa's membership to reach across common barriers such as religion, race, ideology, politics and social class.

Mensa's aims are extremely simple: social and intellectual contact between people all over the world; research on the opinions and attitudes of intelligent people; and the identification and fostering of human intelligence for the benefit of humanity. Mensa recruits its members by seeking them out as objectively as possible.

The author invites those who do well in these tests to apply for membership to:

UK
The Mensa Selection Agency
Bond House
St John's Square
Wolverhampton
England
WV24 AX

USA
American Mensa Ltd
2626 East 14th Street
Brooklyn
NY 11235-3992
USA

NO ONE SPEAKS FOR MENSA

There is one thing I must make crystal clear. I happen to be the International President of Mensa, the society whose members qualify by passing an IQ Test at a high level. My position is honorific, not executive, it does not give me the right or duty to speak for Mensa. No one has that right because Mensa has no collective views. Mensa has a wide and fascinating array of individual views, and those put forward in this book are mine. I speak for myself. Mensa has neither sponsored nor is responsible for this book in any way.

Victor Serebriakoff

1

Self-awareness

Let's settle one thing: this book is about psychology and, in particular, psychometrics or mental measurement. The inquiring layman is bombarded with contradictory views that make him wonder whether he can be sure of anything in this field.

Now, if what you mean by *sure* is *absolutely sure,* then you should know right away that you will learn nothing in this book of which you can be *absolutely* sure. Psychology is just not like that.

In some areas of human knowledge, our information is so certain that we can discount the possibility of error. In most areas, however, the best we can do is to make an educated guess. For example, it is simple to measure accurately the exact size and weight of solid objects such as coal or sugar. Measurements of this sort are easily determined, and you can be sure of the results. But if you want to know the value of your house, you go to a professional to get an estimate. An expert's estimate is better than that of an untrained and inexperienced person, but it is still open to a chance of error.

Almost all the important decisions in life turn out to be of this iffy nature; and it is not surprising, because easily settled decisions are usually obvious and do not need much consideration, no matter how important they are.

Those who read this book want their brains tested. You are reading the book, so you probably question the views of those who tell you that the results of Intelligence Tests are 'absolutely meaningless' or 'socially divisive'. You feel there might be something in them. You are right, there is. I shall try and tell it, as they say, like it is. I shall not hide the faults, doubts, difficulties or the fuzziness of the results of intelligence testing and I shall try to help you to make your way through the smoke-screen of confusion that has drifted over the subject. This frequently comes from the activities of the well-intentioned, kind and compassionate people who passionately want to believe in the Ultimate Fairness of Things.

These people, alas, do not accept the unfortunate *fact* that brains, competence, and problem-solving ability are *unfairly* distributed. So, by the way, are height, eye, hair and skin colour, sex, speed, personal beauty and every other difference between people.

Fairness is, unfortunately, a rarity and like it or not, some people unluckily, are born with mental handicap, while others are retarded. But most of us are around the average and some of us pretty bright. We cannot actually help it. Whatever cards you draw in the genetic or socioeconomic lottery it is nothing to be proud of, but it is nothing to be ashamed of either. Some of the nicest folk are as thick as the Earth's crust. Some of the nastiest people are so bright that a brain surgeon would have to use welder's goggles to operate.

May be you *are* one of those who are committed to the belief that everyone is born with the same chance of being a mathematical genius or a simpleton and that only 'faults in the social system' or 'prejudice', 'labelling' or 'discrimination' can be held responsible for any differences. If you are, I congratulate you on a feat of credulity. But if you are unequal to this brilliant achievement in unsupported belief it will be because you know from your own experience that there *are* great differences between the people you know. Some people are slow on the uptake, do not catch on easily and tend to be interested in simple problems. Others you will have met are quick, sharp, grasp the point of an argument and have a tendency to do better than others in any question where thinking counts.

Parents will know that these differences are noticeable from birth in babies. Some are quick, bright and alert from the earliest age and others less so.

But despite this normal human observation some people cannot square their egalitarian ideals with IQ tests. The very idea of trying to assess human talent and character is anathema – immoral, unjust and wrong. In the Communist world the measurement of talent is ideologically unrespectable and in the developed world the innocence and perfectibility of unspoiled man is a quasi-religious doctrine. Marxists are at one with Freud in thinking that all important human differences are environmental. Our *rights* are equal therefore *we* are equal.

Give me a newborn baby, they say, and with the right treatment I will make him a genius. But they do specify a *human* baby. They never ask for a monkey or puppy or worm, so perhaps they may think there is *something* inborn. Attempts were made in all seriousness to apply this doctrine by bringing up a chimpanzee side by side with human children. When they found that the ape (after a period in the lead) fell behind in mental development, they had to conclude that there may be *some* inherited difference.

Greatly daring, I suspect that if nature rather than nurture is largely responsible for the difference between men and apes, it might be partly responsible for the difference between idiot and the genius, though I do not deny that the true human potential is often not fully realized. A sensible view is that nature sets the ceiling and nurture decides how near to that ceiling we get. The undeniable fact is that human beings are unequal in achievement, even if not in potential. So we still face the question: 'Do we want to know?'

WHY WE WANT TO KNOW

In a primitive farming community where everybody toils for survival with simple tools, the advantage of being able to solve sophisticated problems may be little. But that is not how we have chosen to live in the developed world.

The daily continuance of the immensely complex interrelated commercial and industrial systems, upon which we depend for the thousand things and services we think we need each day, depends on putting a very large number of round and square human pegs into the proper holes. The continuance of our present civilization depends on finding people whose qualities fit closely to an enormous range of highly specified roles. 'Home Heart Transplants', 'Do-It-Yourself Brain Surgery', 'Every Man His Own Industrial Manager', and 'The Amateur Stevedore' are all equally inappropriate book titles. Our complex society works because we have found out how to put the right man into the right job. The fact that we, in the developed world, can do this so well is a sign that somewhere or other, seen or unseen, someone is making judgements about what a person can do and what he cannot do and what his or her character is and how bright he is or she is.

It is safe to predict that all the attempts to abolish the classification of people as to ability will come to nothing: as fast as we throw such 'discrimination' out of the door it will creep back in through the window. At present we 'discriminate' by using human judgement, by examinations, by degrees and by qualifications — which means a lot of senseless education-free 'coaching'. But as they become more perfect, we may find we can use more simple, easily administered, quick and efficient scientific tests, which can be made to be fair, objective, free from nepotism, religious or racial prejudice, influence and the corruption of the old-boy network. Tests save time, money, unfairness, unhappiness, and mistakes. Above all, they are *predictive*.

But intelligence tests are not, as I have said, perfect. They still measure inaccurately the culturally deprived, or those from cultures different from that on which the test was standardized, but they are *less* unfair than anything else. They are only a rough guide, but many experiments have shown that they are better than and less biased than the unaided human judgement. They are better than guesswork, more efficient than trial and error, and they are improving all the time. They were invented as an instrument of social justice, a way of getting through to the inborn capacity of a child despite lack of education. They are attacked primarily by egalitarian downlevellers. There is a great body of experimental evidence that establishes their general validity and very little which contradicts it.

So don't let the kind-hearted social reformers talk you out of your own experience. Don't let yourself be told that your observations are an illusion, that God in His goodness has made us all equal, not only in our *rights* as we should be, but in our potential and ability. We are not robots, built to close tolerances, we are people. All different. And it is our differences which make the world the exciting, fascinating and interesting place that it is. Don't let us be talked into believing we are a lot of mass-produced replicates. We are unique individuals. Our differences are not divisive, they are what makes life interesting.

THE NEED TO KNOW

We need to know how big our feet are if we want to be well shod, and what our height, bust and waistline are if we don't want to look like badly tied-up parcels. So measuring these *physical* differences has its uses.

What about *mental* differences? Why do we want to know these? Well, curiosity. That's not a bad reason. But there is a more important one. The natural inequalities between people in height, weight, sex, intelligence, memory, skill, health, speed over the ground, skill at darts, and personal beauty are not the only inequalities we see around us. The big inequalities are the inequalities of wealth. To generalize one could say that in about one third of the world people are rich and indulgent. Another third are comfortable but have no luxuries. The last third, alas, are underprivileged, they are hard put to make ends meet. It worries us and makes us sad.

So, what causes all this? 'Faults in the social system', 'failure of the idea of the brotherhood of man', 'capitalism', 'imperialist exploiters'? 'God's punishment'? 'The inefficiency and incompetence of the people in the developing countries that simply are not developing'? No one really knows.

There has developed a so-called sociological science which claims to study an entity which is described as 'social inequality'. Taxpayers are paying highly educated professors and students to study 'inequality' and find out what causes it and how to prevent it.

Someone surely needs to say this: inequality is not a state that requires explanation. There is nothing remarkable about it. Historically, it is the natural state of affairs. It is the way we expect people to be in the absence of some strong standardizing or equalizing force. People are born similar but not identical. They are born into widely differing cultures and traditions and from the moment they are born they get more different in every possible way. The expectation is of very wide differences, and that is what we find. What needs study and explanation is the rare and strange phenomenon of *equality* or lessened inequality. In some countries we find that great differences in genetics and environment produce much less difference in wealth, life style, health and well-being than in others.

In poor countries the poorest are living on the verge of starvation while the rich are fabulously so. The difference is maximal. In rich countries almost all have homes, health care and enough to eat. Nearly all can even afford leisure and drugs like alcohol and tobacco. The differences are quite small in comparison.

We may legitimately look for the reasons behind this strange and unlikely phenomenon, a much reduced range of inequality.

Some countries have exploited science, industry, commerce, agronomy and a thousand other arts. They have much higher and more equal standards of living. Inequality remains but it is very much less. Other countries try hard to do the same but consistently fail.

Why so? My guess is this: although there are many individual causes which will vary from country to country, the one consistent and principal difference between the rich countries and the poor countries is the emphasis put on promoting educated intelligent people – or to put it in a simpler way, on the way in which they use their brains. There is a general pattern of life in the advanced countries which, wherever it spreads, seems to enrich the people. Despite every possible local disadvantage they achieve a level of prosperity and general well-being which would have been thought miraculously wonderful by our ancestors only a few hundred years ago.

USING BRAINS

What is the central feature of these wealth-creating cultures, ways of living? It isn't very difficult, simply the principle of 'the best man for the job'. Specialization. Around the world in various cultures and societies there are numerous ways of allocating roles, privilege, influence, power. It is distributed through family connections, through political parties, via Marxist apparatchiks, through power-seeking juntas, through victorious war lords, through complicated ancient tribal forms and practices, by tradition, by primogeniture, nepotism, and in a thousand other ways. None of them, absolutely none of them is 'fair'. But in what we call 'the Western World' something different has grown up. All nations including the rich ones started with the old, simple system, that of a single ruler with a single hierarchy of control. But the system of kings and emperors, tsars, kaisers and dictators does not work for very large nations or organizations. Now in some countries this centralist pattern has been overlaid by something relatively new. Over the last few hundred years a new polyhierarchic organization has grown up – from the roots – not down from the top. Instead of the organizational structure of society being set up and controlled by a central authority, there has evolved a free system by which any person can, if they make the right moves, build up their own institution, firm, society, organization, company. These subsystems fall into competition with each other so that they are like living animals, growing, competing, dying and evolving, thus becoming more adapted to the place in society they aim to take. They become more efficient by performing their supply or distribution or service function better. The universal biological principle of trial and error is at work.

The result has been dramatic but it has been so gradual that it is not easy for us, living in the comfort and plenty of the resulting system, to see how enormous and radical the change has been.

AMPLIFYING INTELLIGENCE

Working in this competitive system, with inefficient variants being wiped out and new experiments tried all the time, there has been an opportunity and stimulus for ability, talent, intelligence to move to those positions in the informational network of society where they can be influential. As the competitive struggle, not so much between individuals but between the firms, institutions and societies they work in, has continued, there has been a rapid and successful evolution of those institutions. Those organizations which are intelligently and skilfully directed tend to survive better than those which are not. Intelligence and other abilities inevitably rise to positions of influence in such a society to the great benefit of everyone in it – and in the long run – to the benefit of other societies as well.

What does this mean? That the progressing nations have access to a great brain lever which multiplies the power of intelligence. Free societies amplify intelligence.

In traditional societies there is much less freedom to change roles within working groups and much less competitive selection with the elimination of the less efficient groups.

Where do the socialist societies stand in this? In uncompetitive societies like the ones in the socialist world, where they have readopted the old centralist pattern (except that power passes after power struggles instead of from father to son) there is a reversion to a monocentric hierarchy. In these societies with a reduced competitive element it is more likely to be the party hack than the bright young entrepreneur who gets promoted. Inefficient ministries, departments and factories go happily on doing a bad job. And everyone suffers.

The price is slower development and a poorer life style because of the failure to amplify intelligence. Society is making a poorer use of its talents.

In a society where the able, the intelligent and the industrious are free to move to positions of influence, things are run better, more efficiently organized, life is easier, everyone gains.

The beauty of this system lies in the fact that while the institutions, firms and companies are in a competitive fight to the death, the people in those firms, associations and companies are fully independent of them. People can move away from a failing company to a successful one. They get another job if their company fails. The companies struggle, grow, survive or die. They evolve, improve or fade out. The people in them move from one to another and, relatively to the rest of the world, a good time is had by all.

Karl Marx said, 'To each according to his needs, from each according to his ability.' Perhaps the greatest failure of the socialist movements around the world has been that they have paid too much attention to the first phrase and not enough attention to the second.

PROBLEMS ATTRACT INTELLIGENCE

'From each according to his ability' is just what the pluralist, free, open society can achieve because it allows talent and ability to rise through the system to positions where it is more influential. The problem-solving ability of the society is concentrated at those places where the problems are most severe; the places where they need the best brains. Solutions find their way towards problems because the *solver* profits.

So, I suggest, we *do* want to know. It *is* important to know people's ability and potential and when we know, to try to use them to the advantage of us all. We can do even better at the task of collectively using our brains if we know what we are doing.

I am one of those who feel that it is a reasonable human right, that all people should have the opportunity to use the talents they have to the full. This is a good principle but it is not enough. With exceptional talent we must go further. Our society must *find*, educate, motivate, train and use *all* exceptionally able people in the positions in which they can do most good for all of us. In an age of high technology, these are the golden ones, as Plato called them, who create prosperity for all.

Let me be frank and reveal my bias. I think that human intelligence is the most important thing we know of in the universe. It is this conviction that has led me to spend so much of my life in building up the international organization of intelligent people, called Mensa, of which I am the present International Hon. President. I believe, passionately, that what is most valuable on this planet is just that power of communicable, conceptual intelligence. That is my chief value, my prejudice. What is yours?

ASHAMED TO BE BRIGHT!

This supreme human quality is not something to be hushed up, hidden in corners and spoken of in whispers. Yet some able, persuasive academics and envy-exploiting politicians have almost convinced the intelligent, industrious and successful, those who can and should contribute most to the common pool, that they should feel ashamed of the difference between themselves and other people.

THE INTERFACE PROBLEM

I have described earlier the way in which the effect of a few intelligent people is amplified by the right kind of society. In that kind of society the discoveries of science are similarly amplified in effect, because they are disseminated throughout that society by that very important section of society, the intelligent well-informed layman.

I refer to that great mass of people throughout society who are literate and numerate, who have a good understanding of what they read, and who are interested in the discoveries of science. It is very sad indeed that scientists tend to undervalue the degree of comprehension that can be obtained by the autodidact, the layman, the intelligent outsider.

This, for instance, is a book by a layman for laymen. The aim is simply to give the intelligent, enquiring layman's view of the subject. By popularizing scientific ideas possible applications for them may be found, which would never occur if all scientists worked through official in-group channels only.

I hope I have convinced you, or at least opened your mind to the possibility, that knowing and assessing human differences is not immoral and can be helpful.

I need hardly urge that it will be useful to any thinking person to get some idea of his position on the intelligence scale.

CHECKING YOUR CHILD'S IQ

Most parents want the best for their children as they grow up, and they have to make decisions that affect the children's lives. Among these decisions are what kind of education a child should have, when it should leave school, and what occupation or vocation it should pursue. These are some of the most important decisions parents will ever make concerning the future of their children. But the information available to parents when they make these important decisions is frequently inadequate. Consequently, the decisions are often far from the best.

One purpose of this book is to provide parents with information that will help them to make better judgements and ultimately, better decisions. The information is not – cannot be – certain. It will be, however, the best guess.

You have every right to question it and to challenge it if it does not seem right, and you will learn how to do so most effectively.

Today it is more important than ever before for parents to have the information necessary to make the best judgements. Some authorities who might be expected to provide this information are reluctant to do so. Many psychologists, for instance, will not tell parents the results of intelligence and aptitude tests because they hold (wrongly, I believe) that parents cannot be trusted with this information. Teachers, doctors and social workers as well sometimes subscribe to the doctrine that 'we know best', suggesting that they alone are equipped to properly interpret and use such test results.

It is principally this outlook that has persuaded me to make available an intelligence test designed specifically for the use of parents. Here is a 'first approximation' of IQ tests with normative data for children.

We cannot really blame the psychologists or the teachers for their refusal to inform parents. They operate under a system of contradictory social, professional, and political pressures. It is fashionable in some quarters to believe that the recognition of mental ability is antisocial and divisive. To select and recognize certain children as having good brain power, it is said, is at the same time to reject others. The 'rejected' children, the theory goes, are 'labelled' and their lower performance in the future is more a result of this labelling than it is due to a basic lack of ability. I do not agree with these views, though they have gained wide acceptance. The intentions of the people who subscribe to these views may be honourable, but as a result, the concerned and educated parent who wants the best information available about his or her children may not be able to obtain it and so will be unable to set the best, most realistic education and vocational standards and aims for them.

The policy of non-disclosure goes even further. In some schools today, even the results of examinations are kept secret or are made available only on demand, lest the children be confronted with the truth that there are others who can better assimilate and articulate ideas. Some teachers carefully 'adjust' reports provided to parents in such a way that every child appears to be of equal ability and promise. This deception denies parents the information they need upon which to base their judgements. They are left with only their own, sometimes biased, personal view of their children's abilities.

The publication of the tests contained in this book will not please some of the educators and psychologists I have described above. There will be many who will fear that the test may be misused, that parents are not sufficiently objective to test their own children, and that they would misinterpret the instructions and the results. Many others claim that this kind of test is meaningless.

I take the position that the overwhelming majority of parents who will be interested in this book will also be sufficiently responsible to use it properly and to interpret the results with common sense. Certainly, it is in their power to influence the result by bending the rules, allowing more time, or being overstrict. They will not be doing their children or themselves favours if they do.

I do not think that many will use this information foolishly and I am confident that the overall effect of publishing these tests will be a positive one. Those parents who misuse the tests will do so to confirm opinions they already hold about the level of their children's intelligence. The worst that will happen is that they will have missed an opportunity to correct their views. The vast majority of parents who really want to know fall into two classes: those, probably the majority, who have already made a reasonably accurate assessment of their child and those who may have incorrectly evaluated their children. Both groups will probably receive corrective information. Those whose views are confirmed will be able to proceed with confidence based on usable evidence and be better able positively to direct and develop their children's future.

If you fail to follow the test instructions, you will be deceiving no one but yourself. The parent or the person who undertakes to conduct these tests must be as careful, responsible, and serious as possible. Correct information will do the most good; wrong information will do no good at all. It is, therefore, of the utmost importance that you read all the instructions with care, making sure that you understand them completely *before* you apply the tests.

We see a decline in the quality of the educational system, which may in part have been caused by ideologies influencing it, opposition to the idea of selection, or trends toward indiscriminate education. These factors have combined to increase the burden of responsibility the parent must carry. It takes as much courage to accept and cope with the truth as it does to seek the truth. For the sake of your children, you must not be dissuaded or discouraged in your pursuit of the best for them despite the fact that you will confront envy and even a conscious effort to stifle excellence and high-quality performance. Insist on knowing the facts about your children and do your best to see that this information is used in the most productive and beneficial way.

If your own perception of your child's intelligence is significantly different from the indication of this test, or if your child's score is very high or very low for its age, then it is most important that you do not rely on the tests but let them stimulate you into seeking professional advice. You will find a psychologist who will test your children and give you not only the results but also a realistic evaluation and interpretation of them.

2

Can Intelligence and Personality be Measured?

MEASURING INTELLIGENCE

Writers in this field are in the surprising position of finding that they have to defend that useful concept 'intelligence' because serious scientists have questioned it. So first, what *is* intelligence? Let us look at how the idea arose.

The Graeco-Roman culture is the source of most of the underlying concepts which have helped our thinking in this, as in many other fields. All human ideas and concepts are subject to an evolution towards sharpened, more predictive and more useful forms.

How did *this* idea develop? Plato was first to see the defect in the earlier Greek word 'nous', an imprecise concept which included the modern concepts of soul, spirit, mind, thinking and mental ability.

Plato's analysis was brilliant. He emphasized that it was convenient to think of the impulsive, emotional side of human nature separately from the other aspects, thinking and reasoning. He saw our good and bad impulses, our urges, passions and appetites as horses restrained by the charioteer, intelligence.

There was, said Plato, a strong but not overwhelming influence of heredity upon intelligence. He wrote: 'Now, since you are all of one stock, although your children will generally be like their parents, sometimes a golden parent may have a silver child, or a silver parent a golden one, and so on with all the other combinations.'

Thus, he anticipated two phenomena now well established, the heredity of intelligence and the tendency for the children of bright parents and of dim parents generally to revert some way back towards the average. This is called the regression to the mean and it will be discussed later.

An insight which came from Aristotle, Plato's pupil, was even more brilliant.

19

He showed us that it is useful to recognize that the rational, controlling part of the mind can be sensibly divided into two aspects, perception and cognition. The observation and recording of information on the one hand – and dealing with it on the other. Data capture and data processing are what the modern computer technologist would call them. Cicero seems to have coined the word 'intelligentsia' which, though it has not got a nice flavour, is with us today as a word which describes the whole class of intelligent people everywhere.

The pioneer lexicographer Samuel Johnson gave the word 'intelligence' four senses. The first is commerce of information (mutual communication, distant or secret). The second is commerce of acquaintance (terms on which men live with one another). The third is spirit (unbodied mind). The fourth is nearest to the modern meaning: understanding, skill. The modern sense of an *inborn* quality is altogether missing in Johnson's usage, which deals with acquired powers only.

Spenser shows a glimpse of the modern sense: 'Heaps of huge words, unhoarded, hideously, they seem to be cheap praise of poetry; and thereby wanting due intelligence, have marred the face of goodly poesy.' Bacon's phrase could be read either way: 'It is not only in order of nature for him to govern that is the more *intelligent* as Aristotle would have it; but there is no less required for government, courage to protect, and above all, honesty.' In France a pioneer of mental testing, Binet, used the word *'habileté'* which is fairly close to 'ability'.

In the Oxford English Dictionary the first meaning given to the word 'intelligence' is the faculty of understanding, intellect. It is the second meaning which is of interest to us for the purposes of this book. Here it is: 'Understanding as a quality *admitting of degree;* superior understanding, quickness of mental apprehension, sagacity' (my italics).

This idea of the *differences* in intelligence and making judgements about them also comes clearly from Quintilian (70 AD): 'It is generally and rightly considered a virtue in a teacher to observe accurately the differences in ability among his pupils, and to discover the direction in which the nature of each particular inclines him. There is an incredible amount of variability in talent, and the forms of minds are no less varied than the forms of bodies.'

As we shall hear, there are some theorists today who feel that judgements about differences in mental capacity are only made so as to 'oppress the poor'. Perhaps that is what Quintilian was doing. Perhaps not.

For nearly 2000 years this useful concept remained much as it had been left by the Graeco-Roman thinkers. It became part of the language in most countries that have been influenced by those cultures. It has proved through the years to be a sensible and useful way of sorting people out and understanding their powers and what can be expected of them.

The concept 'Intelligence' as it came down to us was something about which we had to make a judgement. No one then tried to *measure* the differences. However, in the last few centuries the idea of precise empiric measurement of natural phenomena began to take a real grip on the minds of men in some advancing societies. This changed things, as we shall see.

Francis Galton, who pioneered the science of anthropometry (measuring human qualities), used the word 'intelligence' in an extended sense. He used it to signify the *inborn* problem-solving ability. Galton was the first clearly to establish this by his genetic studies. The older meaning of the word, 'information', is now overshadowed except in military affairs, and the Galton sense is the one usually intended. In other words, the common usage derives from the new technical sense and not from the traditional sense of the word. There is, therefore, no legitimate complaint, because 'intelligence is what intelligence tests measure'. The circularity of this definition is a feeble joke.

The definition of intelligence in an operational sense is relatively simple. It is demonstrable that the ability of people to perform specific tasks varies from one person to another; it is equally obvious that some people are good at some things and some are good at others. What is not so usually known but is equally true is that there is a relation, or rather a correlation (or *measured* relation), between skills and abilities. That is to say, they are 'unfairly' or unequally distributed. There is, alas, no law of compensation, as there is popularly supposed to be, which ensures that those who are good at one thing are poor at another and vice versa. On the contrary, the tendency is for those who are good at one thing to be good at many and those who are bad at one thing to be bad at many. Thus we get, *on the average,* a range from the versatile genius who can not only solve problems well but can paint, draw, think, write and even run better than average to the mentally subnormal who is below average at the majority of tasks.

Stop! I know what my reader has started to say here. I deal with statistical generalizations and not with invariable laws. In the human sciences we are forced to deal with *tendencies.* It is sad how frequently otherwise well-educated people feel they have defeated a statement about a statistical tendency by giving one contrary example. '*You* say', they retort with scorn, 'that children who are good at verbal understanding tend to be good at arithmetic – but I can prove you completely wrong; my Johnny is always top in English but he is useless at arithmetic. So there!' Useless to point out that one specially chosen case does not constitute a sample of great statistical reliability.

Let it be clear that this book lives in the real world of indeterminacy and adopts the simple biological strategy of 'the best guess'.

In the 19th century, universal education became the rule in England. It was only then that teachers, taking in large, very mixed classes from all sections of the community, learned something new and strange. They found that the children that were much above average in one subject or skill seemed to be above average in all the other subjects and skills. If a child is in the top quarter of a class at *anything* you can almost guarantee that the child will be in the top half at nearly *everything*.

It is this observation that led to the whole science (or art) of intelligence testing. Human cognitive ability *clusters* in people. Unfair? Who knows? True? Yes! Like it or not the rule is: 'To them that hath shall be given!'

This clustering tendency led to the possibility of a very simple measure of mental power; we could talk about the *general* mental ability which seemed to underlie the several different abilities and skills. We did not need to work out abilities on a dozen scales. A single underlying scale made it possible to put a single, easily understandable number on cognitive ability.

But what was this quality that teachers began to be able to measure? How, we may ask, can it be defined? Well, not everything we can easily comprehend can be adequately defined but I shall put forward at least an operational definition.

AN OPERATIONAL DEFINITION OF INTELLIGENCE

My operational definition is just this: 'Intelligence is a factor which varies between individuals and is associated with the general level of ability displayed in performing a wide variety of different tasks.' Intelligence in this sense *is* measurable with reasonable accuracy, and it is a strong indication of the general ability or versatility of the subject. It is not simply a measure of your skill at intelligence tests; it is a measure of something definite and fundamental about you which affects and informs everything you do. Intelligence is not a virtue. Since it is largely genetic, it is nothing to be proud of. But it is not a fault either, and nothing to be ashamed of.

A further definition of intelligence

I would like to add another to the many general attempts to define intelligence. I prefer the simple operational one given above, but for the semanticists and lexicographers who are still obsessed with the idea that all human concepts can be entrapped and held within the confines of a precise verbal definition, I add the following.

Intelligence is a biological phenomenon. It is evident in any living thing or system, however primitive. The universe is dispersing, breaking down, and moving from states of greater to lesser order by the ubiquitous increase of entropy, but it contains a number of self-ordering homeostatic entities which act as though they oppose the universal trend to move from order to disorder, from states of low to higher probability. In *this* class of entities there is a trend to build up order, to retain stability and to resist changes in form, to preserve low probability states. This is the class of living things.

In order to resist the action of the change-forces in the universe these entities have to detect and counteract them. Since the process of counteraction often takes time, these entities have also to be able to predict change-threatening forces, and to do this they have to have sense organs and the ability to receive information from the outside universe. They have to store it (in coded form) and transduce it into an appropriate output of instructions to their parts, organs and muscles so that they can resist the tendency of the universe to change their form beyond the level which they can correct. If the change passes beyond this level then a runaway change called death (or decay) sets in.

I define intelligence, therefore, as the capacity in an entity (living thing or artifact) to detect, encode, store, sort and process signals generated in the universe and transduce them into an optimal output pattern of instructions. The word 'optimal' may cause some difficulty here because that is where 'value' creeps in. I would define it as that which is best designed in the longest-term sense to ensure that preservation of the form of the entity concerned through time. It would include 'evolutionary' changes in that form, i.e. those which tend to make the entity an even better homeostatic form-preserving device.

The *measurement* of intelligence would be associated with a number of parameters of the described process. High intelligence would be associated with a large store, accuracy of coding, accessibility of information, long-term prediction, accuracy of probability estimates and ability to generate emergent or original behavioural solutions to problems.

TESTING GENERAL AND SPECIAL ABILITIES

The discovery by Professor Spearman that abilities cluster or correlate was crucial. It led to the notion that there is some general factor underlying the individual differences in ability and contributing to a person's success in a number of skills. Thus Spearman accounted for *both* the individual variations of skill *and* the tendency for abilities to 'cluster' in certain people. His 'theory' is really a simple conceptual framework which helps us to think about human ability more clearly. Each person can be assessed for 'g' (general ability) and a number of 's' (special ability) factors. In any one particular skill your 'g' rating contributes a part and your 's' rating the rest of your score. If you have a high 'g' and a high 's' for say, music, then you will probably be a better musician than if you have the high 's' score with a low 'g' score.

The only way to get at 'g' is by using a number of different tests each of which is a *partial* test of 'g'. That is why we have batteries of different tests.

Each type of test has a different 'g' saturation or 'loading', and verbal ability has the highest 'g' saturation. Most tests reflect this.

A well-designed intelligence test should not, of course, test the educational background of the subject. Even the verbal test items are usually chosen to avoid those items (questions) where the answers would be more likely to be known to a well-educated person. It is the ability of the subject to discern the exact shade of meaning of relatively common words which is measured, and not his knowledge of esoteric ones like 'esoteric'.

The simple case I am making here is that there are, as we can all perceive, great differences between people in their thinking power, the way they select, remember and use information to benefit themselves or their group.

Each of us can judge people within our cultural group and rank them fairly well on the scale of 'braininess' or intelligence. We can rely on our judgement of this and other qualities enough to elect or appoint people to important roles and jobs. In view of this it seems likely that with careful research and selection it should be possible to standardize our judgements as formal tests. I said 'within our group' so there is one important condition. Those who take the tests must be familiar with the language and symbolism of the test. The tests apply to and only to persons in groups like those groups upon whom the standards were set.

Taking your group, those who read this book, that condition is obviously met. If you can read this you belong to the group, literate English speakers, to which the tests apply.

In Chapter 7 I shall extend this justification and go into more detail. I shall deal with the history of IQ testing, the difficulties and the controversies about them.

MEASURING PERSONALITY

I have claimed that we can all make reasonably reliable judgements about how bright the people around us are. We can judge more than that. And we do. We are constantly judging the whole of the character (or personality) of everyone in our circle. Our family and all our colleagues and associates are under our constant appraisal, examination and re-examination. We do not advertise the fact too much but we are all at it. Why are we all so harsh? Because we have been bred to be and we have to be. Mankind is a social creature, people live or die in social groupings upon which each member utterly depends. Our human social contacts are much the most important part of our environment. We need to know them well. We must be able to understand and predict their behaviour if we are to thrive or even survive.

You, my reader, were evolved to be a member of a hunter-gatherer clan. Our species, Man, has been around for millions of years but we are less than 7 millennia from the time before towns, agriculture, or settled life. There can have been little further evolution in that short time.

The hunter-gatherer group depends for its daily life on its members' skilled co-operation and that is possible only if the tribesmen learn to predict each other's behaviour. So we are all born judges of what we call character and what psychometrists (psychologists who measure human traits) call personality.

Making good judgements about personality is quite simple for almost anyone but defining the concept 'personality' is a tough task.

Professor Alice Heim is a psychometrist. She emphasizes the difficulties in her book *Intelligence and Personality*. She feels that it is difficult to separate personality traits from cognitive ones, that is those concerned with conscious thinking and problem solving.

Personality traits are those which are concerned with predictive regularities of behaviour and response which are to do with feelings, desires and emotions and not with cognitive or thinking and planning skills. Alice Heim uses the word 'orectic' to describe such traits.

In fact, we cannot really judge a person's intelligence if we have no idea what their aims and desires are. Why not? Intelligence is measured by the skill with which information is used to optimize behaviour towards some objective. If you do not know the aim or objective you must misjudge the actions. You might think a man's behaviour very stupid and then change your mind when you hear that his objective was suicide. Every IQ tester makes a hidden assumption. The tester assumes that the subject wants to do well in the test. Having said all that we can agree that we can indeed predict peoples' needs and wants quite well so that we can be fairly safe in estimating intelligence.

It was certain that, as soon as it had been established that good and predictive estimates of general intelligence could be made, there should be attempts to use the statistical mathematical methods that had been developed to deal with them for orectic, or personality tests.

My friend, Professor Raymond Cattell, has done a very complete analysis of the human personality traits revealed by research based on both test question-naires and objective behavioural tests. He did not attempt to pre-define the factors he was measuring but used subtle mathematical techniques to see what factors emerged from the accumulated data.

What emerged was a set of 16 predictive factors or personality traits which made it possible to draw the subject's personality profile.

The factors that emerged were a surprise. They did not correspond to the factors with which we are familiar. Those factors like bravery, persistence, deviousness, cheerfulness, came through only in strange ways and in peculiar combinations in the final measures. I have no doubt that the Cattell tests could be used very effectively in personnel selection, for instance, but the problem is that the complex new language has to be thoroughly learned by all those concerned before a set of predictive rules can be built up and the underlying knowledge that has been accumulated used by people on the job. The managers may judge the qualities that they need but they do not know how to say it in the language that emerged from the researches, or pick it out from the personality profiles the tests produced.

The arguments about this are still going. on. On the one hand Professor Eysenck feels that, apart from intelligence, two principal dimensions account for most of the difference. On the other, Cattell has, after a lifetime of work, come to the conclusion that there are sixteen relatively independent factors mentioned which make it possible to determine a complete description of the human personality. Apart from these, there is the Johnson's Temperament Analysis, Guilford's work and many others like them, each of which has its own rigorous statistical background but not too much in the way of common ground between them.

But it is not a valid attack upon this kind of testing to say that the different ways of classifying the human personality are mutually inconsistent. When the human mind begins to look at phenomena it has to classify them first in order to deal with them at all. The laws which emerge are dependent on this original classification. Each set of laws is true in its own field or frame of reference. Eventually, scientists agree on the most useful way of classifying phenomena and from that point forward the science usually grows and flourishes. But in the early, difficult days of a science many different classification methods are tried out before the most effective and predictive is discovered. The 'truth' of any of them is like the truth of any scientific statement. The answers we get depend on the questions we ask. Some questions turn out to be more useful than others, some are the foolish questions which infallibly attract foolish answers.

In trying to measure his own qualities mankind is examining the most complicated thing he knows in the universe, and it is not surprising that science in this field has not made the progress that it has in some others.

The proper utilization and the happiness of people in the developed world today depends on their fitting precisely and well into a thousand different and highly specified roles. We can fit them by a hit-and-miss, trial-and-error method if we choose, but if we are wise we will not neglect even these early discoveries of psychometric science which can help us to do the job wisely, sanely and without prejudice.

Personality *measurement* is the art of finding scalar measures of a person which will be a guide to his or her general behaviour. The measures must, as it were, see beneath the hour-to-hour variability in behaviour, the mood swings and temporary behavioural factors to some lasting general underlying ones which will improve estimates as to how the subject will perform.

I have followed Professor Eysenck's method. He investigated to what extent the way people answer a survey form correlates and predicts the way they are classified by other people, on well-known and accepted measures such as aggressiveness, extraversion, humility, etc. He was looking for permanent features of the character and not at judgements based on single actions. The method worked well and his general conclusion was that many of these known traits, or variables, were fairly stable in any one person.

What came out of his many years of research was that there was a clustering in people of the well-known traits that have found a place in normal language.

Just as with intelligence testing there is a general factor behind the many measured ability factors, so in personality testing there seem to be a number of general personality variables which are revealed by the clustering.

The traits behind the words in the language separate into groups which cluster in people to make these more general factors. Researches with uniovular twins showed that those general traits which revealed themselves were probably largely genetic in origin.

For instance in his book *Know Your Own Personality* he and his collaborator Glen Wilson find the known traits, active, sociable, impulsive, adventurous, expressive, unreflective and irresponsible, tend to cluster in one trait which is called extraversion.

His extensive research showed that questions intended to test these known and named factors obtained answers from large samples which showed that if you have one of these known traits you are more likely to have some or all of the others in that group of traits.

Now the usefulness of this way of classifying people has not really been put to the test because, so far the industrial and commercial world has made little use of such methods. What is lacking is a great deal more work to decide what the scores on these underlying personality factors predict in the way of performance and behaviour on many different jobs.

The person selecting people for work roles does not know whether being extraverted, tender minded, intelligent and emotionally stable is a good or bad qualification for a manager, storekeeper or statistician. But it is very likely that if we did the research we should find that knowledge of the personality profile would be a great advantage to those involved in the difficult task of choosing people for work roles.

Personality testing is still undeveloped but I believe that it will play a more important part in the complex technical world of the future. In the 21st century we may have a world in which optimum role allocation will become ever more important as new techniques and life styles emerge. There are strong signs in the newly invigorated industrial climate that psychometric tests are being used in personnel departments.

I have picked out and produced tests for four personality traits or variables which seem to have been generally accepted and for which there are well validated tests. I shall not write more about them here because I assume that the reader may want to take the tests before he or she actually knows what they are testing for. That is the only way to be sure that the subject under test is not unconsciously distorting answers to get a desired result. The tests are modelled on well validated professional tests and will give a first approximate measure for those who take them according to the instructions. A full explanation of the four factors follows the personality tests in Chapter 5.

3

About the Tests

I must emphasize that the tests in this book are not offered as fully standardized professional instruments. It is not possible for such tests to be published in a general interest book of this kind for two excellent reasons. Firstly, if any such test with the answer key and the interpretation is widely published it becomes invalid for use by professional psychologists because there can be no assurance that subjects did not know the answers beforehand.

Secondly, the cost of the long and complex process of statistical validation on large random samples of the population would make a book like this, which spoils the tests by publication, uneconomic.

Tests which have had the required validation are prepared by universities and are available only to professional psychologists.

However, it is possible to compose tests which use the same general principles as validated tests and to cross-standardize them on smaller samples of those whose results on valid tests are known, such as Mensa members. Such tests can be seen as a layman's introduction to the subject and a reasonably accurate first-guess guide.

These tests should be used in that way. The objection that people may cheat does not apply when people are testing themselves or their children because there is no motive for deception. If used for industrial, clinical or educational purposes they should be taken as a better-than-guesswork indication and professionally checked whenever real doubts arise.

PROFESSIONAL TESTS

Concerning the unobtainable professional tests, clinically, they are vitally important for the psychiatrist and even the neurosurgeon. The psychiatrist needs them to assess the degree of retardation so that he can work out the best treatment for children with Down's syndrome or other defects. There seems to be no argument at all that can sensibly be presented against their use for these purposes. There is also a medical use in assessing the damage from strokes or other brain traumas.

Educationally, intelligence tests in their various forms and under their various names can be an extremely valuable instrument to enable educationalists to get an idea of the educability of the subject. It is possible to make assessments of under-achievement and self-limitation only by such means. The chance for really able children who are found in poor circumstances to get an appropriate education is much increased by their use.

Industrially, intelligence tests are widely used to help management in the enormously difficult task of fitting people comfortably into their roles in a business. It cannot be assumed that employers simply pick out those with the highest IQ. There is also a strong tendency to reject people whose intelligence quotient puts them in too high a category, relative to the job. Experience has shown that such people tend to become restless and leave. It is in their own interests as well as that of the company for very able people to seek positions which make better use of their mental abilities.

These are some of the practical ways in which intelligence tests are useful.

The tests published here are offered as an inexpensive and convenient way to have fun and accept Pope's challenge to 'know thyself' on a near-enough-basis. They are parallel with and based on fully standardized tests. They have been restandardized and cross-checked on Mensa members and candidates who have all been checked on professionally supervised tests.

IMPORTANT NOTE: COPYRIGHT

The copyright for all these tests belongs to or is granted to the author. However, readers may want to test a number of persons on them. The author and the publisher have agreed that a reasonable number of photocopies of test forms, say 20 in all, may be taken by each full price purchaser. These are for private and personal use only. They may not be sold or used for payment. If you want to avail yourself of this facility then you should take the copies before tests are marked in any way, otherwise later users may be able to make out previous markings even after erasure. Further copies of the test forms may be obtained from Brainbox, 27 Zealand Park, Caergeiliog, Anglesey, Gwynedd, UK, at reasonable prices.

THE TESTS

People enjoy doing these tests so I am publishing a variety of different ones based on well-known professional forms. You may find that you get different results on different tests and that will give an indication of the uncertainty which surrounds the subject. It is as foolish to place undue reliance on such results as it is to reject them altogether. It is better to know yourself a little than to know nothing about yourself at all. Here is a list of the tests.

A.   ADULT INTELLIGENCE TESTS

1.   *Cognitive tests*

There are three of these. I divide cognitive skills into three different aspects: word power or Verbal Ability, arithmetic skill or Number Ability and three-dimensional or Space Relations comprehension.

Cognitive Test Battery A   This is the first of two batteries of timed intelligence tests. Each is preceded by an untimed practice test.

Verbal practice test
Verbal test A

Number practice test
Number test A

Spatial practice test
Spatial test A

Cognitive Test Battery B

2.   *THE MAC Advanced Intelligence Test Battery*

This is a further battery of untimed intelligence tests designed for those of higher intelligence.

Odd one out?
Which is the same?
Which is opposite?
Add-ons
Double meanings
Complete it

3.   *Serebriakoff Advanced Culture Fair Test*

This is an untimed non-verbal test based on culture fair tests which are widely used. It is also an advanced test. This is the most difficult test. I designed it myself as a test of what Professor Raymond Cattell calls 'fluid' rather than 'crystalized' intelligence. It should be fairer on those who are not so familiar with English as it is entirely non-verbal. This was also standardized on Mensa members at Cambridge.

B. CHILDREN'S INTELLIGENCE TESTS

These were devised for children aged between 7 and 14 but for younger children if they are very bright. It is important to follow the instructions more exactly when they are used.

1. *Langer Non-Verbal Test*

This is an untimed, non-verbal test which is therefore less sensitive to culture. It was devised for any children from 7 years.

2. *Russell Test For English Speakers*

This is a timed parallel test for English speaking children over 7 years.

C. PERSONALITY TESTS (ADULTS)

Untimed but do them quickly. The factors will be revealed after the test is complete.

1. *Personality Factor 1*
2. *Personality Factor 2*
3. *Personality Factor 3*
4. *Personality Factor 4*

It makes no sense to wish you luck and a good score when you start the tests. I wish you an accurate, predictive and informative result. I wish you better knowledge of yourself. But I do hope that you may justifiably have the same pleasant surprise I had when I applied to join Mensa and found that I had a very high score. That made me try things I never should have dreamed of trying before (such as writing books like this one).

4

The Intelligence Tests

Tests for Adults

COGNITIVE TEST BATTERIES

For each of the cognitive tests here, a preliminary test is given. This is to give you practice so that you do not come to the proper test without some idea of what you are about.

I recommend that some time early on the day that you intend to do the test you should work through the preliminary test fairly quickly – but not so fast that you do it carelessly. Check your answers first before you go on to take the tests.

Testing and timing

IQ tests are designed to be administered under standardized conditions. A trained intelligence tester says exactly the same words in the same tone of voice in the same way and gives everyone the same timing. He also tries to preserve a cool, comfortable, and undistracting background, so that every batch of subjects has the same chance. He may have only variable success in achieving this.

The cognitive tests are designed to take exactly 30 minutes and the result will not mean much if you take more. If you take much less and the results are very good – well, I can pat you on the head, but I haven't worked out how much you should add to your score. It will certainly be higher than the book says. Timing yourself may be some distraction, so, if you are not too embarrassed, get someone else to do it for you.

Peeking

Peeking, or having a preliminary glimpse at the main test questions before you do them, can be good or bad according to your objective. If the object of the exercise is to prove to yourself that you are bright, whether you are or not, then the more you peek the better. There is no harm in it because you are kidding no one but yourself. But if you really want to know, and are tough enough to take it, then peeking is out – it renders the rest of the exercise a complete waste of time. The use of pocket calculators has not been allowed for, so use them only if you want self-deception more than self-knowledge.

Remember it is a speeded test so get as much done as you can. There is no penalty for wrong answers, and it is a good strategy to have a guess even if you don't know. Your guesses may be more guided by intelligence than you think. The obsessive checker is at a disadvantage; leave the checking till you've finished the last question. Don't rush too much. Work at the fastest speed at which you can put down well-considered answers. Don't get bogged down on one question – leave it and come back to it.

The questions are graded for difficulty, so most people will run into trouble somewhere through the list and find they cannot get much further. Don't worry about this – the test is designed to stop everyone somewhere.

Spend a little time over the instructions: you must understand them thoroughly or the thing is no go.

Each question earns one mark, so you can score 50 for each section of the cognitive tests. Now is the time to draw back if you don't want to be sorted or want to go on believing you are a genius. As I said, I cannot wish you luck because the more you have the more you will be deceived, and having said 'know thyself' I have to be consistent.

Those who proceed beyond this point want their brains tested . . .

Cognitive Test Battery A

Test begins here

PRACTICE VERBAL TEST

No time limit (18 questions). Try to practise working quickly. Answers are on page 37.

Analogies 1

This is an analogy: *dark is to light as black is to white.*
Complete each following analogy by underlining two words from those in brackets.

Example: high is to low as (*sky, earth,* tree, plant: sky is analogous to earth)

VP   1   dog is to puppy as (pig, cat, kitten)

VP   2   circle is to globe as (triangle, square, solid, cube)

Similarities

Underline the two words in each line *with the most similar meanings.*

Example: mat, linoleum, floor, *rug* (mat is similar to rug)

VP   3   large, all, big

VP   4   empty, wide, entire, whole

Comprehension

Read the following passage. The spaces may be filled from the list underneath. In each space write the letter of the *word which would best fill the space.* No word should be used more than once and some are not needed at all. The first letter is inserted as an example.

VP   5 and 6   Little (. B. .) of silvery mist (. . . .) to drift through the hollows while the light (. . . . .) after sunset.

(A) eroded, (B) wisps, (C) before, (D) ended, (E) began, (F) faded.

Odd out

In each group of words below underline the two words whose meanings *do not belong with the meanings of the other words.*

Example: robin, pigeon, *spade, fork,* eagle

VP   7   man, cod, herring, boy, flounder

VP   8   nose, mouth, smile, eyes, frown

VP = Practice Verbal Test

Links

Write in the brackets one word which means *the same in one sense as the word on the left, and in another sense the same as the word on the right.* The number of dashes in the brackets corresponds to the numbers of letters missing.

Example: invoice (**B i l L**) beak

VP   9   summit (**T _ P**) spinning-toy

VP   10   spot (_ _ **T**) Dorothy

Analogies II

Complete each analogy by writing in the brackets one word which *ends with the letter printed.*

Example: high is to low as sky is to (e a r t **H**)

VP   11   young is to old as boy is to (_ _ **N**)

VP   12   aeroplane is to bird as submarine is to (_ _ _ **H**)

Opposites

In each line below underline the two words *which are most nearly opposite in meaning.*

Example: heavy, large, light

VP   13   bold, bad, timid

VP   14   tense, terse, serious, relaxed, provoked

Mid-terms

In each row, three terms on the right should correspond to three terms on the left. Insert *the missing mid-term on the right.*

Example: first (second) third : : one (**T w o**) three

VP   15   mile (foot) inch : : ton (**P _ _ _ _**) ounce

VP   16   triangle (square) pentagon : : three (**F _ _ _**) five

Similar or opposite

In each row below underline two words *which mean most nearly either the opposite or the same as each other.*

Examples: 1.   mat, linoleum, rug

              2.   hate, love, affection

VP   17   reply, punish, repute, reward

VP   18   disdain, feign, pretend, flatter

END OF PRACTICE VERBAL TEST

Answers to practice verbal test

VP 1   cat, kitten
VP 2   square, cube (a circle is a flat shape produced from a globe, and a
        square is a flat shape produced from a cube)
VP 3   large, big
VP 4   entire, whole
VP 5   E (began)
VP 6   F (faded)
VP 7   man, boy (human beings, not fish)
VP 8   smile, frown (expressions, not features)
VP 9   top
VP 10   dot
VP 11   man
VP 12   fish
VP 13   bold, timid
VP 14   tense, relaxed
VP 15   pound
VP 16   four
VP 17   punish, reward (opposites)
VP 18   feign, pretend (synonyms)

You have now finished the practice test. Now make sure you have a half hour
free of the risk of interruption for the next timed test.

Test begins here

VERBAL TEST A

Begin with exact timing. 50 questions in a half hour.
Answers on page 86.

Analogies I

There are four terms in analogies. The first is related to the second in the same way that the third is related to the fourth. *Complete each analogy* by underlining two words from the four in brackets.

Example: high is to low as (*sky, earth,* tree, plant)

VA   1   sitter is to chair as (cup, saucer, plate, leg)

VA   2   needle is to thread as (cotton, sew, leader, follower)

VA   3   better is to worse as (rejoice, choice, bad, mourn)

VA   4   floor is to support as (window, glass, view, brick)

VA   5   veil is to curtain as (eyes, see, window, hear)

Similarities

Underline the two words in each line *with the most similar meanings.*

Example: mat, linoleum, floor, *rug*

VA   6   divulge, divert, reveal, revert

VA   7   blessing, bless, benediction, blessed

VA   8   intelligence, speediness, currents, tidings

VA   9   tale, novel, volume, story

VA 10   incarcerate, punish, cane, chastise

VA = Verbal Test A

Comprehension

Read this incomplete passage. The spaces in the passage are to be filled by words from the list beneath. In each space write the letter of the *word which would most suitably fill the space*. No word should be used more than once and some are not needed at all.

VA   11 – 20   A successful author is (. . . .) in danger of the (. . . .) of his fame whether he continues or ceases to (. . . .). The regard of the (. . . .) is not to be maintained but by tribute, and the (. . . .) of past service to them will quickly languish (. . . .) some (. . . .) performance brings back to the rapidly (. . . .) minds of the masses the (. . . .) upon which the (. . . .) is based.

(A) neither, (B) fame, (C) diminution, (D) public, (E) remembrance, (F) equally, (G) new, (H) unless, (I) forgetful, (J) unreal, (K) merit, (L) write.

Odd out

In each group of words below underline the two words whose meanings *do not belong with the others*.

Example: robin, pigeon, <u>space</u>, <u>fork</u>, eagle

VA   21   shark, sea lion, cod, whale, flounder

VA   22   baize, paper, felt, cloth, tinfoil

VA   23   sword, arrow, dagger, bullet, club

VA   24   bigger, quieter, nicer, quick, full

VA   25   stench, fear, sound, warmth, love

Links

Write in the brackets one word which means *the same in one sense as the word on the left and in another sense the same as the word on the right*.

Example: price list (**B** <u>i</u> <u>l</u> **L**) beak

VA   26   dash (**D** _ _ **T**) missile

VA   27   mould (**F** _ _ **M**) class

VA   28   squash (**P** _ _ _ **S**) crowd

VA   29   thin (**F** _ _ **E**) good

VA   30   ignite (**F** _ _ **E**) shoot

Opposites

In each line below underline the two words *that are most nearly opposite in meaning.*

Example: heavy, large, light

VA 31   insult, deny, denigrate, firm, affirm

VA 32   missed, veil, confuse, secret, expose

VA 33   frank, overt, plain, simple, secretive

VA 34   aggravate, please, enjoy, improve, like

VA 35   antedate, primitive, primordial, primate, ultimate

Mid-terms

In each line, three terms on the right should correspond with three terms on the left. Insert *the missing mid-term on the right.*

Example: first (second) third : : one (**T** w o) three

VA   36   past (present) future : : was (**I** _) will be

VA   37   complete (incomplete) blank : : always (**S** _ _ _ _ _ _ _) never

VA   38   glut (scarcity) famine : : many (**F** _ _) none

VA   39   rushing (passing) enduring : : evanescent (**T** _ _ _ _ _ _ _ _) eternal

VA   40   nascent (mature) senile : : green (**R** _ _ _) decayed

Similar or opposite

In each line below underline two words *which mean most nearly either the opposite or the same as each other.*

Examples: (a) mat, linoleum, rug,   (b) hate, affection, love

VA   41   rapport, mercurial, happy, rapacious, phlegmatic

VA   42   object, deter, demur, defer, oblate

VA   43   tenacious, resolve, irresolute, solution, tenacity

VA   44   real, renal, literally, similarly, veritably

VA   45   topography, heap, prime, plateau, hole

Analogies II

Complete each analogy by writing in the brackets one word which *ends with the letters printed*.

Example: high is to low as sky is to (e̲ a̲ r̲ **T H**)

VA   46   proud is to humble as generous is to (_ _ _ _ _ _ **H**)

VA   47   brave is to fearless as daring is to (_ _ _ _ _ _ **ID**)

VA   48   lend is to borrow as harmony is to (_ _ _ _ _ _ **D**)

VA   49   rare is to common as remote is to (_ _ _ _ _ **NT**)

VA   50   skull is to brain as shell is to (_ _ _ **K**)

END OF TEST. 50 QUESTIONS IN HALF AN HOUR.
ANSWERS: page 86.

**Test
begins
here**

PRACTICE NUMBER TEST

No time limit (26 questions). Practise working quickly.
Answers are on page 47.

Equations

In each of the following equations there is *one missing number*, which should
be written into the brackets.

PN   1 $21 - 6 = 3 \times (\ldots)$

PN   2 $48 \div 2 = 20 + (\ldots)$

PN   3 $4 \times 0 \cdot 5 = 0 \cdot 25 \times (\ldots)$

Targets

In each set of missiles there are rules which allow the target number of the
missile to be formed from the numbers in the tail and wings. In the example
the rule is: *add the wing numbers and multiply by the tail number to get the
target number.* Write the answer in the blank target.

Example:

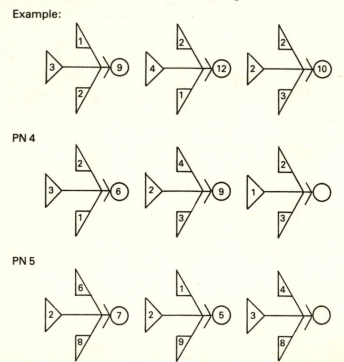

PN 4

PN 5

PN = Practice Number Test

Series I

Each row of numbers below forms a series. Write in the brackets at the end of each line *the number which logically should follow in the series*.

Example: 1, 2, 4, (. .8. .)

PN   6   2, 4, 6, 8, (. . . .)

PN   7   18, 27, 36, (. . . .)

PN   8   81, 64, 49, 36, (. . . .)

Double rows

In each set of numbers below the same rules apply within each set to produce the numbers in the circles. Whether a number is in an upper or a lower row shows which rule applies to that number. In the example, the upper numbers in a set are added and then multiplied by the lower number to give the answer in the circle. Write *the correct number* in each blank circle.

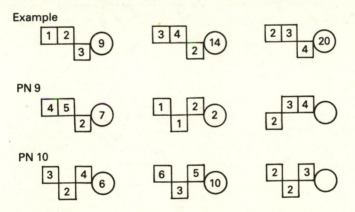

Mid-terms

In each line below the three numbers on the left are related in the same way as the three numbers should be on the right. Write *the missing middle number* on the right.

Example: 2(6)3   : :   3(12)4

PN   11   11(12)13   : :   4(   )6

PN   12   4(9)5   : :   2(   )3

PN   13   25(5)5   : :   24(   )4

Pies

In each diagram below the numbers run in pairs or in series going around or across the diagram. Insert *the missing number* in the blank sector.

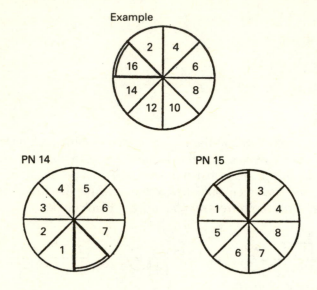

Example

PN 14

PN 15

Matrices

In each square below the numbers run down and across following simple rules. In the example, the numbers in each row are formed by adding 1 to each previous number and the numbers in each column are formed by adding 2 to each previous number. Insert *the missing number* in the blank square.

Example:

1	2	3
3	4	5
5	6	7

PN16

2	4	6
4	6	8
6	8	

PN 17

2	4	8
3	6	12
4	8	

Squares and triangles

In each set of squares the numbers are related by particular rules to produce the number in the triangle. Each row has the same set of rules but the rules change from row to row. In the example, we add the numbers in the first two squares and subtract the number in the third square to give the number in the triangle. Write *the missing figure* into the blank triangle in each row.

Example:

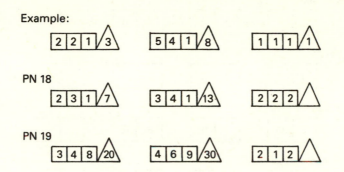

PN 18

PN 19

Rules and shapes

The shapes tell us the rules of arithmetic applying to the number. In each set, the numbers enclosed by shapes are used *to produce the number not completely enclosed. Write in the missing number in each row.*

Example:

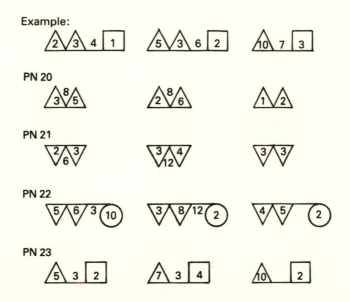

PN 20

PN 21

PN 22

PN 23

Double squares

The numbers in each row run in series. Write *the two numbers which should appear in the blanks on the right-hand double square.* In the example, the left-hand numbers increase by one at each step. The right-hand numbers are multiplied by two at each step.

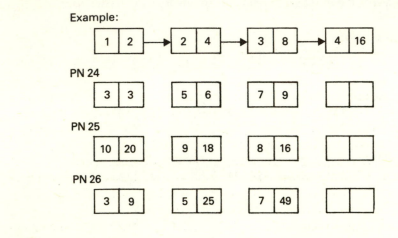

Example:

| 1 | 2 | → | 2 | 4 | → | 3 | 8 | → | 4 | 16 |

PN 24

| 3 | 3 | | 5 | 6 | | 7 | 9 | | | |

PN 25

| 10 | 20 | | 9 | 18 | | 8 | 16 | | | |

PN 26

| 3 | 9 | | 5 | 25 | | 7 | 49 | | | |

END OF PRACTICE TEST.

Answers to practice number test

PN   1   5
PN   2   4
PN   3   8
PN   4   6 (Add numbers in wings and tail)
PN   5   4 (Add numbers in wings and divide the result by the number in the tail)
PN   6   10 (Add twos)
PN   7   45 (Add nines)
PN   8   25 (The numbers in the series are the squares of 9, 8, 7, 6, and the square of 5 is 25)
PN   9   5 (Add numbers in upper row and subtract number in lower)
PN 10   3 (Multiply numbers in upper row and divide by number in lower)
PN 11   5 (5 stands in the normal sequence of counting, between 4 and 6)
PN 12   5 (Add the outer numbers to give the inner)
PN 13   6 (Divide the left outer number by the right outer number)
PN 14   8 or 0 (Add one to each number successively in a clockwise direction)
PN 15   2 (Each pair of diagonally opposite numbers totals nine)
PN 16   10 (Both rows and columns progress by adding twos)
PN 17   16 (Rows progress by doubling. Columns progress by doubling not the original numbers but the numbers which are to be added to make the progression)
PN 18   6 (Multiply the first two numbers and add the third)
PN 19   3 (Multiply the first and third numbers and subtract the second)
PN 20   3 (Numbers enclosed within triangles to be added)
PN 21   9 (Numbers enclosed within reversed triangles to be multiplied)
PN 22   10 (Numbers enclosed within reversed triangles to be multiplied and product divided by numbers within circles)
PN 23   8 (Numbers within squares to be subtracted from numbers within triangles)
PN 24   9 and 12 (The first numbers in successive double squares form a series progressing by adding twos, and the second numbers similarly by adding threes)
PN 25   7 and 14 (The first numbers progress by subtracting ones, and the second by subtracting twos)
PN 26   9 and 81 (The first numbers in successive double squares form a series by adding twos and the second numbers are the squares of corresponding first numbers)

You have now finished the practice test. Now make sure you have a half hour free of the risk of interruption for the timed test.

Test
begins
here

NUMBER TEST A

Begin with exact timing. 50 questions in half an hour.
Answers on page 87.

Equations

In each of the following equations there is *one missing number* which should be written into the brackets.

Example: $2 \times 12 = 6 \times (.\overset{4}{..})$

NA   1 $8 \times 7 = 14 \times (....)$

NA   2 $12 + 8 - 21 = 16 + (....)$

NA   3 $0{\cdot}0625 \times 8 = 0{\cdot}25 \div (....)$

NA   4 $0{\cdot}21 \div 0{\cdot}25 = 0{\cdot}6 \times 0{\cdot}7 \times (....)$

NA   5 $256 \div 64 = 512 \times (....)$

NA = Number Test A

Targets

In each set of missiles there are rules which allow the target number of the missile to be formed from the number in the tail and wings. In the example the rule is: *add the wing numbers and multiply by the tail number to get the target number.* Write the answer in the blank target.

Example:

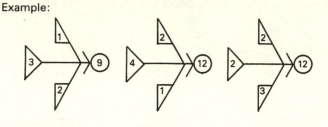

NA 6

 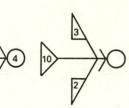

NA 7

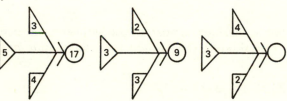

Series I

Each row of numbers forms a series. Write in the brackets *the number which logically follows.*

Example: 1, 2, 4 (. 8 . .)

NA   8   3, 6, 12, 24, (. . . .)

NA   9   81, 54, 36, 24, (. . . .)

NA 10   2, 3, 5, 9, 17, (. . . .)

NA 11   7, 13, 19, 25, (. . . .)

NA 12   9, 16, 25, 36, (. . . .)

Double rows

In each set of numbers below the same rules apply within each set to produce the numbers in the circles. Whether a number is in an upper or a lower row shows which rule applies to that number. In the example *the upper numbers in a set are added and then multiplied by the lower number to give the answer in the circle*. Write the correct number in each blank circle.

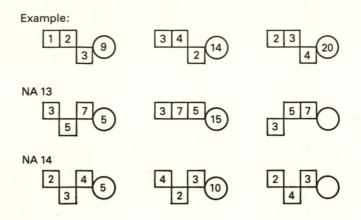

Example:

NA 13

NA 14

Mid-terms

In each line below the three numbers on the left are related in the same way as the three numbers should be on the right. Write *the missing middle number* on the right.

Example: 2 (6) 3　: :　3 (12) 4

NA　15　7 (12) 5　: :　8 (. . . .) 3

NA　16　3 (6) 2　: :　3 (. . . .) 3

NA　17　49 (15) 64　: :　16 (. . . .) 144

NA　18　294 (147) 588　: :　504 (. . . .) 168

NA　19　132 (808) 272　: :　215 (. . . .) 113

Pies I

In each diagram below the numbers run in pairs or in series going across or around the diagram. Insert *the missing number* in the blank sector.

Example:

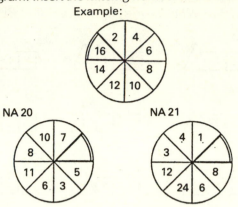

NA 20   NA 21

Series II

Write in the parentheses *the number which belongs at that step in the series.*

NA   22   53, 47, (. . . .), 35

NA   23   33, 26, (. . . .), 12

NA   24   243, 216, (. . . .), 162

NA   25   65, 33, (. . . .), 9

NA   26   3, 4, 6, (. . . .), 18

Matrices I

In each number square below the numbers run down and across following simple rules of arithmetic. Insert *the missing number* in the blank square.

Example:

1	2	3
3	4	5
5	6	7

NA 27

6	7	13
2	5	7
8	12	

NA 28

6	2	12
4	5	20
24	10	

Squares and triangles

In each set of squares the numbers are related by particular rules to produce the number in the triangle. Each row has the same set of rules but the rules change from row to row. Write *the missing number* into each blank triangle.

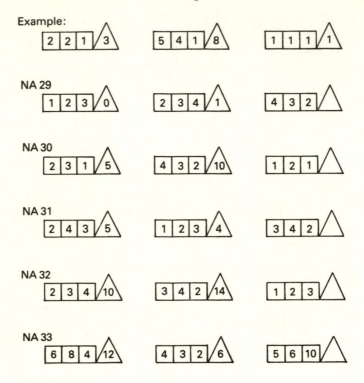

Example:

NA 29

NA 30

NA 31

NA 32

NA 33

Matrices II

Insert *the missing numbers* in the blank squares.

NA 34

1	2	2
2	3	6
2	6	

NA 35

4	2	2
2	2	1
2	1	

Rules and shapes

The shapes tell us the rules of arithmetic applying to the number. In each set, *the numbers enclosed by shapes are used to produce the number not completely enclosed.*

Example:

/2\ /3\ 4 1   /5\ /3\ 6 2   /10\ 7 3

NA 36

/1\ 3 /2\   /3\ 5 /2\   /1\ /4\

NA 37

/6\ 3 \3/   /7\ 3 \4/   /5\ \3/

NA 38

/2\ 6 3   /3\ 15 5   /4\ 3

NA 39

/60\ 5 (12)   /20\ 5 (4)   /5\ (5)

NA 40

\8/4\ 2 /6\   \3/7\ 8 /4\   \7/6\ /5\

NA 41

/6\ 4 8 (3)   /2\ 9 3 (6)   /4\ 3 (2)

Pies II

Write *the missing number* into the space.

NA 42   **NA 43**

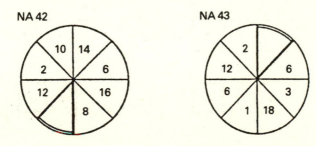

Double squares

The numbers in each row run in series. Write *the two numbers which should appear in the blanks on the right-hand double square*. In the example the left-hand numbers increase by one at each step. The right-hand numbers are multiplied by two at each step.

Example:

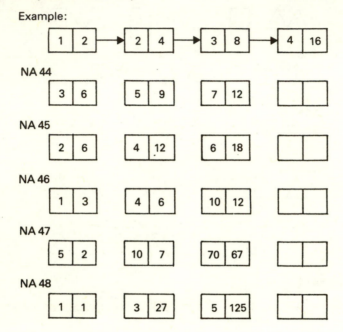

NA 44

NA 45

NA 46

NA 47

NA 48

NA   49   If $42 = A \times (A + 1)$, then A is (. . . .).

NA   50   If $162 \times 98 = B \times B$, then B is (. . . .).

END OF TEST. YOU MAY NOW CHECK YOUR WORK UNTIL THE TIME IS UP. ANSWERS: page 87.

Test begins here

PRACTICE SPATIAL TEST

There is no time limit, but work as quickly as you can. Answers are on page 60.

Flat turning

In each line below underline *the pair of shapes which, if turned around flat, could represent the same shape.*

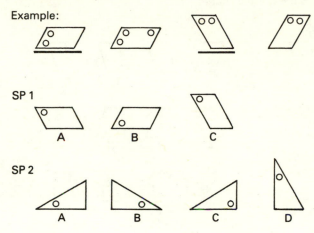

Reflected forms

In each line below, two of the shapes represent mirror images of the same shape. *Underline that pair.*

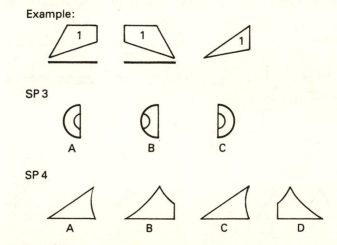

SP = Practice Spatial Test

Reflecting and turning

Imagine that all the shapes in this set are transparent sheets with a heavy black line along one edge and a circle in one corner. In each row, look first at the single shape on the left. If it were lifted off the paper, turned over, laid flat on the paper again and turned around 'head to tail' it would resemble one of the lettered shapes on the right. Write in the circle at the end of each row *which letter shows the correct shape.*

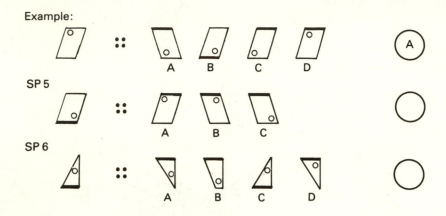

Potter's wheel

In each row, two out of the three shapes on the left represent the same shape turned around – as on a potter's wheel, but not turned over. Underline *the two shapes on the right which are rotated versions of a similar pair on the left.*

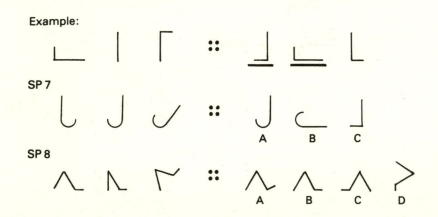

Fitting

The lettered shapes in the top row can be used to form the black shapes below. They may be turned over. Write one letter, or more, in the brackets to the right of each black shape *to show which lettered shape or shapes can be used to form the black shape.*

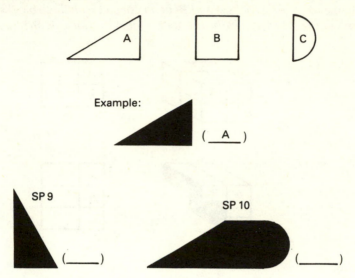

Example:

(__A__)

SP 9

(___)

SP 10

(_____)

Following

The shapes on the left hand form a series. Which of the lettered shapes on the right continues the series? Write *the letter of the correct shape* in the circle.

Example:

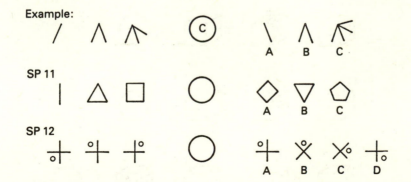

SP 11

SP 12

Counting

Each of these diagrams represents a pile of solid blocks that are all of the same size and shape. If any block is unsupported it is clearly shown as such. Some blocks are lettered. Write a number beside each letter in the column on the right to show how many blocks *touch* each lettered block. A whole face must touch. In the example, *blocks A and B are in contact with three blocks each: now start with SP 13 and fill in the number of faces in contact with blocks A, B and C.*

Example:

A	3
B	3

SP 13

A	
B	
C	

Visualizing

Designs were drawn on some faces of these cubes. No design appears on the face of more than one cube. There are two blank faces on each cube. In each row some of the drawings are the same cube turned around. If a cube *can* be the same as another, assume it *is* the same. Write in the circle at the end of each row *the least number of different cubes represented in the row.* In the example, the second and third drawings are the same cube turned around.

Example:

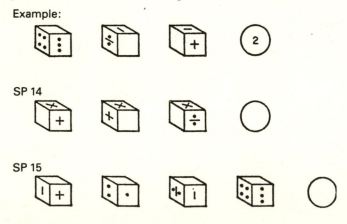

SP 14

SP 15

Analogies

In each row the first shape is related to the second shape in the same way that the third shape is related to the fourth. Underline *the shape on the right which should be the fourth shape.*

Example:

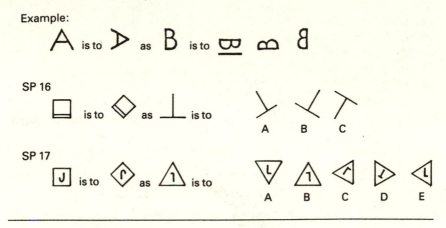

SP 16

SP 17

END OF PRACTICE SPATIAL TEST. Check your answers overleaf.

✔ Answers begin here

Answers to practice spatial test

SP 1 B, C

SP 2 A, D

SP 3 A, C

SP 4 B, D

SP 5 B

SP 6 A

SP 7 A, B

SP 8 B, D

SP 9 A

SP 10 A, B, C

SP 11 C (a line has two points, a triangle three, a square four and a pentagon five)

SP 12 D (the dot moves in a clockwise direction around successive quadrants)

SP 13 A2, B1, C1

SP 14 1

SP 15 2 (the first and third drawings represent one cube and the second and fourth drawings represent another cube)

SP 16 B (the shapes are tilted to the right at an angle of 45°)

SP 17 E (the outlines of the second and fourth shapes are tilted at 45° and the inner shapes are flat turned upside down)

You have now finished the whole practice test. Now make sure you have a half hour free of the risk of interruption for the timed test.

Test
egins
here

SPATIAL TEST A

Begin with exact timing. 50 questions in half an hour. Answers on page 89.
When you are quite ready to start, read the instructions and work as quickly as
you can.

Flat turning

On each line below, underline *the pair of shapes which, if turned around flat,
could represent the same one.*

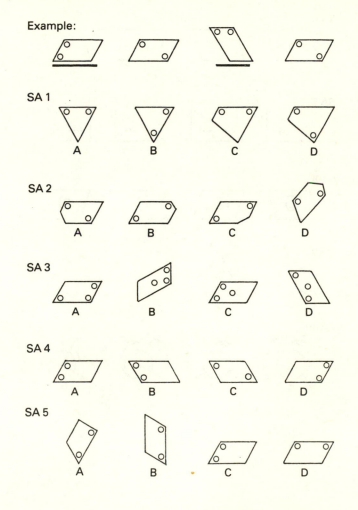

Reflected forms

In each of these lines, two of the shapes represent mirror images of the same shape. *Underline that pair.*

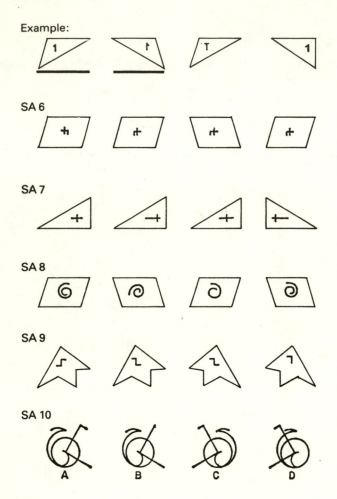

Reflecting and turning

Imagine that all the shapes in this set are transparent sheets with a heavy black line along one edge and a dot in one corner. One of the right-hand set of shapes represents the left-hand one, turned over like a pancake and then turned upside down flat. *Write its letter in the blank circle.*

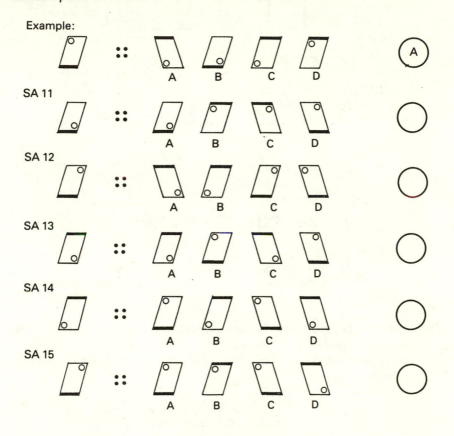

Potter's wheel

In each row, two of the three shapes on the left represent the same shape turned around but not over. Underline *two of the shapes on the right which are rotated versions of the pair on the left.*

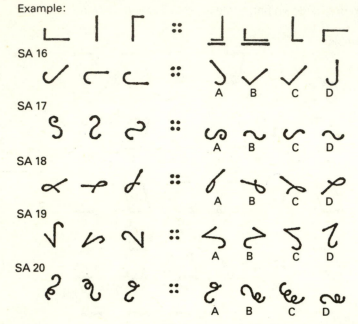

Fitting

The lettered shapes in the top row can be used to form the black shapes below. They may be turned over. Write one letter, or more, in the brackets below each black shape *to show which lettered shape, or shapes, can be used to form the black shape.*

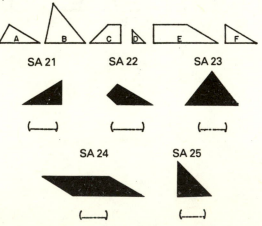

Following

The shapes on the left form a series. *Which of the lettered shapes on the right continues the series?* Write the letter of the correct shape in the circle.

Example:

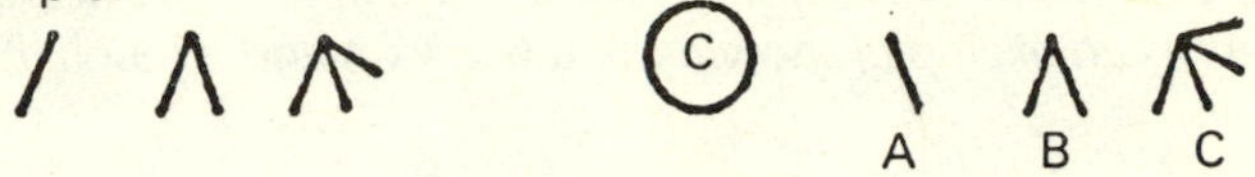

/ ∧ ∧   Ⓒ   \ ∧ ↖
                           A B C

SA 26

    ⌡ ✓ ↳ ⟍   ◯   ↗ ⌠ ↓ ⟍
                                      A B C D

SA 27

    ᘯ ᚠ ᘯ ᚠ   ◯   ᘯ ᚠ ᘯ ᚓ
                                      A B C D

SA 28

    £ ⅃ ⅌ ⅌   ◯   ⅌ ⅁ ⅁ ⅌
                                      A B C D

SA 29

    ʓ ʃ ~   ◯   ⌣ ⌣ ↶ ↶
                                      A B C D

SA 30

    ∟ ⟍ | ⟋   ◯   ⌐ ↙ | ⟋
                                      A B C D

Counting

The piles of blocks shown are solid. Any block without support is shown as such. Each diagram represents a pile of exactly similar blocks. Write a number beside each letter in the column *to show how many other blocks touch the block indicated by each letter. In SA 31 the first two letters have been matched with numbers as an example, showing that blocks A and B touch three other blocks.*

SA 31

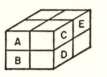

A	3	D	
B	3	E	
C			

SA 32

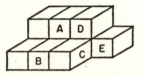

A		D	
B		E	
C			

SA 33

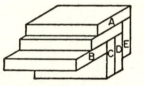

A		D	
B		E	
C			

SA 34

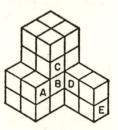

A		D	
B		E	
C			

SA 35

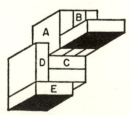

A		D	
B		E	
C			

Visualizing

Designs were drawn on some faces of these cubes. No design appears on the face of more than one cube. There are two blank faces on each cube. In each row some of the drawings are the same cube turned around. If a cube *can* be the same as another, assume it *is* the same. Write in the circle at the end of each row *the least number of different cubes represented in the row*. In the example, the second and third drawings are the same cube turned around.

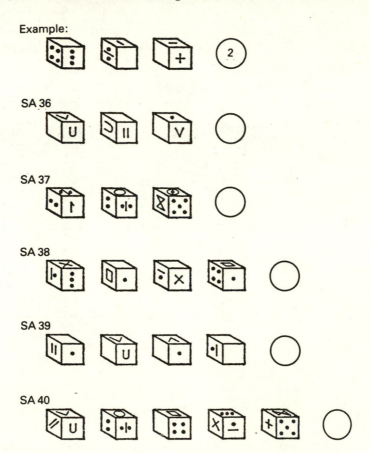

Analogies

In each row (in the figure on the following page) the first shape is related to the second shape in the same way that the third is related to the fourth. Underline *the figure on the right which should be the fourth shape.*

Example:

A is to ▷ as B is to ☷ ∽ ꓭ B

SA 41

L is to ⊥ as J is to

J   U   ⋃   ⋃
A   B   C   D

SA 42

ABCD is to BDCA as XJQL is to JLQX   XQLJ   JXLQ   QLJX
A   B   C   D

SA 43

⊬ is to ⊎ as ·L is to

⊤·   ·⊺   ⌐·   ·L
A   B   C   D

SA 44

◁ ⋎ ◀ is to ⋎ as LPFƐZ is to

P   F   ¿   S
A   B   C   D

SA 45

⯒ is to ⋋ as ⯒ is to

⋊   ⋉   ⋔   ⋊
A   B   C   D

SA 46

∫ is to ∫ as ⟍ is to

⟍   ⟋   ⟋   ⟍
A   B   C   D

SA 47

⌈ is to ⌣ as ⌉ is to

⌐   ⌞   ⌣   ⌐
A   B   C   D

SA 48

⟍ is to ⟨ as ⟨ is to

⟨   ⟩   ⟋   ⟩
A   B   C   D

SA 49

⇢ is to ↑· as ⌐ is to

⌉·   ⌈·   ·⌠   ⌉·
A   B   C   D

SA 50

△|▫ is to ⦸ as ⌐S⌄ is to

x⫿   ⋎   ⌐⫿   ⫽
A   B   C   D

END OF TEST. CHECK YOUR WORK UNTIL TIME IS UP. ANSWERS: page 89.

You have now completed Cognitive Test Battery A (the first cognitive test battery) and you can turn to p. 86 to check your answers. Preferably, before you check up and learn the test principles you can take Test Battery B, the second Cognitive Test Battery. (This will take one and a half hours.) Test Battery B is an alternative battery designed on exactly the same lines as Test Battery A. By taking both batteries before checking you can average the results and get a better estimate of where you stand in cognitive intelligence.

Cognitive Test Battery B

VERBAL TEST B

Test
begins
here

Begin with exact timing. 50 questions in a half hour. Answers are on p. 90.

Analogies I

There are four terms in analogies. The first is related to the second term in the same way that the third is related to the fourth. *Complete each analogy* by underlining two words from the four in brackets.

VB   1   mother is to girl as (man, father, male, boy)

VB   2   wall is to window as (glare, brick, face, eye)

VB   3   island is to water as (without, centre, diagonal, perimeter)

VB   4   high is to deep as (sleep, cloud, float, coal)

VB   5   form is to content as (happiness, statue, marble, mould)

Similarities

Underline the two words in each line *with the most similar meaning.*

VB   6   lump, wood, ray, beam

VB   7   collect, remember, concentrate, gather

VB   8   idle, lazy, impeded, indolent

VB   9   divert, arrange, move, amuse

VB 10   antic, bucolic, drunk, rustic

Comprehension

Read the following passage. The spaces are to be filled by words from the list beneath. In each space write the letter of the *word which would fill the space most sensibly.* The words are to be used once only, and not all are needed.

VB   11–20   There will be (. . . .) end to the troubles (. . . .) (. . . .), or indeed, my (. . .) Glaucon of (. . .) itself, till philosophers become (. . .) in this (. . .) or till those we (. . .) call kings and rulers really and (. . .) (. . .) philosophers.

(A) world, (B) truly, (C) now, (D) no, (E) humanity, (F) become, (G) states, (H) an, (I) of, (J) dear, (K) kings, (L) red.

VB = Verbal Test B

Odd out

In each group of words below underline the two words *which do not belong with the others*.

VB   21   knife, razor, scissors, needle, lance

VB   22   bravery, disgust, faith, energy, fear

VB   23   prosody, geology, philosophy, physiology, physics

VB   24   glue, sieve, pickaxe, screw, string

VB   25   receptionist, draughtsman, psychiatrist, blacksmith, fitter

Links

Write in the brackets one word which means *the same in one sense as the word on the left and in another sense the same as the word on the right.*

VB   26   register (**L _ _ T**) lean

VB   27   hindrance (**T _ _**) link

VB   28   contest (**M _ _ _ H**) equal

VB   27   blockage (**J _ _**) preserve

VB   30   whip (**L _ _ H**) tie

Analogies II

Complete each analogy by writing in the brackets one word which *ends with the letters printed.*

VB   31   thermometer is to temperature as clock is to (_ _ _ E)

VB   32   beyond is to without as between is to (_ _ _ _ _N)

VB   33   egg is to ovoid as Earth is to (_ _ _ _ _ _ ID)

VB   34   potential is to actual as future is to (_ _ _ _ _ _ _ T)

VB   35   competition is to cooperation as rival is to (_ _ _ _ _ _ R)

Opposites

In each line below underline the two words *which are most nearly opposite in meaning.*

VB 36   short, length, shorten, extent, extend

VB 37   intense, extensive, majority, extreme, diffuse

VB 38   punish, vex, pinch, ignore, pacify

VB 39   reply, tell, join, disconnect, refute

VB 40   intractable, insensate, tract, obedient, disorderly

Mid-terms

In each line, three terms on the right should correspond to three terms on the left. Insert *the missing mid-term on the right.*

VB 41   beginning (middle) end : : head (**W** _ _ _ _) foot

VB 42   precede (accompany) follow : : superior (**P** _ _ _) inferior

VB 43   point (cube) line : : none (**T** _ _ _ _) one

VB 44   range-finder (soldier) cannon : : probe (**S** _ _ _ _ _ _) lancet

VB 45   face (body) legs : : nose (**N** _ _ _ _) knees

Similar or opposite

In each line below, underline two words *which mean most nearly either the opposite or the same as each other.*

VB 46   liable, reliable, fluctuating, trustworthy, worthy

VB 47   foreign, practical, germane, useless, relevant

VB 48   relegate, reimburse, legislate, promote, proceed

VB 49   window, lucent, acrid, shining, shady

VB 50   lucubrate, bribe, indecent, spiny, obscene

END OF TEST. CHECK YOUR WORK UNTIL TIME IS UP. ANSWERS: p. 90.

Test
begins
here

NUMBER TEST B

Begin with exact timing. 50 questions in half an hour. Answers are on p. 91.

Equations

In each of the following equations there is *one missing number* which should be written into the brackets.

Example: $2 \times 12 = 6 \times (\ \overset{4}{..}\ )$

NB   1 $5 \times 9 = 15 \times (\ldots)$

NB   2 $16 + 7 - 29 = 5 + (\ldots)$

NB   3 $0{\cdot}225 \times 4 = 0{\cdot}75 \times (\ldots)$

NB   4 $0{\cdot}28 \div 0{\cdot}35 = 0{\cdot}5 \times 0{\cdot}4 \times (\ldots)$

NB   5 $81 + 27 = 243 \times (\ldots)$

Targets

In each set of missiles there are rules which allow the target number of the missile to be formed from the numbers in the tail and wings. In the example the rule is: *add the wing numbers and multiply by the tail number to get the target number.* Write the answer in the blank target.

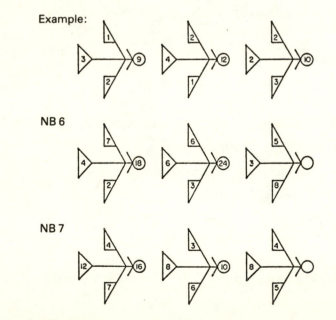

NB = Number Test B

Series I

Each row of numbers below forms a series. Write in the brackets at the end of each line *the number which logically should follow in the series*.

NB   8   2, 6, 18, 54, (. . . .)

NB   9   256, 192, 144, 108, (. . . .)

NB 10   1, 3, 7, 15, (. . . .)

NB 11   6, 13, 20, 27, (. . . .)

NB 12   49, 64, 81, 100, (. . . .)

Double rows

In each set of numbers below the same rules apply within each set to produce the numbers in the circles. Whether a number is in an upper or a lower row shows which rule applies to that number. In the example, *the upper numbers in a set are added and then multiplied by the lower number to give the answer in the circle*. Write the correct number in each blank circle.

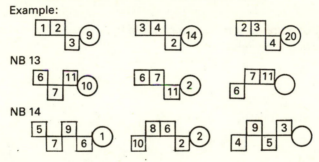

Mid-terms

In each line below the three numbers on the left are related in the same way as the three numbers should be on the right. Write *the missing middle number* on the right.

Example: 2 (6) 3   : :   3 (12) 4

NB 15   4 (11) 7   : :   8 (. . . .) 5

NB 16   3 (12) 4   : :   2 (. . . .) 5

NB 17   661 (122) 295   : :   514 (. . . .) 121

NB 18   205 (111) 239   : :   176 (. . . .) 124

NB 19   784 (112) 336   : :   968 (. . . .) 363

Pies

In each diagram below the numbers run in pairs or series going across or around the diagram. Insert *the missing number* in the blank sector.

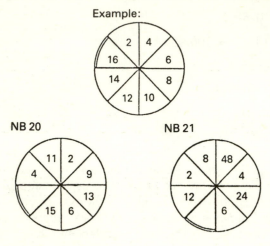

Example:

NB 20   NB 21

Series II

Each row of numbers forms a series. Write in the brackets *the number which logically should be there.*

NB   22   52, 45, (. . . .), 31

NB   23   43, 35, (. . . .), 19

NB   24   416, 390, (. . . .), 338

NB   25   92, 79, (. . . .), 53

NB   26   1, 5, 13, (. . . .), 61

Matrices I

In each number square below the numbers run down and across following simple rules of arithmetic. Insert *the missing number* in the blank square.

Example:

1	2	3
3	4	5
5	6	7

NB 27

3	4	7
7	5	12
10	9	

NB 28

2	5	10
6	3	18
12	15	

Squares and triangles

In each set of squares the numbers are related by particular rules to produce the number in the triangle. Each row has the same set of rules but the rules change from row to row. Write *the missing number* into each blank triangle.

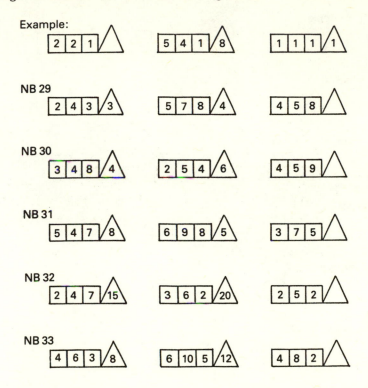

Example:

NB 29

NB 30

NB 31

NB 32

NB 33

Matrices II

Insert *the missing numbers* in the blank squares.

NB 34

10,000	400	16
2,500	100	4
625	25	

NB 35

5	9	17
13	25	49
37	73	

Rules and shapes

The shapes tell us the rules of arithmetic applying to the number. In each set, *the numbers enclosed by shapes are used to produce the number not completely enclosed. Fill in the missing numbers.*

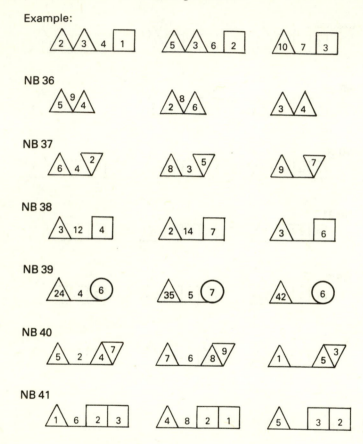

Example:

NB 36

NB 37

NB 38

NB 39

NB 40

NB 41

Pies II

Write *the missing number* into the space.

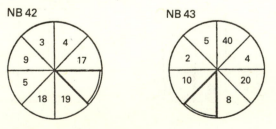

NB 42   NB 43

Double squares

The numbers in each row run in series. Write the two numbers which should appear in the blanks on the right-hand side double square. In the example, *the left-hand numbers increase by one at each step; the right-hand numbers are multiplied by two at each step.*

Example:

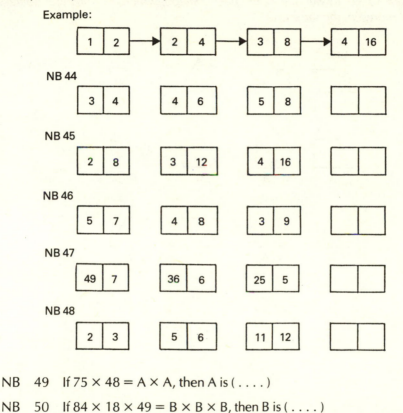

NB 44

NB 45

NB 46

NB 47

NB 48

NB   49   If 75 × 48 = A × A, then A is (. . . .)

NB   50   If 84 × 18 × 49 = B × B × B, then B is (. . . .)

END OF TEST. CHECK YOUR WORK UNTIL TIME IS UP. ANSWERS: p. 91.

Test
begins
here

SPATIAL TEST B

Begin with exact timing. 50 questions in half an hour. Answers are on p. 93.

Flat turning

On each line below underline *the pair of shapes which, if turned around flat, could represent the same one.*

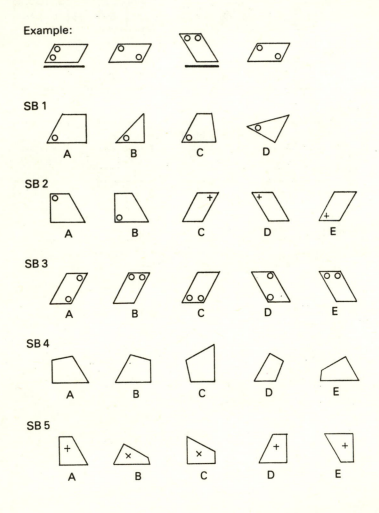

SB = Spatial Test B

Reflected forms

On each of these lines, two of the shapes represent mirror images of the same shape. *Underline that pair.*

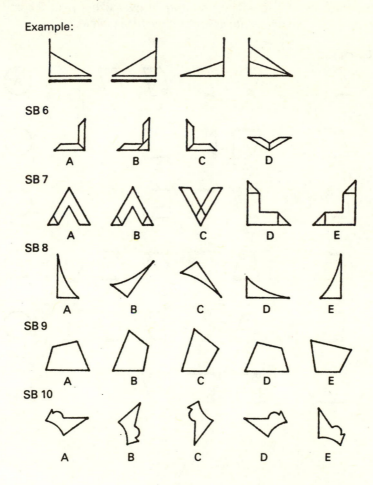

Example:

SB 6

A   B   C   D

SB 7

A   B   C   D   E

SB 8

A   B   C   D   E

SB 9

A   B   C   D   E

SB 10

A   B   C   D   E

Reflecting and turning

Imagine that all the shapes in this set are transparent sheets with a heavy black line along one edge and a dot in one corner. One of the right-hand set of shapes represents the left-hand one, turned over like a pancake and then turned upside down flat. *Write its letter in the blank circle.*

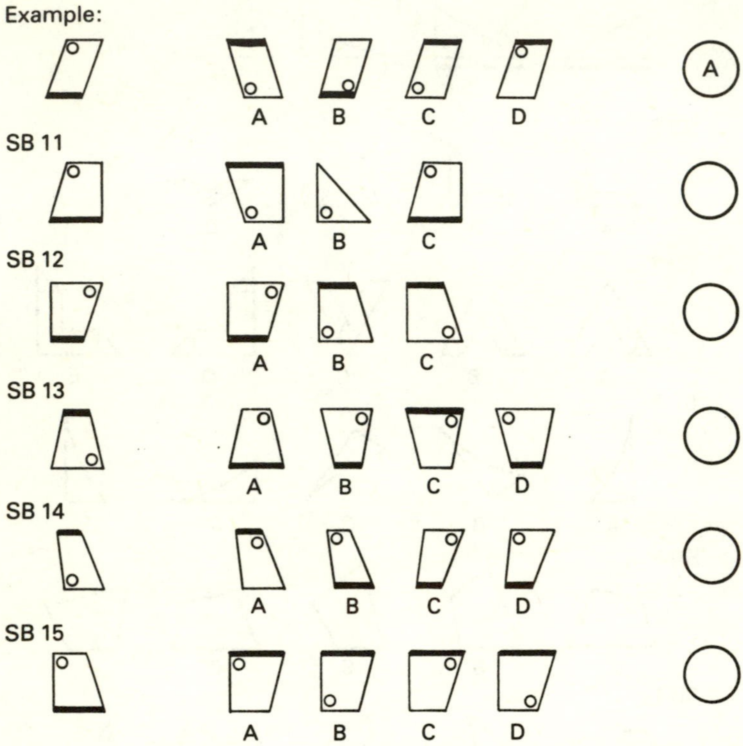

Example:

SB 11

SB 12

SB 13

SB 14

SB 15

Potter's wheel

In each row, two of the three shapes on the left represent the same shape turned around but not over. Underline *two of the shapes on the right which are rotated versions of the pair on the left.*

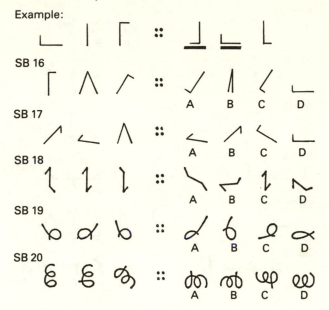

Fitting

The lettered shapes in the top row can be used to form the black numbered shapes below. They may be turned over. Write one letter, or more, in the brackets below each black shape *to show which lettered shape or shapes can be used to make the black shape.*

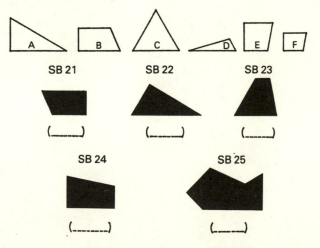

Following

The shapes on the left form a series. *Which of the shapes on the right continues the series?* Write the letter of the correct shape in the circle.

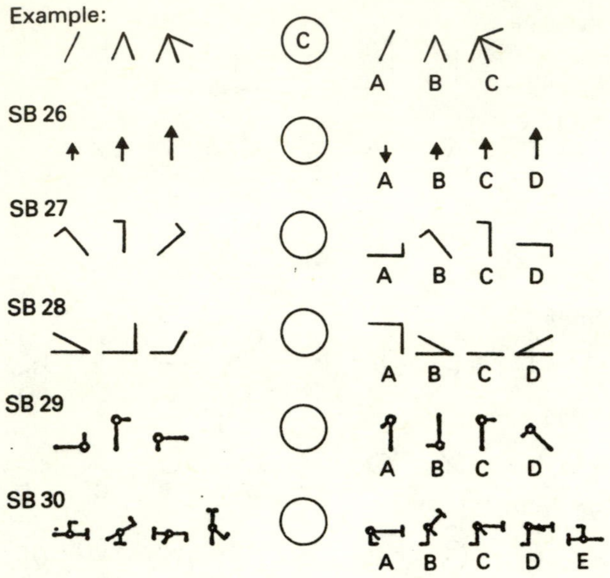

Example:

/ ∧ ∧   Ⓒ   / ∧ ∧
                   A   B   C

SB 26

   ↑ ↑ ↑   ◯   ↓ ↑ ↑ ↑
                          A   B   C   D

SB 27

   ⟍ ⏋ ⟋   ◯   ⌐ ⟍ ⏋ ⌐
                          A   B   C   D

SB 28

   ⟍ ⏌ ⟋   ◯   ⏋ ⟍ ⎯ ⟍
                          A   B   C   D

SB 29

   ⊶ ⌐ ⊶   ◯   ⌐ ⌐ ⌐ ⟍
                          A   B   C   D

SB 30

   ⊶ ⟋ ⊶ ⊦   ◯   ⊶ ⟋ ⊶ ⊶ ⊥
                          A   B   C   D   E

Counting

The piles of blocks shown are solid. Any block without support is shown as such. Each diagram below represents a pile of blocks, all of the same size and shape. Some blocks are lettered. Write a number beside each letter in the column on the right *to show how many blocks touch each lettered block*. The first letter has been matched with a number as an example to show that block A touches three other blocks.

SB 31

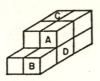

A	3	C	
B		D	

SB 32

A		D	
B		E	
C			

SB 33

A		D	
B		E	
C			

SB 34

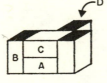

A		C	
B		D	

SB 35

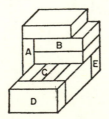

A		D	
B		E	
C			

Visualizing

Designs were drawn on some faces of these cubes. No design appears on the face of more than one cube. There are two blank faces on each cube. In each row some of the drawings are the same cube turned around. If a cube *can* be the same as another, assume it *is* the same. Write in the circle at the end of each row *the least number of different cubes represented in the row*. In the example, the second and third drawings are the same cube turned around.

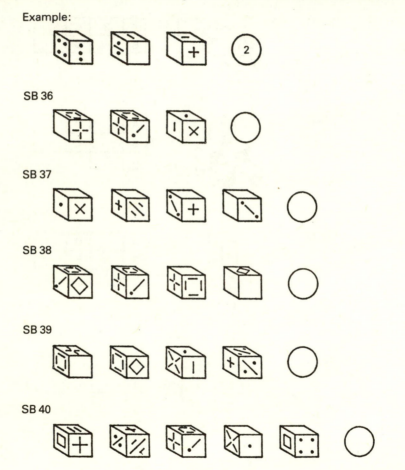

Example:

SB 36

SB 37

SB 38

SB 39

SB 40

Analogies

In each row, the first shape is related to the second shape in the same way that the third is related to the fourth. Underline *the figure on the right which should be the fourth shape.*

Example:

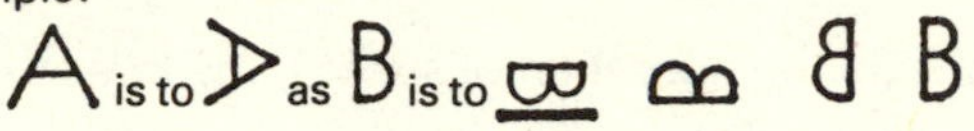

A is to ⟩ as B is to ᗞᗜ ᗝᗜ ᗖ B

SB 41

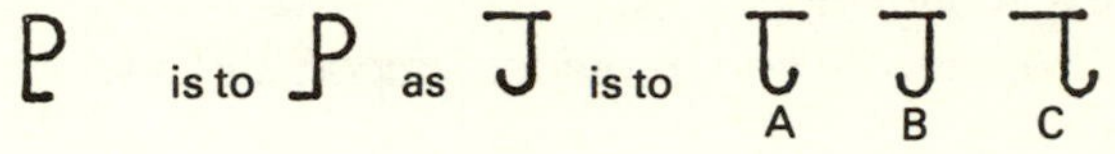

Ρ is to ⌐ᑭ as Ⴑ is to Ⴑ̆ Ⴑ Ⴑ̆
   A   B   C

SB 42

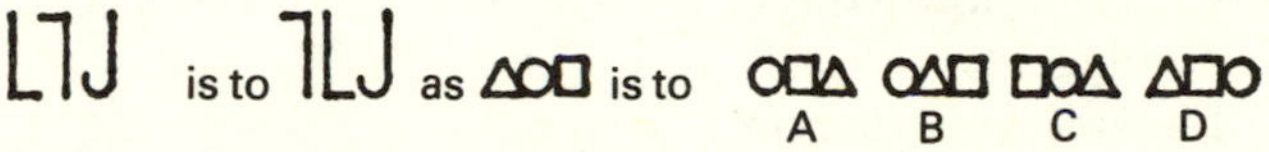

Ⴑ⌐Ⴑ is to ⌐ⴑⴑ as △○□ is to ○□△ ○△□ □○△ △□○
   A   B   C   D

SB 43

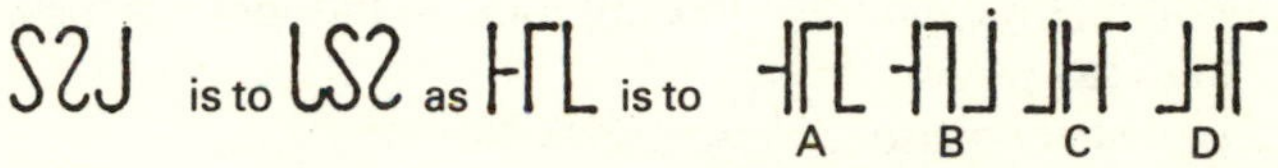

Ⴢ⌐Ⴑ is to ႱႱႢ as ⊢⌐Ⴑ is to ⊣Ⴑ ⊣⌐⌐ Ⴑ⊢ Ⴑ⊢
   A   B   C   D

SB 44

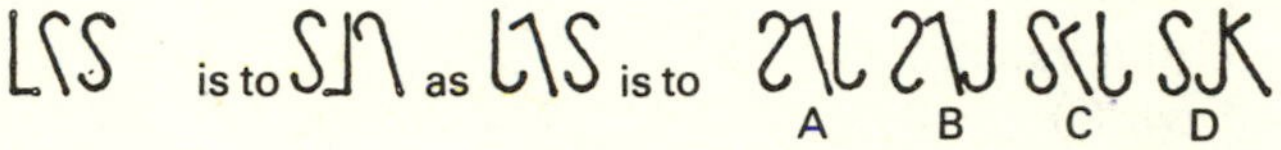

Ⴑ⌐Ⴢ is to Ⴢⴑⴒ as Ⴑⴒⴢ is to ⴒⴢႱ ⴒⴢⴑ Ⴢⴢ Ⴢⴑ
   A   B   C   D

SB 45

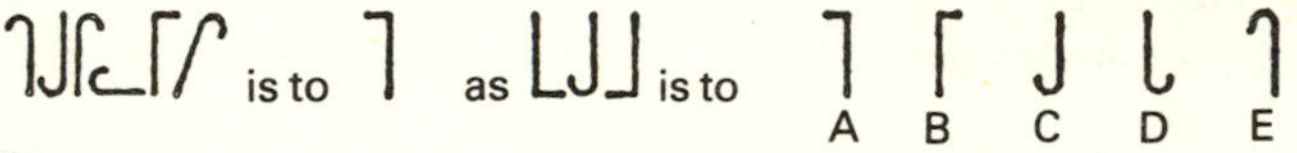

⌐Ⴑ⌐⌐ is to ⌐ as Ⴑⴑⴑ is to ⌐ ⌐ Ⴑ Ⴑ ⌐
   A   B   C   D   E

SB 46

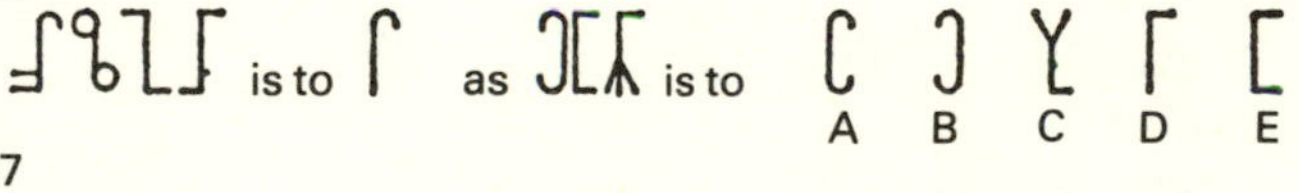

⌐Ⴑ⌐Ⴑ is to ⌐ as Ⴑ⌐⋏ is to Ⴑ ⋏ Ⴘ ⌐ Ⴑ
   A   B   C   D   E

SB 47

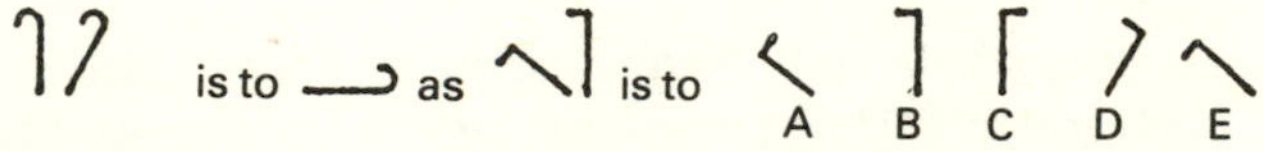

⌐⧸ is to ⌐ as ⋏⌐ is to ⟨ ⌐ ⌐ ⧸ ⟍
   A   B   C   D   E

SB 48

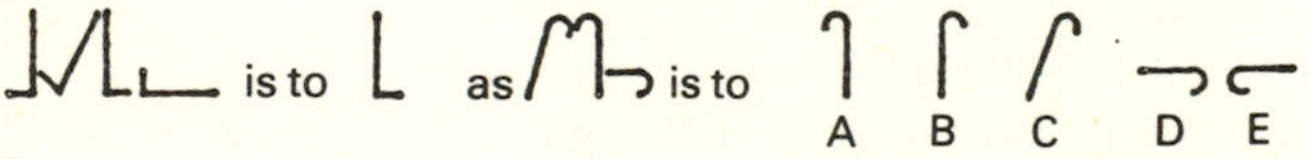

Ⴢ⌐⌐ is to L as ⧸⌐ is to ⌐ ⌐ ⌐ ⟍ ⟍
   A   B   C   D   E

SB 49

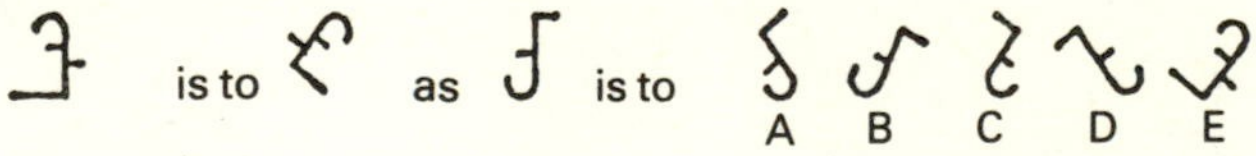

ⴑ is to ⟨ as ∫ is to ⟨ ⟨ ⟨ ⟨ ⟨
   A   B   C   D   E

SB 50

⌐Ⴑ△□Ⴑ is to ∫ as ⴑ□Ⴑ is to ∫ ∫ ⴒ ⟩ ∫
   A   B   C   D   E

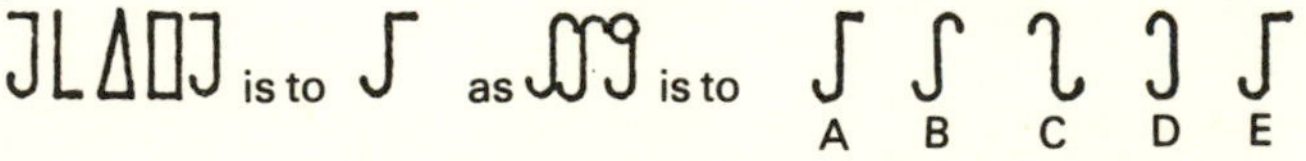

END OF TEST. CHECK YOUR WORK UNTIL TIME IS UP. ANSWERS: p. 93.

Answers and Evaluation (Test Batteries A and B)

COGNITIVE TEST BATTERY A

Answers to verbal test A

Answers
begin
here

VA	1	cup, saucer
VA	2	leader, follower (in the operation of sewing, the thread follows the needle)
VA	3	rejoice, mourn (opposites)
VA	4	window, view (a floor provides support and a window provides a view
VA	5	eyes, window (veils cover eyes as curtains cover windows)
VA	6	divulge, reveal
VA	7	blessing, benediction
VA	8	intelligence, tidings ('intelligence' in the sense of 'news')
VA	9	tale, story
VA	10	punish, chastise
VA	11	F (equally)
VA	12	C (diminution)
VA	13	L (write)
VA	14	D (public)
VA	15	E (remembrance)
VA	16	H (unless)
VA	17	G (new)
VA	18	I (forgetful)
VA	19	K (merit)
VA	20	B (fame)
VA	21	sea lion, whale (both mammals, the others are fish)
VA	22	cloth and tinfoil (the others are made of compressed fibres)
VA	23	arrow, bullet (the others are used in the hand)
VA	24	quick, full (the others mean 'more so')
VA	25	love, fear (the others are detected by the senses)
VA	26	dart
VA	27	form
VA	28	press
VA	29	fine
VA	30	fire
VA	31	deny, affirm
VA	32	veil, expose
VA	33	frank, secretive
VA	34	aggravate, improve
VA	35	primordial, ultimate

VA 36   is
VA 37   sometimes
VA 38   few
VA 39   transient
VA 40   ripe
VA 41   mercurial, phlegmatic (opposites)
VA 42   object, demur (synonyms)
VA 43   tenacious, irresolute (opposites)
VA 44   literally, veritably (synonyms)
VA 45   heap, hole (opposites)
VA 46   selfish
VA 47   intrepid
VA 48   discord
VA 49   present
VA 50   yolk

Answers to number test A

NA   1   4
NA   2   − 17
NA   3   0·5 or ½
NA   4   2
NA   5 $1/_{128}$ (0·0078125)
NA   6   2 (divide the tail number by the sum of the numbers in the wings)
NA   7   11 (multiply together the wing numbers and add the tail number)
NA   8   48 (double the previous number)
NA   9   16 (each number is $2/_3$ the previous number)
NA 10   33 (add to each successive number an amount double the difference between the previous pair of numbers)
NA 11   31 (add sixes)
NA 12   49 (the numbers are, successively, squares of 3, 4, 5, 6 and 7)
NA 13   9 (add upper squares; subtract lower squares)
NA 14   2 (multiply numbers in upper squares; subtract lower squares)
NA 15   11 (add numbers outside brackets to give numbers inside)
NA 16   9 (multiply outer numbers to obtain inner number)
NA 17   16 (inner number is sum of square roots of outer numbers)
NA 18   168 (inner number is largest common factor of outer numbers)
NA 19   656 (inner number is twice the sum of outer numbers)
NA 20   2 (opposite numbers make 13)
NA 21   2 (the product of opposite numbers is 24)
NA 22   41 (each number is 6 less than the preceding one)
NA 23   19 (each number is 7 less than the preceding one)
NA 24   189 (each number is 27 less than the preceding one)

NA 25   17 (each number is half the preceding number after one is added to the preceding number)

NA 26   10 (each number is twice the preceding one, less two)

NA 27   20 (first column plus second gives third. First row plus second gives third)

NA 28   240 (in rows and columns, the first number and second are multiplied to give the third)

NA 29   5 (first two numbers minus the third gives the fourth)

NA 30   1 (the product of the first two numbers minus the third gives the fourth)

NA 31   3 (add the second and third numbers and subtract the first to give the fourth)

NA 32   5 (multiply the first two and add the third)

NA 33   3 (multiply the first two numbers and divide by the third)

NA 34   12 (in rows and columns, the first number multiplied by the second gives the third)

NA 35   2 (in rows and columns, the first number divided by the second gives the third)

NA 36   5 (the sum of numbers in triangles gives the answer)

NA 37   2 (the difference of numbers in triangles)

NA 38   12 (the product of numbers in triangle and square)

NA 39   1 (the number in the triangle is divided by the number in the circle)

NA 40   4 (add numbers in triangles and subtract number in inverted triangle)

NA 41   6 (multiply numbers in the triangle and the square, and divide by the number in the circle)

NA 42   4 (opposite numbers add up to 18)

NA 43   36 (opposite numbers multiplied give 36)

NA 44   9, 15 (the first number in each domino is two more and the second number is three more than in the domino before)

NA 45   8, 24 (the first number in the domino is two more and the second six more than in the domino before)

NA 46   22, 24 (the second number in each domino is twice that in the domino before, and the first number is 2 less than the second)

NA 47   4690, 4687 (the first number in each domino is the product of the numbers in the domino before; the second is three less)

NA 48   7, 343 (the first numbers in the domino are the natural series of odd numbers and the second are their cubes)

NA 49   6

NA 50   126

Answers to spatial test A

SA   1   A, B
SA   2   A, D
SA   3   B, C
SA   4   A, D
SA   5   B, D
SA   6   A, C
SA   7   B, D
SA   8   A, D
SA   9   A, C
SA 10   A, C
SA 11   C
SA 12   A
SA 13   D
SA 14   C
SA 15   D
SA 16   A, D
SA 17   B, D
SA 18   B, D
SA 19   A, C
SA 20   B, D
SA 21   A
SA 22   D, F
SA 23   B
SA 24   E, F
SA 25   C, D
SA 26   B
SA 27   C
SA 28   D
SA 29   D
SA 30   A (the lines resemble clock hands)
SA 31   C3, D3, E3
SA 32   A3, B3, C2, D2, E1
SA 33   A2, B2, C3, D3, E3
SA 34   A3, B5, C4, D3, E2
SA 35   A4, B4, C5, D4, E2
SA 36   one
SA 37   two (the first two represent the same cube)
SA 38   two (the first and third, and the second and fourth have the same
         design on one face and so must be the same cube in each case)
SA 39   two (the first three represent the same cube)

SA 40   three (the different designs *could* be the opposite three faces of two pairs and a single, therefore we assume that they *are*)

SA 41   D

SA 42   A

SA 43   B (the feature face of the shape is turned from left to right and then put at the opposite end)

SA 44   C (the second shape is the same as the odd one from the first set of shapes)

SA 45   D

SA 46   C

SA 47   A

SA 48   D

SA 49   B

SA 50   B (long form tilted, loose features move to centre)

COGNITIVE TEST BATTERY B

Answers to verbal test B

VB   1   father, boy

VB   2   face, eye

VB   3   centre, perimeter

VB   4   cloud, coal (one is found high above earth, the other deep within it)

VB   5   statue, marble (these are examples of form and content)

VB   6   ray, beam

VB   7   collect, gather

VB   8   lazy, indolent

VB   9   divert, amuse

VB 10   bucolic, rustic

VB 11   D

VB 12   I

VB 13   G

VB 14   J

VB 15   E

VB 16   K

VB 17   A

VB 18   C

VB 19   B

VB 20   F

VB 21   needle, lance (the others have sharp *edges*)

VB 22   disgust, fear (emotions; the others are virtues)

VB 23   prosody, philosophy (aspects of literary culture; the others are sciences)
VB 24   sieve, pickaxe (these separate things; the others fix them together)
VB 25   receptionist, psychiatrist (main work is dealing with people; the others deal with things)
VB 26   list
VB 27   tie
VB 28   match
VB 29   jam
VB 30   lash
VB 31   time
VB 32   within
VB 33   spheroid (ovoid means egg-shaped; a spheroid is the shape of the earth)
VB 34   present
VB 35   partner
VB 36   shorten, extend
VB 37   intense, diffuse
VB 38   vex, pacify
VB 39   join, disconnect
VB 40   intractable, obedient
VB 41   waist
VB 42   peer
VB 43   three (points have no dimensions, cubes three and lines one)
VB 44   surgeon (probes and lancets are tools of surgeons as weapons are of soldiers)
VB 45   navel (approximate centre of body)
VB 46   reliable, trustworthy (synonyms)
VB 47   germane, relevant (synonyms)
VB 48   relegate, promote (opposites)
VB 49   lucent, shining (synonyms)
VB 50   indecent, obscene (synonyms)

Answers to number test B

NB 1   3
NB 2   − 11
NB 3   1·2
NB 4   4
NB 5 $^4/_9$ (0·4 recurring)
NB 6   43 (multiply wing numbers and add tail number)
NB 7   12 (multiply wing numbers and subtract tail number)

NB   8   162 (each number is three times that before)
NB   9   81 (each number is three-quarters that before)
NB   10   31 (each number is twice that before, plus one)
NB   11   34 (each number is seven more than that before)
NB   12   121 (the series is: $7 \times 7, 8 \times 8, 9 \times 9, 10 \times 10$ and 11×11)
NB   13   12 (add upper numbers and subtract lower numbers)
NB   14   3 (add upper numbers and subtract lower numbers)
NB   15   13 (the inner number is the sum of the outer numbers)
NB   16   10 (the inner number is the product of the outer numbers)
NB   17   131 (the inner number is one-third of the difference between the outer numbers)
NB   18   75 (the inner number is a quarter of the sum of the others)
NB   19   121 (the inner number is the largest number which is a factor of the outer numbers)
NB   20   8 (opposite numbers add up to 17)
NB   21   1 (the product of opposite numbers is 48)
NB   22   38 (each number is 7 less than that preceding)
NB   23   27 (each number is 8 less than that preceding)
NB   24   364 (each number is 26 less than that preceding)
NB   25   66 (each number is 13 less than that preceding)
NB   26   29 (each number is twice that before, plus three)
NB   27   19 (in columns and rows, the third number is the sum of the first two)
NB   28   180 (in columns and rows, the third number is the product of the first two)
NB   29   1 (add the first two numbers and subtract the third)
NB   30   11 (multiply the first two numbers and subtract the third)
NB   31   1 (add the first and third numbers and subtract the second)
NB   32   12 (multiply the first two numbers and add the third)
NB   33   16 (multiply the first two numbers and divide by the third)
NB   34   1 (divide by 2 going down and divide by 5 going across after taking the square roots)
NB   35   145 (after subtracting one from all numbers, rule is: multiply by 3 going down and multiply by 2 going across)
NB   36   7 (add numbers within the triangles)
NB   37   2 (the middle number is the difference between numbers in the triangles)
NB   38   18 (the middle number is the product of the others)
NB   39   7 (divide the first number by the third)
NB   40   3 (subtract the fourth number from the sum of the first and third)
NB   41   30 (the second number is the product of the others)
NB   42   13 (the sum of opposite numbers is 22)
NB   43   1 (the product of opposite numbers is 40)

NB 44   6, 10 (the first number in each domino is one more, and the second
        two more than in the domino before)
NB 45   5, 20 (the first number in each domino is one more than in the
        domino before, the second number is four times the first)
NB 46   2, 10 (the first number in each domino is one less, and the second
        one more than in the domino before)
NB 47   16, 4 (the second number in each domino is one less than in the
        domino before; the first number is the square of the second)
NB 48   23, 24 (the second number in each domino is twice the number in
        the domino before; the first number is one less than the second)
NB 49   60
NB 50   42

Answers to spatial test B

SB   1   B, D
SB   2   C, E
SB   3   B, C
SB   4   A, C
SB   5   A, E
SB   6   A, C
SB   7   D, E
SB   8   A, E
SB   9   A, D
SB 10   A, D
SB 11   A
SB 12   C
SB 13   B
SB 14   D
SB 15   B
SB 16   A, D
SB 17   A, B
SB 18   B, D
SB 19   B, C
SB 20   A, C
SB 21   B
SB 22   A
SB 23   D, C
SB 24   E, F
SB 25   A, B, D
SB 26   D
SB 27   A

SB 28   C

SB 29   B

SB 30   C

SB 31   B2, C3, D4

SB 32   A1, B1, C2, D3, E2

SB 33   A1, B3, C3, D3, E3

SB 34   A4, B2, C4, D2

SB 35   A5, B3, C5, D4, E6

SB 36   two (the first two represent the same cube)

SB 37   two (the first represents a cube different from the rest)

SB 38   one

SB 39   three (the first two represent the same cube)

SB 40   four (the first and second represent the same cube)

SB 41   C (the foot of the shape is turned from one side to the other)

SB 42   B (the first and second units in the shape change places)

SB 43   C (the last unit becomes the first and is transformed into its mirror image)

SB 44   D (the first unit becomes second and is transformed into its mirror image; the last unit becomes first, and the second unit becomes last and its head is turned around)

SB 45   D (the shape most unlike the rest is transformed into its mirror image)

SB 46   D (pick out the head of the shape whose head differs from its foot)

SB 47   D (the series proceeds by units successively turning in a clockwise direction)

SB 48   A (pick out the shape least resembling the others in virtue of laterality, or terms of mirror images)

SB 49   C (the first shape is transformed into the second shape by turning it in a clockwise direction through 45° after it has been transformed into a mirror image)

SB 50   D (pick a shape which has a twin and turn its head from one side to the other)

COGNITIVE TEST RESULTS (FOR ADULTS ONLY)

To get your IQ (or percentile) from your score, whether you did one or both Test Batteries:

(1)   Add up the number of questions you got completely right on the Verbal Test(s) and enter it on the form overleaf. If you did both A and B tests enter both scores.

(2)   Now do the same for the Spatial Test(s).

(3)   Now do the same for the Number Test(s).

(4)   The verbal score has to be multiplied by three and then added to the other scores to make up the final raw score (either for one test or for both).

(5)   Now refer to the Results Table on p. 97.

The Results Table allows you to read from raw score to results as IQ or percentile rating.

There are two columns for the raw score against IQ and percentile, one for those who took both A and B tests and one for those who took only one of them.

Read from the appropriate column across to the IQ and percentile score.

Find the score nearest above your own score and read across to the correct column (1 test or 2 tests). Read out IQ and percentile.

The percentile rating tells you what proportion of the test sample population would have scored as well as you did or lower. For example, if you are on the 90th percentile then 90% of people score the same or less than you. Only 10% score higher. If you are on the 50th percentile (IQ 100) then you have exactly the average score.

The Intelligence Quotient or IQ is a confusing technical expression which should never have become popular. Strictly, it applies to children and only by extrapolation to adults. It is the mental age multiplied by 100 divided by the actual age. If a child of 10 can perform as well as the average child of 15, its IQ is

$$\frac{15 \times 100}{10} = 150$$

The average IQ is (naturally, therefore) 100.

Unfortunately, the different psychologists produce different results from Binet's primitive scheme, so that an IQ score means different things on different tests according to the standard deviation.

A preferable way of judging IQ is by percentile rating. Your percentile rating is that percentage of the general population (upon whom the test was standardized) which your performance equals or excels. This will be explained later.

Test total form ————————————————————————————

                                                        Raw score

                                    Number Test   A   [   ]
                                                  B   [   ]
                                    Spatial Test A   [   ]
                                                  B   [   ]

Verbal test   A   [   ]
              B   [   ]

Verbal total   [   ]   X 3   =   [   ]

Total Raw score   [   ]

IQ = [   ]   Percentile = [   ]

Raw score

One test	Both tests	IQ	Per-centile
5	11	81	10th
9	19	82	12th
13	27	83	13th
17	35	84	14th
21	43	85	16th
25	50	86	18th
29	58	87	20th
33	66	88	21st
37	74	89	23rd
41	82	90	25th
45	90	91	27th
48	97	92	30th
52	105	93	32nd
56	113	94	34th
60	121	95	37th
64	129	96	40th
68	137	97	42nd
72	144	98	45th
76	152	99	47th
80	160	100	50th
84	168	101	52nd
88	176	102	55th
92	184	103	58th
95	191	104	60th
99	199	105	63rd
103	207	106	66th
107	215	107	68th
111	223	108	70th
115	231	109	73rd
119	238	110	76th
123	246	111	77th
127	254	112	79th

Raw score

One test	Both tests	IQ	Per-centile	
131	262	113	81st	
135	270	114	82nd	
139	278	115	84th	
142	285	116	86th	
146	293	117	87th	
150	301	118	88th	
154	309	119	90th	
158	317	120	91st	
162	325	121	92nd	
166	332	122	93rd	
170	340	123	94th	
174	348	124	94th	← *Worth a try for Mensa*
178	356	125	95th	
182	364	126	96th	
186	372	127	96th	
189	379	128	97th	
193	387	129	97th	
197	395	130	98th	
201	403	131	98th	
205	411	132		
209	419	133		
213	426	134		*Mensa level*
217	434	135		
221	442	136		
225	450	137		
229	458	138	99th	
233	466	139		
236	473	140		
240	481	141		
244	489	142		
248	497	143		
250	500	144		

THE MAC ADVANCED INTELLIGENCE TEST

This is an untimed or *Power* Test, and it was designed to measure the higher levels of intelligence. This makes it impossible to standardize on the normal population and was standardized on Mensa applicants, a highly selected sample. It must be taken for what it is worth. It has been keyed in to the test scores of those applicants and should provide a fairly good guide at the upper levels. Although designed to test high cognitive ability, it has questions of graded difficulty. Eveyone should be able to start each test but very few should be able to finish any of them. The question is not 'Can you finish?' but 'How far can you get?'

The battery comprises seven tests, each probing different abilities. You will be allowed as much time as you like but you should time yourself on each test because that may affect your final result.

Go through each test in order. Do not hurry. Read each question carefully and go ahead at a fast but comfortable speed. Do not waste too much time if you are stumped – pass on and come back to that question later. It is worthwhile to guess if you do not think you can answer surely. There is no penalty for wrong answers. If you alter your answer make sure you have made it clear which answer you settle on. Doubtful answers are not counted.

The tests are:

Test 1   Find the odd one out

Test 2   Which means the same?

Test 3   Which is opposite?

Test 4   Add on words

Test 5   Double meanings

Test 6   Complete the sentences

Test 7   Conceptual problems

Test
begins
here

Test 1:   Find the odd one out

Test 1 is aimed at testing the most important human ability, classification, the supreme trick of conceptual intelligence which collects things into named mental slots to help thinking.

Here you are given five words. You have to think about the various ways of classifying them. Some ways of looking at them leaves one of them, the 'odd one out'. There is one, simple fairly obvious way, the other ways are obscure or tortuous. You have to find the odd one out by the simplest rule. There is a quality or attribute which four of the words in each question share which is *not* shared by the odd one out.

Underline the word whose meaning does not fit in with the others, the odd one out.

Example: knife, fork, spoon, *hat,* cup.

Answer: 'hat', the others are tableware.

  (1)   A bird, B plane, C bee, D car, E butterfly

  (2)   A look, B glance, C stare, D wink, E observe

  (3)   A rain, B snow, C sleet, D lightning, E hail

  (4)   A cotton, B wool, C nylon, D flax, E silk

  (5)   A lifeless, B languid, C torpid, D numb, E sensitive

  (6)   A throw, B kick, C hurl, D toss, E pitch

  (7)   A beech, B ash, C spruce, D willow, E sycamore

  (8)   A cerise, B scarlet, C magenta, D crimson, E saffron

  (9)   A gelding, B bitch, C doe, D ewe, E filly

(10)   A distemper, B anthrax, C martingale, D spavin, E rinderpest

(11)   A dignified, B stately, C sublime, D august, E grand

(12)   A pearl, B agate, C sapphire, D emerald, E ruby

(13)   A funambulist, B acrobat, C clown, D fool, E virago

(14)   A triturate, B powder, C granulate, D titrate, E pulverize

(15)   A daffodil, B tulip, C snowdrop, D chrysanthemum, E gladiolus

Test 2:   Words which mean the same

This tests your comprehension of language. There are six words in each question, two of the words are closer in meaning than any other pair. Find the two words which mean nearly the same. Underline them.

Example: walk, run, drive, *stroll,* fly, sit.

Answer: 'walk' and 'stroll' are closest in meaning.

  (1)   A soon, B almost, C nearly, D partly, E often, F portion

  (2)   A forgo, B forget, C detest, D leave, E possess, F abhor

  (3)   A inhuman, B brutal, C manly, D careful, E compassionate, F celestial

  (4)   A ill, B peculiar, C odd, D weary, E stilted, F funny

  (5)   A ghostly, B gruesome, C comely, D thin, E horrible, F tasteless

  (6)   A wanton, B mediocre, C repulsive, D absurd, E ludicrous, F meaningful

  (7)   A everything, B blended, C many, D main, E complete, F entire

  (8)   A befriended, B watched, C fetched, D escorted, E accompanied, F joined

  (9)   A combat, B fulfil, C oppose, D exist, E affect, F apply

 (10)   A resistance, B allowance, C reason, D impedance, E affliction, F effect

 (11)   A relevant, B saucy, C absurd, D pertinent, E impatient, F intrusive

 (12)   A afternoon, B countryside, C gloaming, D daytime, E heathland, F twilight

 (13)   A pettifog, B quibble, C render, D assist, E demonstrate, F destroy

 (14)   A iambic, B obscene, C perverse, D wayward, E mean, F argumentative

 (15)   A hat, B split, C manager, D stable, E dubious, F trifid

Test 3:   Opposites

This is again a test of clear conceptual comprehension and grasp of meaning. Two of the words in each question mean more exactly the opposite of each other than any other pair. They mean the reverse of each other. Find the two 'opposites' and underline them.

Example: curved, long, *big, small*, broad.

Answer: 'big' and 'small' are the most *opposite*.

  (1)   A rotate, B ascent, C plunge, D approach, E descent

  (2)   A leak, B withdraw, C overflow, D approach, E escape

  (3)   A derail, B unsettle, C float, D dislodge, E sink

  (4)   A calm, B inactive, C relaxed, D employed, E numbed

  (5)   A sever, B wrench, C unseat, D join, E pluck

  (6)   A bluff, B blunt, C hard, D stinging, E acute

  (7)   A operatic, B discordant, C cantabile, D syncopation, E melodic

  (8)   A think, B learn, C calculate, D forego, E forget

  (9)   A filibuster, B opportunist, C assailant, D adversary, E partner

 (10)   A meagre, B fluent, C mean, D superfluous, E copious

 (11)   A alive, B dull, C slothful, D inert, E bemused

 (12)   A detach, B rally, C scatter, D debunk, E enthuse

 (13)   A patriotic, B animated, C seditious, D agitated, E motivated

 (14)   A toddler, B flapper, C stripling, D adolescent, E dotard

 (15)   A silky, B unshaven, C suave, D rounded, E coarse

 (16)   A loosen, B pay, C demand, D receive, E invoice

 (17)   A peccable, B seedy, C honoured, D saintly, E loving

 (18)   A cummerbund, B sash, C bandolier, D peruke, E buskin

 (19)   A stocky, B homunculus, C stubby, D giant, E squat

Test 4:   Add on words

This is a test of how well your mind works in scan and recall. It checks how well ordered your mental filing system is. There is a word which fits on *after* the first word to make another word. Also the word you are seeking fits on *before* the second word to make another sensible word. The number of hyphens tells you how many letters are missing. Sometimes a letter or two of the missing word is given as a clue. Write in the missing letters above the hyphens so as to make up the missing word.

Example: house *hold* all

(1)   green   _ _ _ _ _   wife

(2)   letter   p _ _ _ s   ups

(3)   pin   t _ _ _ e   cloth

(4)   broad   c _ _ _   away

(5)   fly   w _ _ _ _   wright

(6)   pick   _ _ _ _ _ _   book

(7)   pad   _ _ _ k   smith

(8)   leader   _ _ _ _   mate

(9)   with   _ _ _ _   all

(10)   spin   d _ _ _ t   wood

(11)   farm   _ _ _ _ _   fast

(12)   mud   _ _ _ k   spur

(13)   honey   _ _ _ _   light

(14)   dung   _ _ _ _   top

(15)   wood   _ _ _ _ _ _   hole

(16)   flame   _ _ _ _ _   reader

(17)   inter   _ _ _ _   thing

Test 5:   Double meanings

This tests similar abilities to Test 4. Find the middle word. You are looking for a word which has the same meaning as the first word *in one sense* and the same meaning as the second word *in another sense*. Fill in the missing letters. Some are already filled in as a clue.

Example: breathes heavily _ a _ _ _ underclothes

Answer: The answer is 'pants' because to breathe heavily is to pant and pants are underclothes also.

(1)	creep	_ _ e _ _	rob
(2)	look	_ _ _ _ _	time-piece
(3)	pound	b _ _ t	patrol
(4)	hyphen	d _ _ _	run
(5)	learn	_ _ _ _ y	room
(6)	lose	_ _ _ _	hut
(7)	waste	_ _ _ _ s _	deny
(8)	wilderness	_ _ _ _ _ _	leave
(9)	flop	_ _ _ _ _ _ _ r	fish
(10)	climb	_ _ _ _ _	horse
(11)	heave	_ _ _ _ h	tar
(12)	vulgar	_ _ _ _ _ _	heath
(13)	lots	_ _ _ _ _ _ _	books
(14)	black	_ _ _ _ _	bird
(15)	saffron	_ _ _ _ _	fruit
(16)	teacher	_ o _ _ _	charabanc
(17)	maw	_ _ _ _ h	voice
(18)	nincompoop	b _ _ _ _	bird
(19)	component	_ _ _ _ _ _	agent

Test 6:   Completion

Here we are testing comprehension and your sense of the appropriate. There are three incomplete sentences. You are offered five alternative words for each space left vacant. The task is to find the most *appropriate* word for each space. You are looking for the *combination* that best fits so as to make sense. Write the letter which is in front of the correct word in each space.

Completion

Complete the quotations from the selection of words shown in the *Alternatives* given below.

I want to go .... 1 .... from the .... 2 ...., where the .... 3 ....
doesn't crouch over me like a .... 4 .... waiting to .... 5 ....

The .... 6 .... genius is a .... 7 .... of large .... 8 .... powers, ... 9
.... determined to some .... 10 .... direction.

The .... 11 .... of .... 12 .... constitution are .... 13 .... lost when
the .... 14 .... power is .... 15 .... by the executive.

Alternatives

(1)   A near, B east, C far, D west, E pontificating

(2)   A hurricane, B winter, C tornado, D lightning, E thunder

(3)   A cold, B desert, C heat, D heavens, E stars

(4)   A mouse, B stag, C mole, D snow-leopard, E rabbit

(5)   A pounce, B stagger, C rush, D sleep, E forget

(6)   A lost, B missing, C evil, D true, E desperate

(7) A mind, B thought, C charge, D wave, E spread

(8) A general, B overt, C bland, D changed, E altered

(9) A separately, B accidentally, C fondly, D tentatively, E haltingly

(10) A lost, B particular, C piscatorial, D mythological, E rosy

(11) A kernels, B principles, C personalities, D principals, E imagination

(12) A autonomous, B chartered, C licensed, D free, E effortless

(13) A irrevocably, B indispensably, C imperatively, D spontaneously, E awkwardly

(14) A legislative, B codification, C chartered, D consultative, E spasmodic

(15) A accredited, B usurped, C deputed, D cured, E accepted

Test 7:   Problems

Now comes the crunch. This is where we sort out the men from the boys (or the women from the girls).

If you reach these questions undiscouraged, good! They are meant to discriminate among the top dogs. There are ten tricky questions which test your logical powers, your memory, comprehension and your quickness on your mental feet. Watch out for catches.

Again you are given a number of alternative answers to choose from. Write down the letter of the correct answer in the space provided in the table overleaf.

Problems

(1)   A man purchased a car for £560 and sold it for £725. He was then told that he had sold too cheaply so he bought the car back for £750 but could sell it for only £725. How much profit or loss had he made?

(2)   Mr Allen has a green door, Mr Ball does not have a red door, Mr Clark has a white door if Mr Ball has a red door, Mr Doe has a black door if Mr Allen has a green door, Mr Edge has a red door. Which one of these statements might be true?

(A)   Mr Allen has a red door.

(B)   Mr Ball has a white door.

(C)   Mr Clark has a white door.

(D)   Mr Doe has a black door.

(E)   Mr Edge has a black door.

(3)   A frog is at the bottom of a 30 ft deep well. He climbs up 3 ft and slips back 2 ft each day. How many days will it take him to reach the top?

(4)   One man's watch showed 6.10, another 6.25, another 6.40, yet another 6.55. If the correct time was 6.30, what was the average amount of time fast or slow that showed on all the watches?

(5)   A boat is anchored in the harbour, over its side is a rope ladder with the last rung just touching the water. The rungs are 200 mm apart. When the tide comes in it rises 1600 mm. How many rungs are covered?

(6)   A man bought a number of eggs at a shop. $^2/_3$ were cracked, $^1/_2$ were bad, $^1/_4$ were both cracked and bad, 2 were O.K. How many eggs did the man buy?

(7)   A cyclist cycles 10 miles to town A at 4 miles per hour. He does the return journey at 6 miles per hour. How many minutes does he take to do both journeys?

(8)   A factory owner decided to give each of his employees a bonus. As he was a chauvinist he decided to give each man £1 and each woman 40p. Then he had second thoughts. As he had 100 employees it would cost too much even though there were more women than men. He would wait until 60% of the men were away on a course and give the bonus only to those remaining. How much did it cost him?

(9)   In a Sports Centre 70% play squash, 75% play tennis, 80% play badminton, 85% play table-tennis. What is the minimum percentage that play all four sports?

(10) A man has 3 white socks, 3 black socks, 3 pink socks, and 3 blue socks in his drawer. What is the minimum number of socks that he must take out of the drawer to make up 3 pairs assuming that he cannot see the colours?

Alternative answers   *Your answer*

(1)   A loss £50, B loss £25, C nil, D profit £25, E profit £50   ....

(2)   A, B, C, D, E   ....

(3)   A 27, B 28, C 29, D 30, E 31   ....

(4)   A 2½ mins slow, B 5 mins slow, C 10 mins fast,
      D 5 mins fast, E 7½ mins fast   ....

(5)   A 9, B 8, C 7, D 6, E 0   ....

(6)   A 24, B 36, C 48, D 60, E 72   ....

(7)   A 220 mins, B 230 mins, C 240 mins, D 250 mins,
      E 260 mins   ....

(8)   A £400, B £500, C £600, D £700, E £800   ....

(9)   A 10%, B 15%, C 20%, D 25%, E 30%   ....

(10) A 6, B 7, C 8, D 9, E 10   ....

ANSWERS AND EVALUATION (MAC BATTERY)

Answers to the tests

Test 1

(1) D	(2) D	(3) D	(4) C
(5) E	(6) B	(7) C	(8) E
(9) A	(10) C	(11) C	(12) A
(13) E	(14) C	(15) D	

Test 2

(1) B, C	(2) C, F	(3) A, B	(4) B, C
(5) B, E	(6) D, E	(7) E, F	(8) D, E
(9) A, C	(10) A, D	(11) A, D	(12) C, F
(13) A, B	(14) C, D	(15) B, F	

Test 3

(1) B, E	(2) B, D	(3) C, E	(4) B, D
(5) A, D	(6) B, E	(7) B, E	(8) B, E
(9) D, E	(10) A, E	(11) A, D	(12) B, C
(13) A, C	(14) A, E	(15) C, E	(16) B, D
(17) A, D	(18) D, E	(19) B, D	

Test 4

(1) house	(2) press	(3) table
(4) cast	(5) wheel	(6) pocket
(7) lock	(8) ship	(9) hold
(10) drift	(11) stead	(12) lark
(13) moon	(14) hill	(15) pigeon
(16) proof	(17) play	

Test 5

(1) steal	(2) watch	(3) beat
(4) dash	(5) study	(6) shed
(7) refuse	(8) desert	(9) flounder
(10) mount	(11) pitch	(12) common
(13) volumes	(14) raven	(15) lemon
(16) coach	(17) mouth	(18) booby
(19) factor		

Test 6

(1)	C	(2)	B	(3)	A	(4)	D
(5)	A	(6)	D	(7)	A	(8)	B
(9)	A	(10)	B	(11)	B	(12)	D
(13)	A	(14)	D	(15)	B		

Test 7

(1)	E	(2)	D	(3)	B	(4)	C
(5)	E	(6)	A	(7)	D	(8)	A
(9)	A	(10)	D				

Scoring the MAC Advanced Intelligence Test

Adults

Check your answers and count the number of questions you got right. Be strict. If you made more than one guess you get no mark.

The Table which follows gives an estimate of your IQ rating and your millile rating against your score. Take your millile figure from 1000 and that is the number of people per thousand who may be expected to score better than you did in the test. For example, only five people in a thousand will score better than someone on the 995th millile.

For very high level tests the usual standardization techniques do not apply because there are so few subjects in the samples. This test must be seen as informed guesswork. The millile rating may give an impression of false precision so the results should be taken as a rough guide or ranking of how you stand in relation to the large Mensa group who tried the test.

If you get a millile rating anywhere near 950 you are at the level at which preliminary Mensa candidates are asked to take a supervised test. If you are much above 980 then you are at Mensa level.

For very bright children or older ones

Test the child as per instructions. Take the age of the child in months. Divide 180 by this number to make a decimal fraction (e.g. 12 years 2 months = 146 months. 180/146 = 1.233).

Multiply the child's IQ score on the test by this to give the child's adjusted IQ (e.g. scored IQ say 100 × 1.233. Adjusted IQ = 123).

The MAC Advanced Intelligence Test score table

Score	IQ	Millile	Score	IQ	Millile
22	97	425	50	120	910
23	97	458	51	120	919
24	98	469	52	121	926
25	99	495	53	122	934
26	100	500	54	123	941
27	101	514	55	124	947
28	102	557	56	125	952
29	102	575	57	125	958
30	103	596	58	126	962
31	104	617	59	127	966
32	105	638	60	128	971
33	106	658	61	129	974
34	106	678	62	129	977
35	107	698	63	130	980 ← Mensa level
36	108	717	64	131	982
37	109	735	65	132	984
38	110	738	66	133	987
39	111	769	67	134	988
40	111	786	68	134	990
41	112	801	69	135	991
42	113	816	70	136	992
43	114	830	71	137	994
44	115	841	72	138	995
45	116	857	73	139	995
46	116	866	74	139	996
47	117	881	75	140	996
48	118	889	76	141	997
49	119	891	77	142	997

Score	IQ	Millile	Score	IQ	Millile
78	143	998	87	150	
79	143	998	88	151	
80	144	998	89	152	
81	145	999	90	153	
82	146		91	153	!!!
83	147		92	154	
84	148	!!!	93	155	
85	148		94	156	
86	149				

THE SEREBRIAKOFF ADVANCED (CULTURE FAIR) TEST

This test is recommended for those who do very well on the other tests. By itself, it can be seen as a culture fair test. It tests your understanding of space relationships, pattern and design. It also tests your reasoning power and your ability to grasp underlying principles despite deliberate distraction. These arrays are bi-logical – like a crossword puzzle they make sense in two dimensions, down and across. Some are very difficult.

The Test was standardized against a Mensa sample. The level is quite high. It is not suitable for those below average. There is no time limit.

Instructions

Test
begins
here

Try to work out the plan, or scheme, or order behind the way the central tiles are placed so as to find out which of the surrounding scattered tiles fits reasonably and logically into the space in the array.

Go through the 36 tests. There are eight 'tiles' in the central 3 × 3 array which have an inner bi-logical order. But one tile is missing. You will find it among the other ones which are scattered around. Find the missing tile among the lettered ones and write the letter above the tile against the question number on the answer page. Turn the book sideways so that you can see four puzzles each time you turn a page.

The answer page

Write the letter by the missing tile after each question number.

Question number	Answer letter	Question number	Answer letter
1	. . . . . .	19	. . . . . .
2	. . . . . .	20	. . . . . .
3	. . . . . .	21	. . . . . .
4	. . . . . .	22	. . . . . .
5	. . . . . .	23	. . . . . .
6	. . . . . .	24	. . . . . .
7	. . . . . .	25	. . . . . .
8	. . . . . .	26	. . . . . .
9	. . . . . .	27	. . . . . .
10	. . . . . .	28	. . . . . .
11	. . . . . .	29	. . . . . .
12	. . . . . .	30	. . . . . .
13	. . . . . .	31	. . . . . .
14	. . . . . .	32	. . . . . .
15	. . . . . .	33	. . . . . .
16	. . . . . .	34	. . . . . .
17	. . . . . .	35	. . . . . .
18	. . . . . .	36	. . . . . .

EXAMPLE

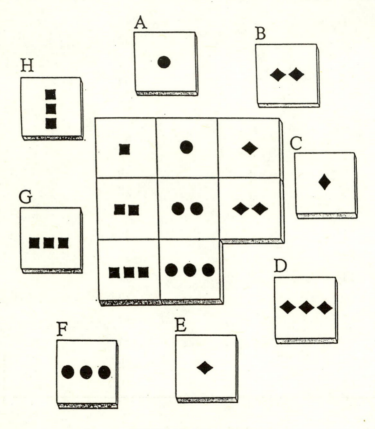

THE MISSING TILE IS D

TEST No. 1

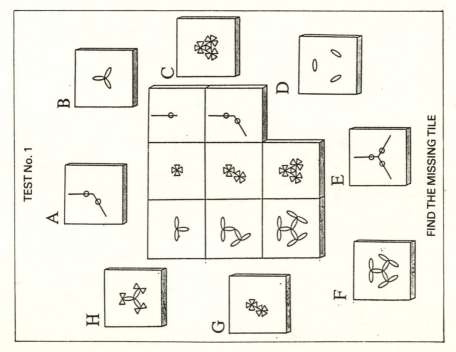

FIND THE MISSING TILE

TEST No. 2

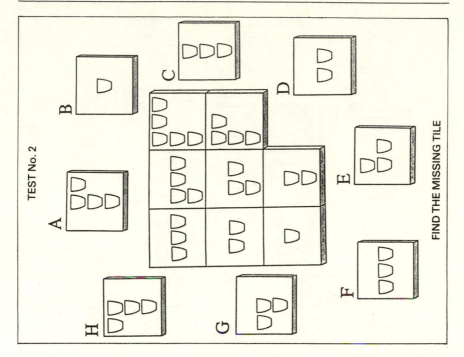

FIND THE MISSING TILE

TEST No. 4

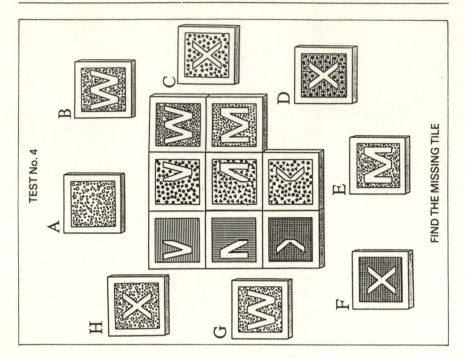

FIND THE MISSING TILE

TEST No. 3

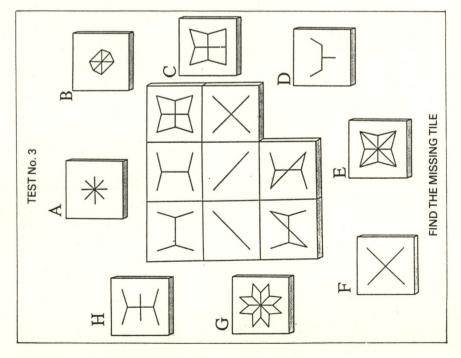

FIND THE MISSING TILE

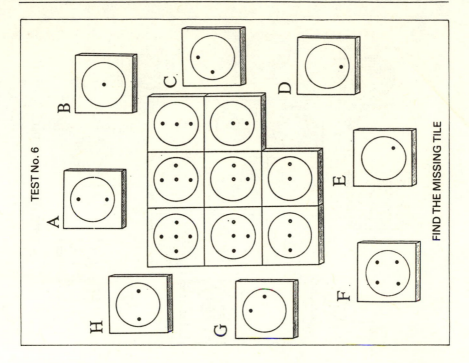

TEST No. 6

FIND THE MISSING TILE

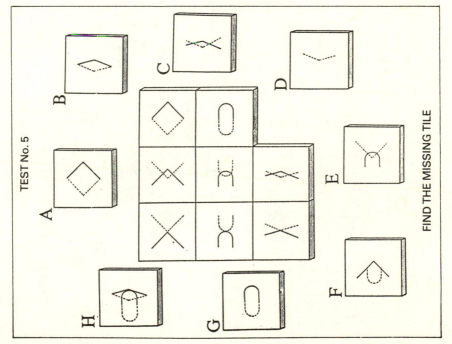

TEST No. 5

FIND THE MISSING TILE

TEST No. 8

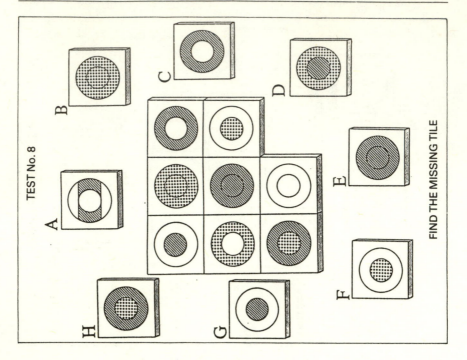

FIND THE MISSING TILE

TEST No. 7

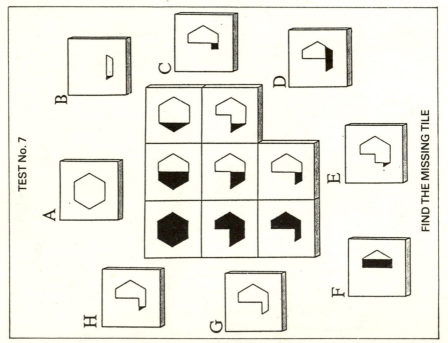

FIND THE MISSING TILE

TEST No. 10

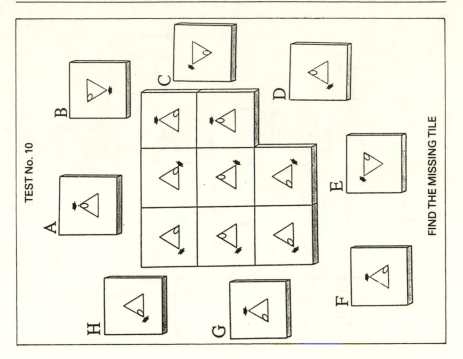

FIND THE MISSING TILE

TEST No. 9

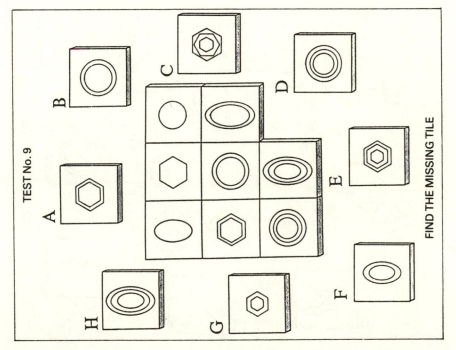

FIND THE MISSING TILE

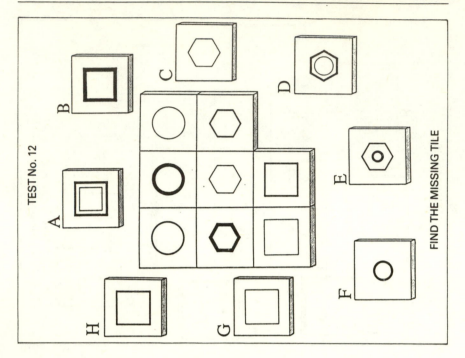

TEST No. 12

FIND THE MISSING TILE

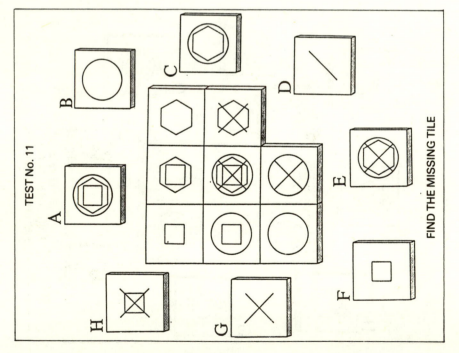

TEST No. 11

FIND THE MISSING TILE

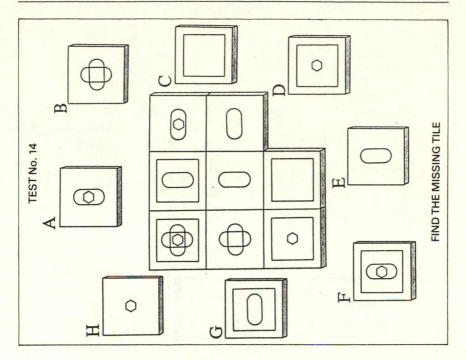

TEST No. 14

FIND THE MISSING TILE

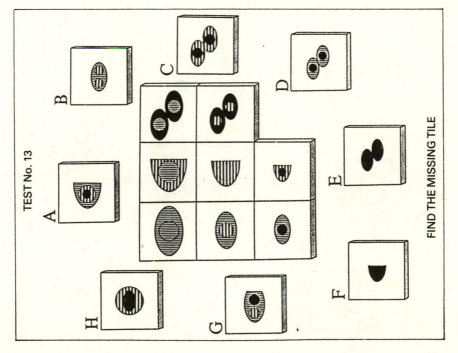

TEST No. 13

FIND THE MISSING TILE

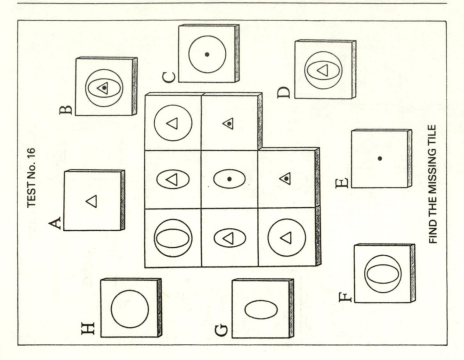

TEST No. 16

FIND THE MISSING TILE

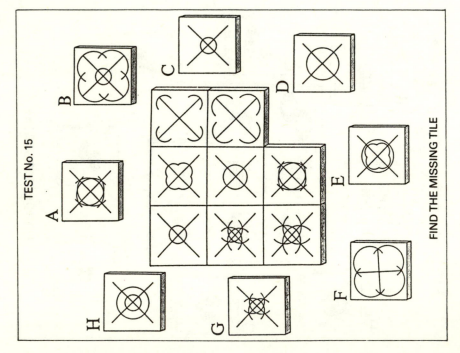

TEST No. 15

FIND THE MISSING TILE

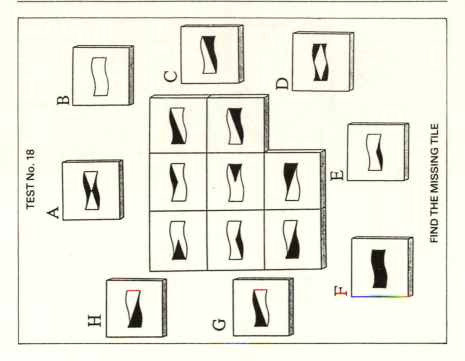

TEST No. 18

FIND THE MISSING TILE

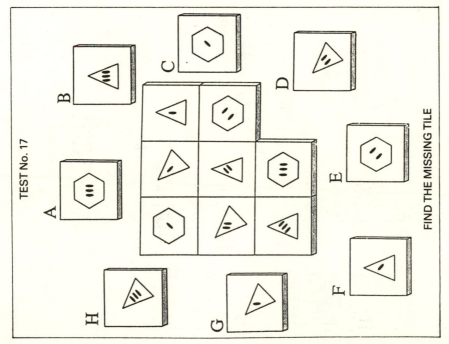

TEST No. 17

FIND THE MISSING TILE

TEST No. 20

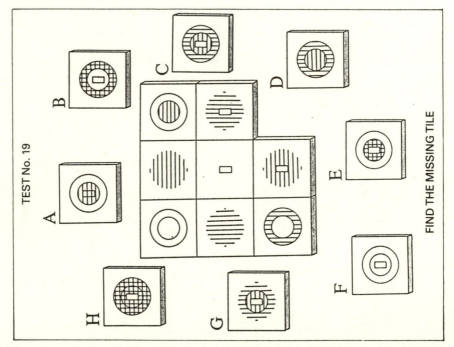

FIND THE MISSING TILE

TEST No. 19

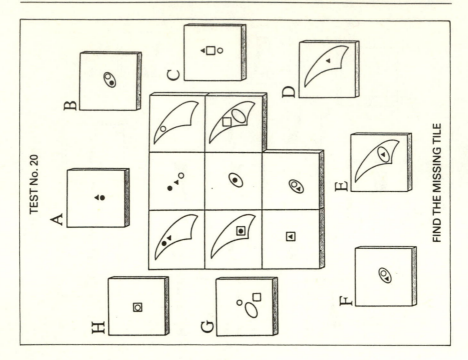

FIND THE MISSING TILE

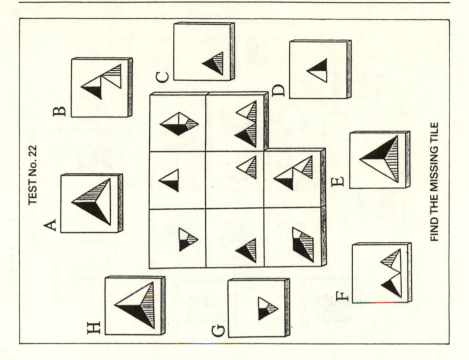

TEST No. 22

FIND THE MISSING TILE

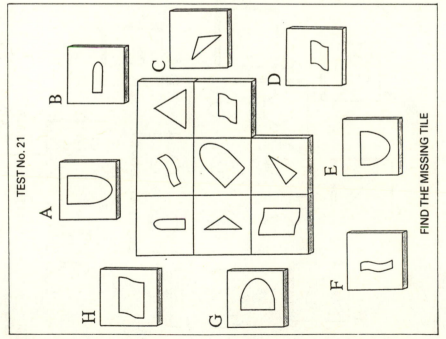

TEST No. 21

FIND THE MISSING TILE

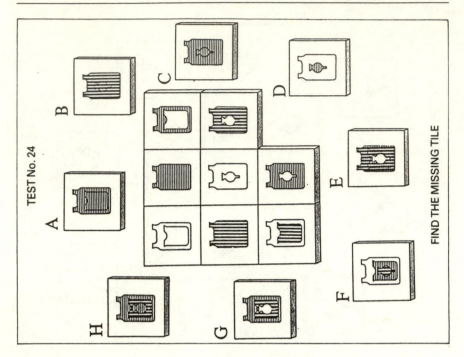

TEST No. 24

FIND THE MISSING TILE

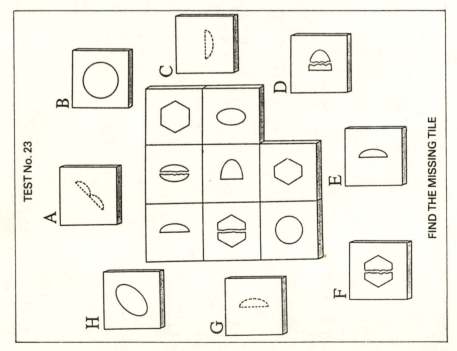

TEST No. 23

FIND THE MISSING TILE

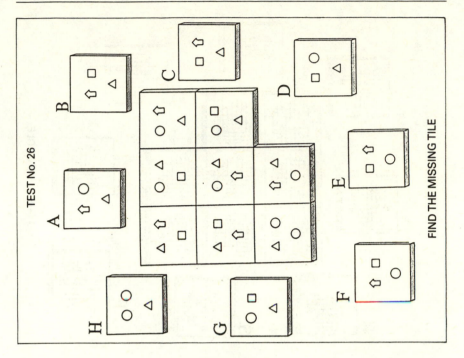

TEST No. 26

FIND THE MISSING TILE

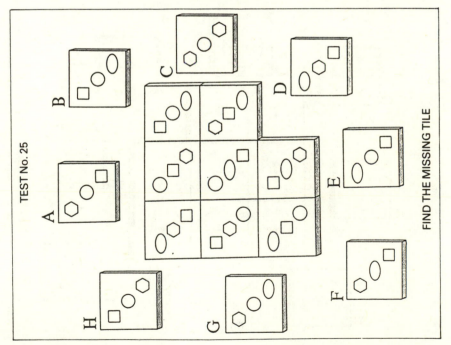

TEST No. 25

FIND THE MISSING TILE

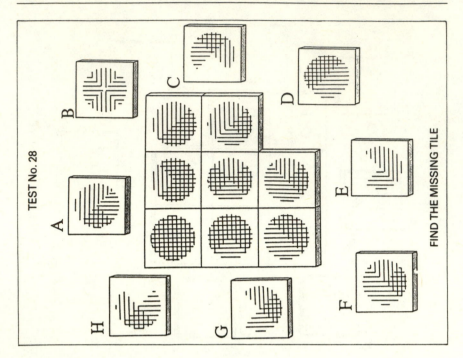

TEST No. 28

FIND THE MISSING TILE

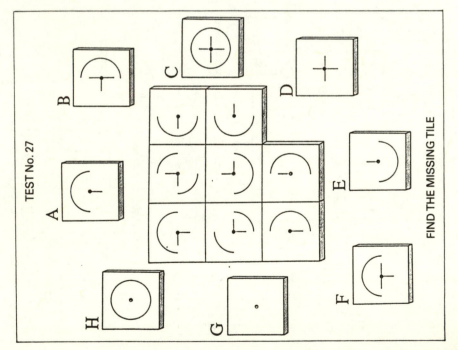

TEST No. 27

FIND THE MISSING TILE

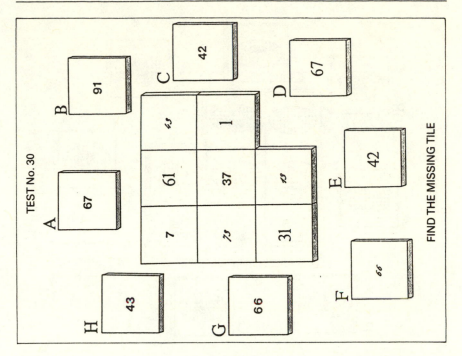

TEST No. 30

FIND THE MISSING TILE

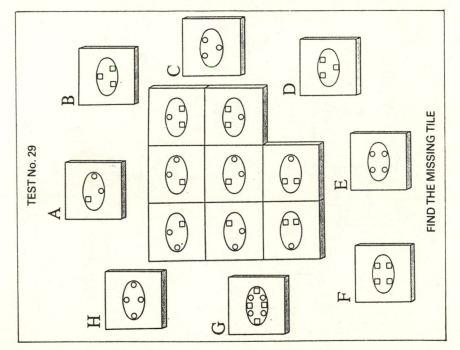

TEST No. 29

FIND THE MISSING TILE

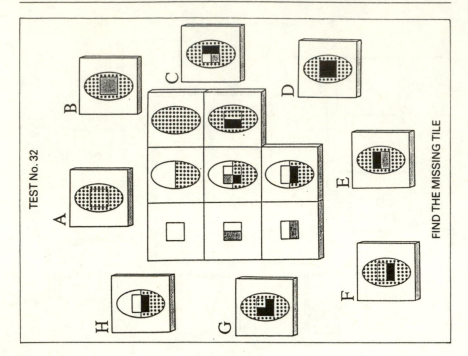

TEST No. 32

FIND THE MISSING TILE

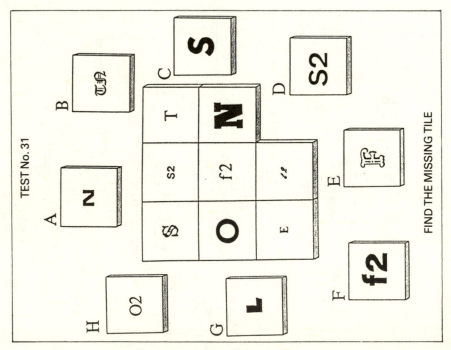

TEST No. 31

FIND THE MISSING TILE

TEST No. 34

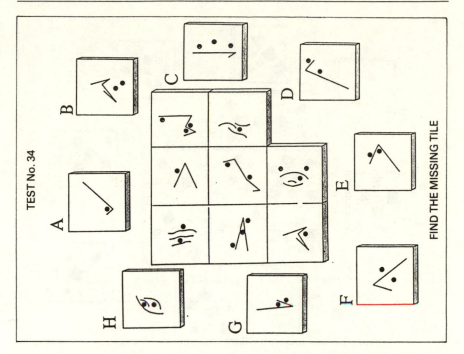

FIND THE MISSING TILE

TEST No. 33

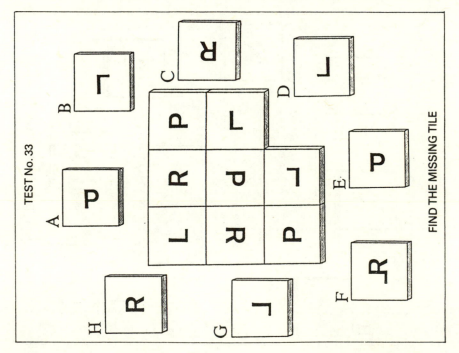

FIND THE MISSING TILE

TEST No. 36

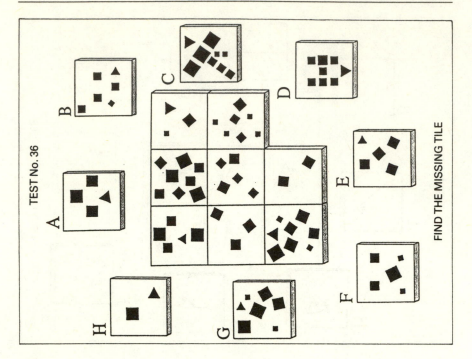

FIND THE MISSING TILE

TEST No. 35

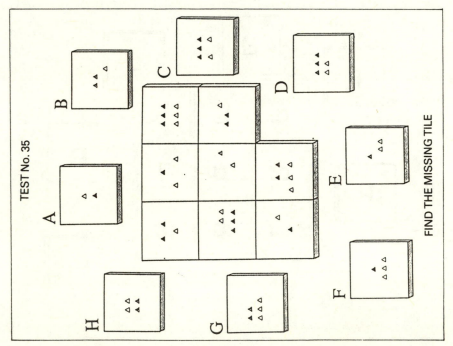

FIND THE MISSING TILE

Answers to the Serebriakoff Advanced Culture Fair Test

The question number is followed by the letter of the correct tile.

(1)	E	(2)	C	(3)	E	(4)	H
(5)	B	(6)	B	(7)	H	(8)	D
(9)	E	(10)	G	(11)	G	(12)	B
(13)	E	(14)	C	(15)	D	(16)	C
(17)	H	(18)	F	(19)	C	(20)	G
(21)	G	(22)	H	(23)	D	(24)	G
(25)	F	(26)	A	(27)	G	(28)	G
(29)	F	(30)	D	(31)	E	(32)	E
(33)	C	(34)	E	(35)	E	(36)	B

Total correct ....

Scoring the Serebriakoff Advanced Culture Fair Test

Adults

Check your answers and tick, then count the number of questions you got right. Be strict. If you made more than one guess you get no mark.

The Table which follows gives an estimate of your IQ rating and your millile rating against your score. Take your millile figure from 1000 and that is the number of people per thousand who may be expected to score better than you did in the test. For example, only five people in a thousand will score better than someone on the 995th millile.

For very high level tests the usual standardization techniques do not apply because there are so few subjects in the samples. This test must be seen as informed guesswork. The millile rating may give an impression of false precision so the results should be taken as a rough guide or ranking of how you stand in relation to the large Mensa group who tried the test.

If you get a millile rating anywhere near 950 you are at the level at which preliminary Mensa candidates are asked to take a supervised test. If you are much above 995 then you scored better than most Mensans.

For very bright children or older ones

Test the child as per instructions. Take the age of the child in months. Divide 180 by this number to make a decimal fraction (e.g. 12 years 2 months = 146 months. 180/146 = 1.233).

Multiply the child's IQ score on the test by this to give the child's adjusted IQ. (e.g. scored IQ 100 × 1.42. Adjusted IQ = 123).

Note: The millile rating for a score gives the number of persons per thousand who do not exceed that score.

Serebriakoff Test score table

Score	IQ	Millile	Score	IQ	Millile
4	97	440	21	130	980 ◄──
5	99	492	22	132	985
6	101	544	23	134	989
7	103	595	24	136	993
8	105	644	25	138	995
9	107	692	26	140	996
10	109	753	27	142	998
11	111	745	28	144	999
12	113	813	29	146	
13	115	846	30	148	
14	117	870	31	150	
15	119	899	32	152	!!
16	121	925	33	154	
17	123	938	34	156	
18	125	952	35	158	
19	126	963	36	160	
20	128	971			Mensa level

Tests for Children

Here are two tests for children. They will show two different approaches. I have mentioned a valid criticism of intelligence tests. The results depend on the cultural affinity between the subject and the group upon which the test was first standardized. The more contrast between the subject's language and culture and that of the standardization group the less valid is the result. However, the more intelligent the child the less this matters.

To answer the fair but unavoidable criticism in multicultural societies, Professor Raymond Cattell and others have developed what are called Culture Free or Culture Fair or non-verbal tests. These use only diagrams and figures because these are common to many language groups and cultures. Words belong to a particular language and to subcultures within language groups. Tests ought to be restandardized for each of these sub-cultures. However, since word-skill or verbal tests are, within a language group, the strongest indicator of intelligence, the wordless Culture Fair tests tend to measure a slightly biased aspect of general intelligence. They suit children who are good at space and number relations rather than those who have word-power.

But remember the two foolish and damaging mistakes people make about this. The first mistake is made by those who ignore these linguo-cultural effects, and the second mistake is made by those who say that because of them tests are 'meaningless'. Within the many very large homogeneous groups they are very useful indeed.

I give two tests here, one of each type. The results will be different and will indicate whether the child has a word-skill or a maths/engineering bias.

THE LANGER NON-VERBAL TEST

First we have the test devised by my collaborator Dr Steven Langer, a qualified psychologist who standardized the tests on Chicago schoolchildren. This is the Langer Culture Fair Intelligence Test For Children.

The place where you test your child should be quiet, well lighted, and well ventilated. Just you and your child should be in the room; there should be no interference from or comments by other children.

Your child should have a pencil and paper in case he or she wishes to calculate anything before giving you an answer. You also should have a pencil. When your child makes its final decision as to the answer it wishes to give and indicates that answer to you, circle the picture or number your child has chosen.

The total uninterrupted time you should allow to administer this test should be between 20 and 50 minutes, including the time it takes for you to give directions to your child. However, remember this is not a timed test, so it is

only a suggested time period, not a rigid limit; take additional time if necessary. It is important that you do *not* rush your child or make him or her anxious about time limitation, especially if he or she needs encouragement to finish the questions.

It is essential that the child understand the directions before beginning the questions. A certain amount of flexibility in giving directions is permissible. You will know best how to be sure your child understands the directions without clues to the answers. The directions may be repeated as often as necessary, with *minor* variations each time. Use your judgement to decide when your child understands what is required and is ready to begin.

If your child has not yet reached the age of 10 years 6 months, have him or her answer *only* questions 1 – 43.

If your child is at least 10 years 6 months old, but under 14 years 6 months old have him or her answer questions 11 – 53.

If your child is 14 years 6 months old or older, have him or her answer *only* questions 16 – 55.

Some children do not take tests well and become easily discouraged and distracted. Therefore, if necessary, you should encourage your child to attempt to answer each question. Do not, however, pressure the child by belabouring any one question too long. If the child feels that a question is too hard for him or her to answer, pass it by temporarily until the child has attempted to answer all the questions for his or her age. Then return to any questions the child has not answered as yet. If the child cannot answer all the questions for his or her age, encourage your child to guess.

First, you should explain to the child that this is an interesting quiz, like a game, but that your child should try hard to see how well he or she can do. It is important to eliminate any sense of anxiety. You may need to take some time to build up interest and ensure positive motivation. Be very patient and very encouraging. Be careful not to give the slightest clue to the answer by expression, word, or sound. Do not answer questions aimed at getting your opinion or give answers that would influence your child's decision in choosing an answer. Just repeat the question. The child is allowed only one choice among the answers given for each question. Reassure the child by saying that he or she may take any amount of time necessary; the child should have confidence in his or her answer.

Your child will undoubtedly give a number of wrong answers. Accept them without comment. Do *not* ask the child any questions such as, 'Are you sure that's the right answer?' However, if the child *volunteers* that he or she thinks an answer may be wrong, encourage him or her to think about it a moment longer and then decide whether he or she feels it's right or wrong. Thereafter, accept the child's decision as to what the correct answer is, and mark the test accordingly.

The test

When you are sure the child is ready to begin, start the test by reading aloud the test instructions.

After the child decides, circle the picture or letter he or she indicates as the answer he or she has chosen.

"In each of the following questions, there will be five pictures or drawings. *Four* of the pictures or drawings *go together in some way* or are the same in some way. *One* of the pictures or drawings *does not go with the other four* -- it is different in some way."

● "*Which one* of the five drawings in Question 1 *does not go with the other four?*"

(1)

When your child has answered Question 1, ask:

● "Which *one* of the five drawings in Question 2 does *not* go with the other four?"

(2)

Now say:

● "Which one of *these* does *not* go with the other four?"

(3)

Then say:

● "And which of *these?*"
    before each question through Question 15.

(4)

(5)

(6)

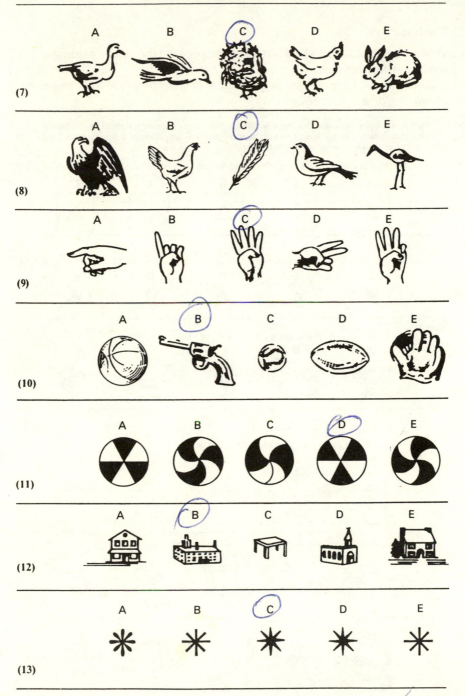

A   B   C   D   E

(14)

A   B   C   D   E

(15)

Before Question 16, say:

● "Here is a picture of some blocks. How many blocks are there in this picture?"

	A	B	C	D	E
(16)	1	2	3	4	5

Before Question 17, say:

● "Here is another picture of some blocks. In this picture, there are two layers of blocks. How many blocks are there in this picture? Remember that the blocks in the top layer have to have a block under each of them."

	A	B	C	D	E
(17)	6	8	9	10	11

Before Question 18, say:

● "In this question, there are five numbers. The numbers are all getting larger. *Four* of them *get larger* according to some *rule* or *plan* or *pattern*. However, there is one *extra* number that does *not* fit the rule. Which *one* does not fit the rule?"

	A	B	C	D	E
(18)	2	4	6	8	9

Before Question 19, say:

● "This question is like the last question. However, here the numbers are becoming *smaller* according to some *rule* or *plan* or *pattern*. Which *one* extra number does *not* fit the rule?"

	A	B	C	D	E
(19)	14	12	11	10	8

Before Question 20 and up to and including Question 24, it is not necessary to repeat the complete instructions. Just say:

● "And how about these numbers?"

	A	B	C	D	E
(20)	10	12	15	20	25
(21)	27	23	19	15	12
(22)	15	30	45	60	65
(23)	12	9	6	4	3
(24)	3	9	27	55	81

Before Question 25, say:

"The following questions are like some that you've already done. In each of the following questions, there will be five pictures or drawings. *Four* of the pictures or drawings go together *in some way* or are the same *in some way*. *One* of the pictures or drawings does *not go* with the other four — it is *different* in some way."

● "Which *one* of the five drawings in Question 25 does *not* go with the other four?"

Before Question 26, up to and including Question 41, say:

● "And how about in this question?"

(30)   A   B   C   D   E

(31)   A   B   C   D   E

(32)   A   B   C   D   E

(33)   A   B   C   D   E

(34)   A   B   C   D   E

(35)   A   B   C   D   E

(36)   A   B   C   D   E

(37)   A   B   C   D   E

(38)   A   B   C   D   E

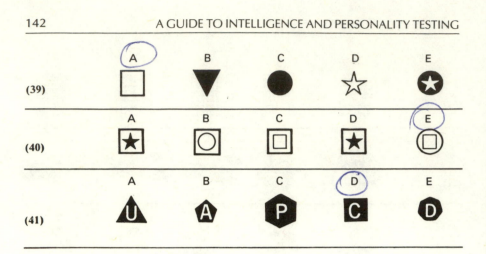

Before Question 42, say:

● "This question is like two that you did before. However, it is harder to answer. How many blocks are there in this picture? Remember that *each* block in *each* layer above the bottom one has to be supported by one or more blocks under it."·

	A	B	C	D	E
(42)	27	28	29	30	31

Before Question 43, say:

● "And how about this one?"

	A	B	C	D	E
(43)	68	69	70	71	73

Before Question 44, say:

● "Question 44 is like some questions that you have answered before. Four of the numbers get larger according to some *rule* or *plan* or *pattern*. However, there is one *extra* number that does *not* fit the rule. Which one does *not* fit the rule?"

	A	B	C	D	E
(44)	3	5	7	11	21

Before Question 45, and up to and including Question 55, say:

● "And how about this one?"

	A	B	C	D	E
(45)	29	22	18	15	8

	A	B	C	D	E
(46)	3	6	10	15	**19**
(47)	4.6	6.9	9.2	18.4	**36.8**
(48)	**8.6**	9.9	10.1	11.2	12.5
(49)	2	**4**	8	12	48
(50)	6,561	**3,321**	81	9	3
(51)	3	6	8	**13**	18
(52)	$2\frac{3}{4}$	$1\frac{3}{4}$	**$1\frac{1}{2}$**	1	$\frac{1}{2}$
(53)	$\frac{1}{2}$	$3\frac{1}{2}$	4	**$7\frac{1}{2}$**	11
(54)	3.00	2.54	**1.73**	1.32	1.15
(55)	$\frac{35}{36}$	$\frac{17}{18}$	**$\frac{33}{36}$**	$\frac{31}{36}$	$\frac{13}{18}$

END OF TEST

Answers and Evaluation (Langer Non-Verbal Test)

Answers to the test

The following is a list of the correct answers to the preceding test.

(1)	D	(20)	B	(39)	E
(2)	C	(21)	E	(40)	C
(3)	D	(22)	E	(41)	A
(4)	B	(23)	D	(42)	C
(5)	B	(24)	D	(43)	B
(6)	D	(25)	C	(44)	E
(7)	E	(26)	C	(45)	C
(8)	C	(27)	B	(46)	E
(9)	A	(28)	C	(47)	B
(10)	B	(29)	A	(48)	C
(11)	C	(30)	B	(49)	C
(12)	C	(31)	B	(50)	B
(13)	A	(32)	A	(51)	B
(14)	C	(33)	D	(52)	C
(15)	D	(34)	D	(53)	B
(16)	C	(35)	E	(54)	B
(17)	B	(36)	B	(55)	C
(18)	E	(37)	A		
(19)	C	(38)	D		

Marking the test

In the preceding list of correct answers, the letter given next to each question number indicates the correct response to that specific question. Using a pen or pencil of a different colour ink or lead than the one you used when marking your child's answers, go through the test and circle the question number for each question your child has answered correctly. Remember, the child is allowed only one final answer to each question. In the event two answers have been marked for any single question, that question must be marked as having been answered incorrectly. After you have circled all the questions the child answered correctly, go back and *count the number of questions you have circled as having been answered correctly in the group of questions designated as the questions to be answered for your child's age level.* The total you get is your child's raw score.

Now turn to the interpretation tables on pp. 146–148. Pick out the correct table for your child's age:

Table 1   If the child is between 6½ years and 10½ years

Table 2   If the child is between 10½ years and 14½ years

Table 3   If the child is over 14½ years

On the appropriate table, locate the row corresponding to your child's age when tested. Using your child's raw score (the number of correct answers), go across the row from left to right, stopping at the number just equal to or nearest below your child's raw score. At the *bottom* of that column, you will see your child's approximate percentile rating on this test, and this rating represents your child's position in relation to the standardization group.

The percentile rating figure represents the percentage of the standardization sample that *scored lower* than your child. For example, the 2 at the bottom of the column means that only 2% of the children would score lower; the 98 at the bottom of the column means that 98% scored lower, or only 2% scored as well or better.

At the *very bottom* of the column that has the number just equal to or nearest below your child's raw score, you will see a number that represents an approximation of the IQ score for your child.

If the percentile achieved is very high, very low, or considerably different from your own estimation of your child's intelligence, you would be well advised to seek professional testing for your child and should not regard these initial test results as definitive.

We hope that you now have a better idea of your child's potential and capacity and that you will use your knowledge for the benefit of your child, your family, and society in general.

Table 1   IQs of children aged 6 years 6 months – 10 years 6 months

Child's age	Raw score (on questions 1 – 43)												
	7	10	11	14	15	16	17	18	19	20	21	24	26
6 years 6 months – 6 years 9 months	7	10	11	14	15	16	17	18	19	20	21	24	26
6 years 9 months – 7 years	9	11	12	15	16	17	18	19	19	20	21	25	26
7 years – 7 years 3 months	10	11	12	16	17	18	19	20	21	22	24	26	27
7 years 3 months – 7 years 6 months	11	12	14	17	18	19	20	21	22	23	26	26	28
7 years 6 months – 7 years 9 months	12	14	16	19	20	21	22	22	23	25	27	28	29
7 years 9 months – 8 years	13	15	17	19	20	21	22	23	24	25	28	29	30
8 years – 8 years 3 months	14	16	18	20	21	22	23	23	24	25	28	30	31
8 years 3 months – 8 years 6 months	14	17	19	20	21	22	23	24	25	26	28	30	32
8 years 6 months – 8 years 9 months	15	18	19	20	22	22	23	24	25	26	28	31	32
8 years 9 months – 9 years	16	18	20	21	22	23	24	25	26	27	29	31	33
9 years – 9 years 3 months	17	18	20	21	22	23	24	25	26	27	29	33	34
9 years 3 months – 9 years 6 months	18	19	20	21	22	23	25	26	27	28	29	33	34
9 years 6 months – 9 years 9 months	18	19	21	22	23	24	25	26	29	30	31	33	34
9 years 9 months – 10 years	19	20	22	23	24	25	26	28	29	31	32	34	35
10 years – 10 years 3 months	19	20	22	23	24	25	27	29	30	32	34	35	36
10 years 3 months – 10 years 6 months	19	21	23	25	26	27	29	31	32	33	35	36	37
Percentile	2	5	10	20	30	40	50	60	70	80	90	95	98
Approximate IQ equivalent	65	73	79	86	91	96	100	104	109	114	121	127	133

Table 2 IQs of children aged 10 years 6 months – 14 years 6 months

Child's age	Raw score (on questions 11 – 53)												
10 years 6 months – 10 years 9 months	8	11	13	17	18	19	20	21	22	23	24	25	27
10 years 9 months – 11 years	9	12	15	17	18	19	21	22	23	25	26	27	28
11 years – 11 years 3 months	10	12	15	17	18	20	21	22	23	25	28	30	31
11 years 3 months – 11 years 6 months	10	13	16	17	19	21	22	23	24	27	28	30	31
11 years 6 months – 11 years 9 months	12	13	16	17	20	21	22	23	25	27	30	31	32
11 years 9 months – 12 years	12	13	17	18	20	21	22	23	25	27	30	31	32
12 years – 12 years 3 months	13	14	17	18	20	21	22	24	25	27	29	31	33
12 years 3 months – 12 years 6 months	13	15	17	18	21	22	23	24	26	28	29	31	33
12 years 6 months – 12 years 9 months	14	15	18	19	21	22	23	24	26	28	29	31	33
12 years 9 months – 13 years	14	15	18	19	21	22	23	25	27	28	29	31	34
13 years – 13 years 3 months	14	16	18	20	21	22	24	25	27	28	29	31	34
13 years 3 months – 13 years 6 months	15	16	19	20	22	23	24	26	27	28	30	31	34
13 years 6 months – 13 years 9 months	15	17	19	21	22	23	24	26	27	28	30	32	35
13 years 9 months – 14 years	16	18	20	21	22	24	25	26	27	29	31	32	35
14 years – 14 years 3 months	17	19	20	21	23	24	25	26	27	29	32	33	35
14 years 3 months – 14 years 6 months	18	19	20	22	23	24	26	27	28	29	32	34	36
Percentile	2	5	10	20	30	40	50	60	70	80	90	95	98
Approximate IQ equivalent	65	73	79	86	91	96	100	104	109	114	121	127	133

Table 3   IQs of children aged 14 years 6 months – 16 years or older

Child's age	Raw score (on questions 16 – 55)												
14 years 6 months – 15 years	11	12	13	14	17	19	20	21	23	24	26	27	29
15 years – 15 years 6 months	12	13	14	15	18	20	21	21	24	25	27	28	29
15 years 6 months – 16 years	12	13	14	16	19	20	22	22	25	26	28	28	29
16 years or older	13	14	14	17	19	21	22	23	25	26	28	29	30
Percentile	2	5	10	20	30	40	50	60	70	80	90	95	98
Approximate IQ equivalent	65	73	79	86	91	96	100	104	109	114	121	127	133

How this test was developed

Over a period of time, an item bank was developed of non-verbal items specifically designed to test the ability of children to recognize similarities and differences, to determine mathematical progressions, and to deal with quantities and spatial relationships.

Subsequently, these items were arranged judgementally by order of difficulty, and a preliminary test was prepared.

Since it was designed to be a power test (testing a person's ability to answer questions regardless of the amount of time spent in the process), and since the time allotted for taking the test had to be limited to the time available during a normal classroom period, the test was administered initially to a small group of first and second graders (6–7 year olds) to determine how many items we could reasonably expect all (or almost all) students in the lower grades to complete within a classroom period.

Thereafter, a subtest was developed that consisted of questions selected in ascending order of assumed difficulty and limited to the maximum number of items that could be completed during one period. This subtest was administered to the first four grades of elementary school (roughly ages 6 – 10). The results were analysed item by item and non-predictive items were either eliminated or revised.

The final group of questions was rearranged by order of difficulty based on the analysis of the results of the subtest. The least difficult items were set aside temporarily, and the next, more difficult group of items was added to the original test. It then became a second, more difficult subtest, which was administered to grades five to eight (roughly ages 10 – 14). The results from the second subtest were analysed as they were for the first subtest. Again, non-predictive items were either eliminated or revised. A third, even more difficult subtest was then created.

To 'test the test', it was administered to a group of high school students who were classified as mentally retarded. In view of this, the lowest level subtest (questions 1 — 43 of the test appearing in this book) was administered. The mean (average) score of this high school group was 23·1, approximately equal to the median for children 8 years – 8 years 9 months of age.

To 'test the test' further, the highest level subtest (questions 16 – 55 of the test) was administered to a group of Mensa members. The mean (average) score of this group was 30·4, equivalent to the 98th percentile of the oldest age group of high school students tested.

The mentally retarded students tested were not included in the normative sample since their scores would tend to make the percentile figures a little bit low. However, since the normative data were obtained in a group testing situation and you are administering the test on a one-to-one basis, this will compensate for what would otherwise be a minor discrepancy.

The same procedure was followed with high school students, using the third subtest. After the results of the third subtest were analysed and refined, a fourth subtest was administered to a group of Mensa members so that those items that discriminated *against* individuals with high IQs could be identified and eliminated.

When the item analysis phase of the study was completed, the first two (overlapping) subtests were administered to all the students in an elementary school (grades one to eight) with over 900 students in a middle class and upper working class area. The third, and most difficult, subtest was administered to three classes in each school grade in each of three different high schools. The classes were selected so that, for each grade in each school, one class represented a high achievement group, one an average achievement group, and one a low achievement group.

The test was developed in Illinois, with the assistance and cooperation of Mr William E. Augustus, superintendent of schools, Thornton Township High School District No. 205; Dr Harold C. Scholle, superintendent of schools, Elmwood Park Community Unit School District No. 401; Mr. John L. Corwin, principal, Elm School; Mr Ronald Habish, principal, Elmwood School; Mr Raymond R. Libner, principal, Elmwood Park High School; Mr Robert L. Littlehale, principal, John Mills School; Dr Robert A. McKanna, principal, Thornridge High School; Dr Robert C. Mitchell, principal, Thornwood High School; Mr John H. Smith, principal, Thornton High School; and their respective staff and students. Without their assistance and cooperation, the development of this test would not have been possible. Our thanks are due and gratefully rendered.

THE RUSSELL ENGLISH LANGUAGE INTELLIGENCE TEST FOR CHILDREN

The second children's test is the Russell English Language Intelligence Test For Children. It is a timed test.

This is a 'parallel' test by another collaborator, Kenneth Russell, a puzzle expert and inventor. The test was constructed by choosing items closely similar to those in an unpublishable but carefully standardized children's test which is now out of use. It will give a first approximation estimate.

This test is suitable for literate and numerate anglophone children between the ages of 7 and 14. It can be administered by supervisors or parents who may read and explain the test but it is intended as a written test where the children read the directions themselves.

These tests for children should be used with care and caution. Children's IQ or percentile ratings tend to remain fairly constant as they grow older but there are exceptions. A very small proportion of children spurt or lag in IQ with time. It is best for each child to take a number of tests at intervals to get a better estimate. A single test is better than none but not too much reliance is to be placed on it. The test measures *general intelligence* only. The child may have special abilities which seem inconsistent with its score. These should be watched for and developed.

If you are supervising the test follow these rules.

(1)   Do it at a time when you will be uninterrupted for an hour. Each child must have a rubber and a pencil sharpened both ends.

(2)   If there is more than one child, photocopy the test form and make sure the children are all identified on the form which they use.

(3)   Tell the children to read the directions carefully and see they do. Then read them aloud slowly.

(4)   For older or forward children you can leave them to go ahead when you give the signal to start.

(5)   With younger or backward ones you may take them through the tests yourself, reading the text and repeating it. But be careful not to 'coach' or give the slightest indication verbally or by your expression. Do not answer any question that can help with the answer and keep a poker face because children are marvellous at reading expressions. If you fail to observe these rules you are engaged in time-wasting self-deception. So be strict.

(6)   Pencils down at the end of time (45 minutes).

Test begins here

The Test

Directions: the child should read this

Read these directions very carefully. Then begin at the beginning and go straight through. The first questions are very easy. Answer with care. They are straightforward – no catches. The later questions get harder. Do not worry. No one can do them all in the time. You have 45 minutes. You must work it out for yourself. No questions! Children must not ask. Supervisors must not answer – or the whole thing is a waste of time.

Do not start the test until you are told or until the timing starts if you are testing yourself.

Start time ....

Finish time ....

(Test supervisor or child marks time and starts test)

Write your answers to these sums. Some of them are ADD, like this 3 + 5 = 8.
Some are TAKE AWAY, like this 4 − 2 = 2.

(1)   6 + 3   = 9   (10)   17 − 4   = 13

(2)   8 − 5   = 3   (11)   18 − 9   = 9

(3)   6 − 2   = 4   (12)   29 + 16 = 45

(4)   9 − 3   = 6   (13)   28 − 17 = 11

(5)   6 + 21 = 27   (14)   27 − 16 = 11

(6)   6 − 3   = 3   (15)   25 − 23 = 2

(7)   11 − 4 = 7   (16)   27 − 12 = 15

(8)   25 + 8 = 33   (17)   23 − 11 = 12

(9)   14 − 6 = 8

Here are some sentences. There is a word left out where the dots . . . .
are.

Some of these words are the ones that were missed out. See if you can see
which words were missed in each sentence. Write it in over the dots.

Example:

Words: TO, COT

Sentence: I like . . TO . sing.

Answer: I like . . TO . sing.

Sentence: A baby sleeps in a . . . . . .

Answer: A baby sleeps in a . COT . .

The answers are here. Choose the right ones.

WASH,	AND,	BIG,	ARE,	SAIL,	TO,
HAPPY,	FRUIT,	TWO,	THAN,	IS,	MAKES,
DIN,	LOVE				

(18)   Red . . . . . blue are colours.

(19)   Most days I go . . . . . school.

(20)   Men build ships to . . . . . in.

(21)   Giants are bigger . . . . . dwarfs.

(22)   An apple is a kind of . . . . . .

(23)   We have chairs to . . . . . on.

(24)   A butterfly has . . . . . wings.

(25)   Ice . . . . . cold.

(26)   Cows and sheep . . . . . farm animals.

(27)   Rain . . . . . the grass greener.

(28)   We use soap to . . . . . with.

You have to answer these questions. The answers are hidden in the word list below. Write the right answer in over the dots.

Example:

Answers (1) FORK, (2) HAT, (3) KNIFE.

Questions: What do you cut your food with? . .KNIFE . .

Answers

AIRPORT,   TREE,   SHEARS,   THERMOMETER,   HAT,
KEY,   LACES,   DAMSON,   TRICYCLE,   STRING,   JOKE,
BLACKSMITH,   KITCHEN,   COAL-MINE,   FRUIT,   CHAIR,
COMPASSES,   ESCALATOR.

Here are the questions:

(29)   What do we use to draw a circle? . . . .

(30)   What are used to tie football boots? . . . .

(31)   Where do we go to catch an aeroplane? . . . .

(32)   What do we call a three-wheeled bike? . . . .

(33)   Who makes shoes for horses? . . . .

(34)   What are used to cut the wool from sheep? . . . .

(35)   What do we tie around a parcel? . . . .

(36)   What do we call the room where meals are cooked? . . . .

(37)   What instrument measures the temperature of a room? . . . .

(38)   Where does coal come from? . . . .

(39)   What do we use to unlock a door? . . . .

(40)   What do we call apples, lemons and peaches? . . . .

(41)   What is a moving staircase called? . . . .

Look carefully at these words:

bean, <u>make</u>, tool, <u>bake</u>, <u>take</u>, tall.

Make, bake, take, all end in the same sound so they are underlined.

Underline three words in each of the following sets which sound the same.

(42)   fit, tie, sit, seat, hit

(43)   book, bash, mash, hush, dash

(44)   head, hand, red, bread, hear

(45)   leak, mean, seek, beak, lean

(46)   book, round, look, took, bowl

(47)   clay, day, why, pray, clown

(48)   rule, fool, fowl, stool, roll

(49)   sigh, fig, dye, lie, mine

The alphabet is like this:

A B C D E F G H I J K L M N O P Q R S T U V W X Y Z

Try to answer these questions: Write the answer on the dotted line.

(50)   What letter comes midway between H and P?   . . . .

(51)   What letter comes next but one after S?   . . . .

(52)   What letter comes next but one before Z?   . . . .

(53)   What letter comes before the letter which comes before M?   . . . .

(54)   What letter comes after the letter which comes after H?   . . . .

(55)   What letter is the 7th letter after the one which comes
       midway between E and S?   . . . .

(56)　What letter comes just after the 7th letter after H?　　　　　........

(57)　Suppose the 1st and 3rd letters of the alphabet were
　　　interchanged, also the 2nd and 4th, then the 5th and 7th,
　　　then the 6th and 8th and so on, what letter would come 16th?　........

(58)　If the 3rd letter of the alphabet were crossed out, then the
　　　6th, 9th, 12th, etc. which would be the 5th not crossed out?　........

(59)　If the letters were crossed out as in the last question,
　　　what would be the last two letters?　　　　　........

　　Look carefully at these words:

dark, full, <u>big</u>, <u>small</u>, road, <u>large</u>

Big and large mean the same and small is the opposite. In the following sets of words underline the two words which mean the same and also underline the word which means the opposite (you underline three words in each set).

(60)　dull, polish, gloomy, peer, bright, wind

(61)　happy, sad, down, pleased, shape, show

(62)　fast, feast, loom, slow, quick, look

(63)　loud, soft, touch, noisy, hard, tease

(64)　loser, eager, victor, keen, winner, take

(65)　tired, sleep, energetic, weary, feed, gone

(66)　open, door, wand, closed, shut, full

(67)　obese, thin, tiny, fat, tall, fen

(68)　still, left, motionless, moving, wound

(69)　pull, push, swing, take, tug, slice

(70)　stop, try, level, halt, start, stare

　　In these lines of numbers there is a rule which tells which number comes next. See if you can see the rule and then write in the next two numbers each time.

Example:　1, 2, 3, 4, (　), (　)

Answer:　1, 2, 3, 4, (5), (6)

Example:　3, 6, 9, 12, (15), (18)

Now try with these:

(71)   1, 7, 2, 7, 3, (7 4 7), (5 7 6 7)

(72)   128, 64, 32, 16, 8, (   ), (   )

(73)   7, 4, 9, 16, 11, (   ), (   )

(74)   26, 13, 14, 7, (   ), (   )

(75)   4, 5, 7, 8, 10, (   ), (   )

(76)   1, 3, 7, 13, 21, (   ), (   )

(77)   2, 3, 30, 31, 310, (   ), (   )

(78)   48, 24, 12, 6, 3, (   ), (   )

(79)   2, 4, 6, 5, 7, (   ), (   )

Look at these words:

coal, black (dew, grass, twig, green, forest)

Coal is black and grass is green so 'grass' and 'green' are underlined.

Next, look at these words:

hand, glove (finger, face, foot, neck, arm, sock)

A glove is worn on the hand and a sock on the foot, so 'foot' and 'sock' are underlined.

Now you underline the right two words in each of the following lines:

(80)   roof, house (hat, arm, show, head, finger)

(81)   time, clock (room, radio, garden, baby, music)

(82)   fur, mink (lion, wool, silk, sheep, gun)

(83)   old, antique (gold, water, sand, precious, bad)

(84)   give, receive (fetch, purchase, sell, carry, clean)

(85)   dwarf, giant (estuary, stream, boat, river, land)

(86)   gaggle, geese (owls, tigers, band, flock, sheep)

A man selling potatoes and carrots offers his potatoes at 10p a pound and his carrots at 15p a pound. I buy an exact number of pounds of vegetables and I pay with the coins receiving no change.

ANSWER
HERE

Now answer these questions:

(87)   What is the greatest weight of vegetables that I can buy with 50p?........

(88)   What is the greatest weight that I can buy with 10p?   ....

(89)   How much money will I need to buy two pounds of potatoes and two pounds of carrots?   ....

(90)   What is the greatest number of pounds of potatoes that I can buy with two coins only?   ....

(91)   If I can use one coin only must I buy potatoes or carrots?   ....

Now try these:

Jane is five years old.
Kay is nine years old.

(92)   How many years ago was Kay twice as old as Jane?   ....

(93)   In how many years will Jane be two-thirds the age of Kay?   ....

(94)   How old was Kay when she was three times Joan's age?   ....

(95)   How old will Jane be when Kay is three times Jane's present age? ....

A number of cubes each with an edge of one inch are stuck together to form a solid cube of edge 3 inches. Then this large cube is painted red on the top, and green on the bottom and four sides.

(96)   How many cubes are not painted at all?   ....

(97)   How many cubes have red paint on them?   ....

(98)   How many have green paint on them?   ....

(99)   How many have both red and green on them?   ....

(100) How many cubes are half coloured?   ....

This is a cube:

---

swers
egin
here

Answers and Evaluation (The Russell English Language Intelligence Test)

Here are the answers to the questions. Each item is either quite right or wrong. One mark for a correct answer. No penalties for errors. No half marks. In questions 12 – 18 spelling errors do not count as long as you are sure the intentions are correct. Ignore anything not an answer written by the child. If there are alternative answers to a question it counts as an error.

(1)	9		(36)	KITCHEN
(2)	3		(37)	THERMOMETER
(3)	4		(38)	COAL-MINE
(4)	6		(39)	KEY
(5)	27		(40)	FRUIT
(6)	3		(41)	ESCALATOR
(7)	7		(42)	FIT, SIT, HIT
(8)	33		(43)	BASH, MASH, DASH
(9)	8		(44)	HEAD, RED, BREAD
(10)	13		(45)	LEAK, SEEK, BEAK
(11)	9		(46)	BOOK, LOOK, TOOK
(12)	45		(47)	CLAY, DAY, PRAY
(13)	11		(48)	RULE, FOOL, STOOL
(14)	11		(49)	SIGH, DYE, LIE
(15)	2		(50)	L
(16)	15		(51)	U
(17)	12		(52)	X
(18)	AND		(53)	K
(19)	TO		(54)	J
(20)	SAIL		(55)	S
(21)	THAN		(56)	P
(22)	FRUIT		(57)	N
(23)	SIT		(58)	G
(24)	TWO		(59)	Y, Z
(25)	IS		(60)	DULL, GLOOMY, BRIGHT
(26)	ARE		(61)	HAPPY, SAD, PLEASED
(27)	MAKES		(62)	FAST, SLOW, QUICK
(28)	WASH		(63)	LOUD, SOFT, NOISY
(29)	COMPASSES		(64)	LOSER, VICTOR, WINNER
(30)	LACES		(65)	TIRED, ENERGETIC, WEARY
(31)	AIRPORT		(66)	OPEN, CLOSED, SHUT
(32)	TRICYCLE		(67)	OBESE, THIN, FAT
(33)	BLACKSMITH		(68)	STILL, MOTIONLESS, MOVING
(34)	SHEARS		(69)	PULL, PUSH, TUG
(35)	STRING			

(70)   STOP, HALT, START
(71)   (7), (4)
(72)   (4), (2)
(73)   (64), (13)
(74)   (8), (4)
(75)   (11), (13)
(76)   (31), (43)
(77)   (311), (3110)
(78)   (1½), (¾)
(79)   (9), (8)
(80)   HAT, HEAD
(81)   MUSIC, RADIO
(82)   WOOL, SHEEP
(83)   GOLD, PRECIOUS
(84)   PURCHASE, SELL
(85)   STREAM, RIVER

(86)   FLOCK, SHEEP
(87)   FIVE POUNDS
(88)   ONE POUND
(89)   50p
(90)   20
(91)   POTATOES
(92)   ONE YEAR
(93)   THREE YEARS
(94)   SIX
(95)   ELEVEN
(96)   1
(97)   9
(98)   45
(99)   12
(100) 8

The Russell Test score tables

Look under the heading of the child's age (take whichever age is closest). Then read IQ against score.

M = Mensa level.

	Age 7 years			Age 7½ years	
Score	IQ	Percentile	Score	IQ	Percentile
7	79	10	7	78	9
9	83	13	9	82	12
11	87	20	11	86	18
13	91	27	13	90	25
15	95	37	15	93	32
17	99	47	17	97	42
19	103	58	19	101	52
21	107	68	21	104	60
23	111	77	23	108	70
25	115	84	25	112	79
27	119	90	27	116	86
29	123	94	29	119	90
31	127	96	31	123	94
33	131	98M	33	127	96
35	135	⎫	35	130	98M
37	139	⎪	37	134	⎫
39	143	⎪	39	138	⎪
41	147	⎬ 99	41	141	⎪
43	151	⎪	43	145	⎪
45	155	⎪	45	149	⎬ 99
47	159	⎪	47	153	⎪
49	163	⎪	49	156	⎪
51	167	⎭	51	160	⎪
			53	164	⎪
			55	167	⎭

Age 8 years			**Age 8½ years**		
Score	IQ	Percentile	Score	IQ	Percentile
7	78	9	9	80	9
9	81	10	11	83	13
11	85	16	13	87	20
13	88	21	15	90	25
15	92	30	17	93	32
17	95	37	19	97	42
19	98	45	21	100	50
21	102	55	23	103	58
23	105	63	25	106	66
25	109	73	27	110	76
27	112	79	29	113	81
29	116	86	31	116	86
31	119	90	33	119	90
33	123	94	35	123	94
35	126	96	37	126	96
37	130	98M	39	129	97
39	133		41	132	M
41	137		43	136	
43	140		45	139	
45	144		47	142	
47	147		49	146	
49	151	} 99	51	149	
51	154		53	152	} 99
53	158		55	155	
55	161		57	159	
57	164		59	162	
59	168		61	165	
			63	168	

Age 9 years			Age 9½ years		
Score	IQ	Percentile	Score	IQ	Percentile
9	79	9	9	79	9
11	82	12	11	82	12
13	86	18	13	85	16
15	89	23	15	87	20
17	92	30	17	90	25
19	95	37	19	93	32
21	98	45	21	96	40
23	101	52	23	99	47
25	104	60	25	102	57
27	107	68	27	105	63
29	110	76	29	108	70
31	113	81	31	111	77
33	116	86	33	114	82
35	120	91	35	117	87
37	123	93	37	120	91
39	126	96	39	123	94
41	129	97	41	125	95
43	132	M	43	128	97
45	135		45	131	M
47	138		47	134	
49	141		49	137	
51	144		51	140	
53	147		53	143	
55	150	99	55	146	99
57	153		57	149	
59	157		59	152	
61	160		61	155	
63	163		63	158	
65	166		65	161	
67	169		67	163	
			69	166	
			71	169	

Age 10 years			Age 10½ years		
Score	IQ	Percentile	Score	IQ	Percentile
11	81	10	11	80	9
13	84	14	13	83	13
15	86	18	15	85	16
17	89	23	17	88	21
19	92	30	19	91	27
21	95	37	21	93	32
23	97	42	23	96	40
25	100	50	25	99	47
27	103	58	27	101	52
29	106	66	29	104	60
31	109	73	31	107	68
33	111	77	33	109	73
35	114	82	35	112	79
37	117	87	37	114	82
39	120	91	39	117	87
41	122	93	41	120	91
43	125	94	43	122	93
45	128	97	45	125	95
47	131	98M	47	128	97
49	134	⎫	49	130	98M
51	136	⎪	51	133	⎫
53	139	⎪	53	136	⎪
55	142	⎪	55	138	⎪
57	145	⎪	57	141	⎪
59	147	⎪	59	144	⎪
61	150	⎬ 99	61	146	⎪
63	153	⎪	63	149	⎪
65	156	⎪	65	151	⎬ 99
67	159	⎪	67	154	⎪
69	161	⎪	69	157	⎪
71	164	⎪	71	159	⎪
73	167	⎭	73	162	⎪
			75	165	⎪
			77	167	⎭

Age 11 years			Age 11½ years		
Score	IQ	Percentile	Score	IQ	Percentile
11	79	9	11	79	9
13	82	12	13	81	10
15	84	14	15	84	14
17	87	20	17	86	18
19	89	23	19	88	21
21	92	30	21	91	27
23	95	37	23	93	30
25	97	42	25	96	40
27	100	50	27	98	45
29	102	55	29	101	52
31	105	63	31	103	58
33	107	68	33	105	63
35	110	76	35	108	70
37	112	79	37	110	76
39	115	84	39	113	81
41	117	87	41	115	84
43	120	91	43	117	87
45	122	93	45	120	91
47	125	95	47	122	93
49	127	96	49	125	95
51	130	98M	51	127	96
53	132	⎱	53	130	98M
55	135		55	132	⎱
57	137		57	134	
59	140		59	137	
61	143		61	139	
63	145	99	63	142	
65	148		65	144	
67	150	⎰	67	146	99
69	153		69	149	
71	155		71	151	⎰
73	158		73	154	
75	160		75	156	
77	163		77	158	
79	165		79	161	
81	168	⎭	81	163	
			83	166	
			85	168	⎭

Age 12 years			Age 12½ years		
Score	IQ	Percentile	Score	IQ	Percentile
13	81	10	13	80	9
15	83	13	15	82	12
17	85	16	17	84	14
19	87	20	19	87	20
21	90	25	21	89	23
23	92	30	23	91	27
25	94	34	25	93	32
27	97	42	27	96	40
29	99	47	29	98	46
31	101	52	31	100	50
33	104	60	33	102	55
35	106	66	35	104	58
37	108	70	37	107	68
39	111	77	39	109	73
41	113	81	41	111	77
43	115	84	43	113	81
45	118	88	45	116	86
47	120	91	47	118	88
49	122	93	49	120	91
51	125	95	51	122	93
53	127	96	53	124	94
55	129	97	55	127	96
57	131	98M	57	129	97
59	134	⎫	59	131	98M
61	136		61	133	⎫
63	138		63	136	
65	141		65	138	
67	143		67	140	
69	145		69	142	
71	148		71	144	
73	150	99	73	147	
75	152		75	149	
77	155		77	151	99
79	157		79	153	
81	159		81	156	
83	162		83	158	
85	164		85	160	
87	166		87	162	
89	169	⎭	89	164	
			91	167	
			93	169	⎭

Age 13 years			**Age 13½ years**		
Score	IQ	Percentile	Score	IQ	Percentile
15	82	12	15	81	10
17	84	14	17	83	13
19	86	18	19	85	16
21	88	21	21	87	20
23	90	25	23	89	23
25	92	30	25	91	27
27	94	34	27	93	32
29	96	40	29	95	37
31	99	47	31	97	42
33	101	52	33	99	47
35	103	58	35	102	55
37	105	63	37	104	60
39	107	68	39	106	66
41	109	73	41	108	70
43	111	77	43	110	73
45	114	82	45	112	79
47	116	86	47	114	81
49	118	88	49	116	86
51	120	91	51	118	88
53	122	93	53	120	91
55	124	94	55	122	93
57	126	96	57	124	94
59	129	97	59	126	96
61	131	98M	61	128	97
63	133	⎫	63	130	98M
65	135		65	132	⎫
67	137		67	134	
69	139		69	136	
71	141		71	139	
73	143		73	141	
75	146		75	143	
77	148		77	145	
79	150	⎬ 99	79	147	⎬ 99
81	152		81	149	
83	154		83	151	
85	156		85	153	
87	158		87	155	
89	161		89	157	
91	163		91	159	
93	165		93	161	
95	167	⎭	95	163	⎭

| | Age 14 years | |
Score	IQ	Percentile
15	80	9
17	82	12
19	84	14
21	86	18
23	88	21
25	90	25
27	92	30
29	94	34
31	96	40
33	98	45
35	100	50
37	102	55
39	104	60
41	106	66
43	108	70
45	110	76
47	112	79
49	114	82
51	116	86
53	118	88
55	120	91
57	122	93
59	124	94
61	126	96
63	128	97
65	130	98M
67	132	
69	134	
71	136	
73	138	
75	140	
77	142	
79	144	
81	146	99
83	148	
85	150	
87	152	
89	154	
91	156	
93	158	
95	160	

5

The Personality Tests

Here is another type of test. It has nothing to do with intelligence. There are no right or wrong answers to the questions.

Do the tests first and read about them afterwards, otherwise your answers may be affected by what you read.

I shall call this first test Personality Factor No. 1. Try to answer quickly and spontaneously without giving the matter too much thought. It is your emotional reaction that is being checked, not your thought processes; so do not bother with doubts or possible illogicalities. Answer impulsively and quickly and pass on.

PERSONALITY FACTOR 1

Circle your answer as A or B:

(1) Would you prefer to be a research scientist (A) or a Member of Parliament (B)?   A or B

(2) Do you feel that many recognized professions or occupations which are accepted as honest do more harm to the country (A) than good (B)?   A or B

(3) Which is more important in a literary critic, to be tolerant and encouraging (A) or carefully discriminating (B)?   A or B

(4) If you had the choice of working as a receptionist (B) or at interesting work in an office of your own (A) which would you choose?   A or B

(5) Should a doctor put his feelings aside in deciding about the treatment of his patients (A), or should his feelings be one of his main guides (B)?   A or B

169

(6) Do you find it easy (B) or hard (A) to modify or adapt your behaviour and everyday relationships according to the company you meet?   A or B

(7) On vacation would you prefer to spend most of your time reading and on solitary walks (A) or would you prefer to spend most of your time meeting people (B)?   A or B

(8) Would you endure being a hermit easily (A) or with difficulty (B)?   A or B

(9) Would you prefer to marry a person who was (A) a thoughtful companion or (B) very sociable?   A or B

(10) Are most people probably (B) or doubtfully (A) worthy of real trust?   A or B

(11) Do you like (A) or dislike (B) organizing parties in general?   A or B

(12) Would you prefer being a travelling salesman (B) or a book-keeper in an office (A)?   A or B

(13) Would you describe yourself as usually looking on the bright side of life (B) or being more cautious (A)?   A or B

(14) Would you prefer to be a high civil servant (A) or a member of the government (B)?   A or B

(15) Do you usually enjoy (B) or not enjoy (A) big noisy parties?   A or B

(16) Would you find it difficult (A) or easy (B) to make a public speech?   A or B

(17) In a dramatic production where would you be happier, working backstage (A) or as a leading actor (B)?   A or B

(18) Are you very ready (B) or more reserved (A) at making a suitable reply in most general conversations?   A or B

(19) Are you usually quick (B) or slow (A) at making new friends in a new situation?   A or B

(20) Would you describe yourself, in most of your activities, as being full of energy (B) or lacking in energy (A)?   A or B

Now count your As and Bs. Write down your score. We will refer to them at the end of this section on p. 186.

Total score: A . . . . ,   B . . . .

Now go on to the next test. Do not look at the key yet.

PERSONALITY FACTOR 2

Again, you are asked to do the test first and check the result afterwards. Peek if you want – but if you do, don't bother to check your result as it may be meaningless. Once again you should be in a decisive and uncontemplative frame of mind and go through the questions quickly and firmly, deciding how you feel about things rather than going into the logic or hesitating between one decision and another. The test should be completed in about 10 minutes, but it is of no great significance if you take more or less time.

Test begins here

(1) As far as you know have you ever (A) or never (B) walked in your sleep?   A or B

(2) Have you (A) or have you not (B) been away from work because of illness for a longer time than most people?   A or B

(3) Do you (A) or do you not (B) have a tendency to feel confused if you are interrupted when working?   A or B

(4) Are you (A) or are you not (B) fond of some hard exercise every day?   A or B

(5) Remember the last time you began to learn a new skill: did you (B) or did you not (A) feel confident?   A or B

(6) Have you (A) or have you not (B) felt strongly about everyday trivial irritations?   A or B

(7) Have you ever (A) or have you never (B) worried for hours afterwards about situations which felt humiliating to you?   A or B

(8) Would many people (A) regard you as a sensitive person, or not (B)?   A or B

(9) Do you (B) or do you not (A) usually get to sleep easily and sleep well?   A or B

(10) Would many people (A) consider you to be shy, or not (B)?   A or B

(11) Do you (A) or do you not (B) feel much put out or disturbed if someone you know fails to greet you?   A or B

(12) Do you (A) or do you not (B) sometimes feel happy and sometimes feel sad without any real cause?   A or B

(13) Do you (A) or do you not (B) find yourself day-dreaming often, when you should be working?   A or B

(14) Can you (A) or can you not (B) remember having any nightmares in the last five years?   A or B

(15)   Have you (A) or have you not (B) a real fear of heights or lifts or tunnels or going out of doors?   A or B

(16)   Do you (B) or do you not (A) usually behave calmly and efficiently in an emergency?   A or B

(17)   Do you (A) or do you not (B) believe yourself to be an emotional person in many of the situations of everyday life?   A or B

(18)   Do you (A) or do you not (B) frequently worry about your health?   A or B

(19)   Can you remember (A) or can you not remember (B) definitely annoying anyone in the last year?   A or B

(20)   Do you (A) or do you not (B) perspire much without exercise?   A or B

(21)   Within the last five years can you (A) or can you not (B) remember your mind going blank in the middle of doing a job?   A or B

(22)   Within the last year have you met as many as three people that you have detected as being definitely unfriendly towards you (A), or not (B)?   A or B

(23)   Have you ever (A) or have you never (B) been short of breath without taking exercise?   A or B

(24)   Are you generally tolerant of other people's odd little ways (B) or not (A)?   A or B

(25)   Are there (A) or are there not (B) any normal everyday situations in which you feel definitely self-conscious?   A or B

(26)   Do you often feel unhappy (A) or not (B)?   A or B

(27)   Have you (A) or have you not (B) more than once suffered from diarrhoea in the last two years?   A or B

(28)   Are you usually self-confident (B) or not (A)?   A or B

(29)   Have you (A) or have you not (B) any reason to believe that you cannot manage the situations of life as easily as most people?   A or B

(30)   Do you (A) or do you not (B) use aspirin, codeine, sedatives, pep pills, sleeping pills or other drugs more than once a month nowadays?   A or B

Now count your As and Bs as before and write down your score.

Total score: A . . . .   B . . . .

PERSONALITY FACTOR 3

In each square there are printed lines; use these as a basis for a separate, original drawing of something recognizable. Draw clearly but quickly. Do not bother with details. You have only five minutes to complete all the drawings.

Creativity (five-minute test)

Test
begins
here

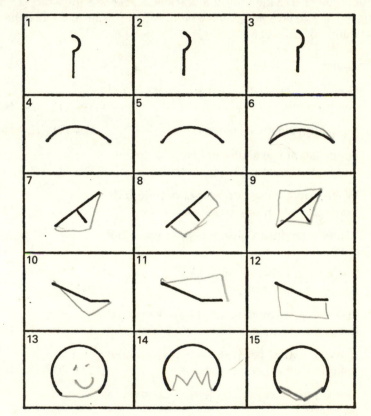

PERSONALITY FACTOR 4

How to take the test

As before you must go through the questions quickly and, without too much reflection; give your immediate reaction to the question. The tests work from instinctive answers you give, not from the truth or otherwise of the actual statements.

If your answer is YES then ring the bracketed letter after the word YES, if it is NO ring the bracketed letter after the word NO. If you are in doubt or hesitant ring the query (?). That is all.

Test
begins
here

Questionnaire

(1)	Does your life have to be full of changes and much varied?	Yes (Y)	(?)	No (X)
(2)	Are you an ambitious person?	Yes (Y)	(?)	No (X)
(3)	Politicians are generally sincere and do their best for the country. Do you think this is so?	Yes (X)	(?)	No (Y)
(4)	When doing things, do you choose to hide from others the motives behind them?	Yes (Y)	(?)	No (X)
(5)	Rather than dream of success, do you work hard to achieve it?	Yes (Y)	(?)	No (X)
(6)	Would you rather be alive and a coward or dead and a hero?	Yes (Y)	(?)	No (X)
(7)	Would you be more upset at loss of material things than hearing of illness of a friend?	Yes (X)	(?)	No (Y)
(8)	Do you always get your own way without regard for other people's opinions?	Yes (Y)	(?)	No (X)
(9)	Do you feel vengeful if a person does you a bad turn?	Yes (Y)	(?)	No (X)
(10)	Do you worry about work whilst on holiday?	Yes (Y)	(?)	No (X)
(11)	Do you compare your performance with other workmates?	Yes (Y)	(?)	No (X)
(12)	When you get into a heated discussion, do you find it difficult to calm down and stop?	Yes (Y)	(?)	No (X)
(13)	Are romantic stories among your reading material?	Yes (X)	(?)	No (Y)

(14)   Do you take short cuts in order to make
       progress at work?   Yes (Y)   (?)   No (X)

(15)   Do you set your sights too low because you
       are afraid of failure?   Yes (X)   (?)   No (Y)

(16)   If given the chance, would you like to witness
       an execution?   Yes (Y)   (?)   No (X)

(17)   Are you rather cool in dealing with other
       people?   Yes (Y)   (?)   No (X)

(18)   Do you prepare thoroughly for examinations?   Yes (Y)   (?)   No (X)

(19)   Do you sometimes tell white lies?   Yes (Y)   (?)   No (X)

(20)   Are you a dancing fan?   Yes (X)   (?)   No (Y)

(21)   If somebody sat in front of you and obstructed
       your view, would you ask them to remove
       their hat?   Yes (Y)   (?)   No (X)

(22)   Would you enjoy travelling at 150 mph in a
       racing car?   Yes (Y)   (?)   No (X)

(23)   Did English Literature take precedence over
       General Science in your preferences at
       school?   Yes (Y)   (?)   No (X)

(24)   Do you think that most politicians cannot be
       believed?   Yes (Y)   (?)   No (X)

(25)   Do you hold very strong opinions, more so
       than most people?   Yes (X)   (?)   No (Y)

(26)   Do you flatter people to enable you to get on
       in life?   Yes (Y)   (?)   No (X)

(27)   Did you always do as instructed when you
       were young?   Yes (X)   (?)   No (Y)

(28)   Did you enjoy playing with guns?   Yes (Y)   (?)   No (X)

(29)   Would you rather be a dentist than a dress
       designer?   Yes (Y)   (?)   No (X)

(30)   Do you place achievement amongst the most
       important things?   Yes (Y)   (?)   No (X)

(31)   Do you strive hard to get ahead?   Yes (Y)   (?)   No (X)

(32) Do you stand on an escalator rather than walk on it?   Yes (X) (?) No (Y)

(33) Would you feel it best not to respond if a person was rude to you?   Yes (Y) (?) No (X)

(34) Do you prefer climates of even temperature?   Yes (X) (?) No (Y)

(35) Would you ask someone to refrain from smoking if it worried you?   Yes (Y) (?) No (X)

(36) Do you like watching aggressive sports on television?   Yes (Y) (?) No (X)

(37) Is love more important than success?   Yes (Y) (?) No (X)

(38) If you were in a queue, would you react if a person went to the front out of turn?   Yes (Y) (?) No (X)

(39) Have you ever experienced the feeling of wanting to kill someone?   Yes (Y) (?) No (X)

(40) Would you be in charge if you were on a committee?   Yes (Y) (?) No (X)

(41) If you disapproved of a friend's behaviour, would you ensure that he was aware of your feelings?   Yes (X) (?) No (Y)

(42) Some drugs cause hallucinations. Would you take any such drugs?   Yes (Y) (?) No (X)

(43) Do you try new innovations or stick to tried and true methods?   Yes (Y) (?) No (X)

(44) Do you get angry with people so that you shout at them?   Yes (Y) (?) No (X)

(45) Do you make a creative contribution to society?   Yes (Y) (?) No (X)

(46) Do you enjoy your daily work?   Yes (X) (?) No (Y)

(47) Do you see things in grey, rather than black and white?   Yes (X) (?) No (Y)

(48) Do you hesitate to ask strangers questions?   Yes (X) (?) No (Y)

(49) Do you long for excitement?   Yes (Y) (?) No (X)

(50) Do you believe that there are better reasons for marriage than being in love?   Yes (Y) (?) No (X)

(51) Would you travel to a different part of the world to live? Yes (X) (?) No (Y)

(52) Do you mix with people who can help you? Yes (Y) (?) No (X)

(53) Would you consider it too dangerous to take up mountain climbing? Yes (X) (?) No (Y)

(54) Do you get people onto your side by telling them what they want to hear? Yes (Y) (?) No (X)

(55) Do you hesitate to take a conspicuous seat in a lecture room? Yes (X) (?) No (Y)

(56) Do you know the difference between right and wrong? Yes (Y) (?) No (X)

(57) Do you prefer ordinary sex? Yes (X) (?) No (Y)

(58) Do you try to shock people? Yes (Y) (?) No (X)

(59) Do you believe in 'every man for himself'? Yes (Y) (?) No (X)

(60) Do you think that fools and their money are soon parted and are you pleased that they are? Yes (Y) (?) No (X)

(61) Do you like buying things? Yes (X) (?) No (Y)

(62) Does other people's ignorance appal you? Yes (Y) (?) No (X)

(63) Do you always do things today rather than leave them until tomorrow? Yes (Y) (?) No (X)

(64) Would you like to learn to be a pilot? Yes (Y) (?) No (X)

(65) Do you have a burning ambition to be of great importance in the community? Yes (X) (?) No (Y)

(66) Do you watch pornographic videos? Yes (Y) (?) No (X)

(67) Do you dislike foreigners? Yes (X) (?) No (Y)

(68) When reading newspaper reports, do you get annoyed at what some politicians say? Yes (X) (?) No (Y)

(69) Do you advocate force where necessary? Yes (X) (?) No (Y)

(70) Do you like painting children's picture books? Yes (X) (?) No (Y)

(71) Do you enjoy taking part in physical activity of a rough nature? Yes (Y) (?) No (X)

(72) Do you feel sorry for injured birds?   Yes (X)   (?)   No (Y)

(73) When you are busy can you listen to other
     people at the same time?   Yes (Y)   (?)   No (X)

(74) Are you inclined to be a lazy person?   Yes (X)   (?)   No (Y)

(75) Have you ever modelled yourself on
     somebody?   Yes (Y)   (?)   No (X)

(76) Do you take excessive pride in your work?   Yes (Y)   (?)   No (X)

(77) Do you avoid disaster scenes on television?   Yes (X)   (?)   No (Y)

(78) Can you persuade people?   Yes (Y)   (?)   No (X)

(79) Are you a leader in a group of people?   Yes (Y)   (?)   No (X)

(80) Do you give the true reason when asking
     somebody to do something for you?   Yes (X)   (?)   No (Y)

(81) Do you think that most people are good?   Yes (X)   (?)   No (Y)

(82) Are you a skilled organizer?   Yes (Y)   (?)   No (X)

(83) Do you plan what you are going to say?   Yes (Y)   (?)   No (X)

(84) Do you dislike snakes?   Yes (X)   (?)   No (Y)

(85) Do you sometimes have cruel fantasies?   Yes (Y)   (?)   No (X)

(86) Do you believe that people with extreme
     political views should inflict those views on
     others?   Yes (X)   (?)   No (Y)

(87) Do you believe that there is only one religion
     and that basically all religions are the same? Yes (Y)   (?)   No (X)

(88) Is it essential that you succeed in your life? Yes (Y)   (?)   No (X)

(89) Do you concentrate on one great cause?   Yes (Y)   (?)   No (X)

(90) Do you agree with or compromise with
     opponents?   Yes (Y)   (?)   No (X)

(91) Do you get annoyed when people do not
     admit that they are wrong?   Yes (Y)   (?)   No (X)

(92) Do you always take shoddy goods back for
     exchange?   Yes (Y)   (?)   No (X)

(93) Are you more interested in science than
     personal relationships?   Yes (Y)   (?)   No (X)

(94)   Do you like being the focus of attention?   Yes (Y)   (?)   No (X)

(95)   Do you fear boredom?   Yes (Y)   (?)   No (X)

(96)   Are you aware of the beauty surrounding
       you?   Yes (Y)   (?)   No (X)

(97)   Would you like to be an astronaut?   Yes (Y)   (?)   No (X)

(98)   Do you believe that playing is more important
       than winning?   Yes (X)   (?)   No (Y)

(99)   Do you put down people who are conceited?   Yes (Y)   (?)   No (X)

(100) Would you go to a wife-swapping party?   Yes (Y)   (?)   No (X)

(101) Are you often furious with other people?   Yes (Y)   (?)   No (X)

(102) Are you drawn to unfortunate people?   Yes (X)   (?)   No (Y)

(103) Do you horse around when at the swimming
       baths?   Yes (Y)   (?)   No (X)

(104) Are you scared of the dark?   Yes (X)   (?)   No (Y)

(105) Do you state your opinions with vehemence?   Yes (Y)   (?)   No (X)

(106) Do you hurt other people in obtaining your
       desires?   Yes (Y)   (?)   No (X)

(107) Do you think that pacifists are cowards?   Yes (X)   (?)   No (Y)

(108) Do you dislike spicy foreign food?   Yes (X)   (?)   No (Y)

(109) Are you scared of spiders and worms, etc?   Yes (X)   (?)   No (Y)

(110) Do you really believe it is always best to be
       honest?   Yes (X)   (?)   No (Y)

(111) Do you try to understand the other person's
       point of view?   Yes (X)   (?)   No (Y)

(112) Does it annoy you when experts are wrong?   Yes (Y)   (?)   No (X)

(113) Would you like to be a lion hunter?   Yes (Y)   (?)   No (X)

(114) Do you disregard other people's feelings?   Yes (Y)   (?)   No (X)

(115) Are you unsure about who to vote for?   Yes (X)   (?)   No (Y)

(116) Are you easily startled?   Yes (X)   (?)   No (Y)

(117) Would you appear on television?   Yes (Y)   (?)   No (X)

(118)   Do you like to pick up furry animals?   Yes (X)   (?)   No (Y)

(119)   Do you prefer to take orders?   Yes (X)   (?)   No (Y)

(120)   Does your intuition tell you whether a person
        is trustworthy?   Yes (X)   (?)   No (Y)

(121)   Do you get bored easily?   Yes (Y)   (?)   No (X)

(122)   Do you argue when you know you are
        wrong?   Yes (Y)   (?)   No (X)

(123)   Would you help somebody?   Yes (X)   (?)   No (Y)

(124)   Do you like practical jokes?   Yes (X)   (?)   No (Y)

(125)   Are you satisfied with your salary?   Yes (X)   (?)   No (Y)

(126)   Do you refrain from placing your trust in
        other people?   Yes (Y)   (?)   No (X)

(127)   Are you scared of people of authority?   Yes (X)   (?)   No (Y)

(128)   Are you emotional when watching a film?   Yes (X)   (?)   No (Y)

(129)   Do you prefer Mozart to Wagner?   Yes (X)   (?)   No (Y)

(130)   Do you obey 'signs'?   Yes (X)   (?)   No (Y)

(131)   Do you think about falling in love?   Yes (X)   (?)   No (Y)

(132)   Do you believe that we can learn a lot from
        other cultures?   Yes (X)   (?)   No (Y)

(133)   Do you find it hard to say 'No' to a salesman?   Yes (X)   (?)   No (Y)

(134)   Does talking about your work excite you?   Yes (X)   (?)   No (Y)

(135)   Can you easily find excuses?   Yes (Y)   (?)   No (X)

(136)   Do you like a peaceful life?   Yes (X)   (?)   No (Y)

(137)   Do you take risks?   Yes (Y)   (?)   No (X)

(138)   Do you break crockery when annoyed?   Yes (X)   (?)   No (Y)

(139)   Are you envious of other people's success?   Yes (Y)   (?)   No (X)

(140)   Do you indulge in political protest?   Yes (X)   (?)   No (Y)

(141)   Do you read science fiction?   Yes (Y)   (?)   No (X)

(142)   Do you blame the other person when things
        go wrong?   Yes (Y)   (?)   No (X)

(143)   Do you stay in the background at parties?   Yes (X)   (?)   No (Y)

(144)   Do you try to convert others to your religion?   Yes (Y)   (?)   No (X)

(145)   Does your work keep you awake at night because you find it so interesting?   Yes (Y)   (?)   No (X)

(146)   Does the sight of blood make you feel queasy?   Yes (Y)   (?)   No (X)

(147)   Do you chastise people who offend you?   Yes (Y)   (?)   No (X)

(148)   Do you mix with people who are unpredictable and rather non-conformist?   Yes (Y)   (?)   No (X)

(149)   Do you avoid thrilling rides at the fun fair?   Yes (X)   (?)   No (Y)

(150)   Would you fight for your rights or would you give them up easily?   Yes (Y)   (?)   No (X)

(151)   Do you always tell the truth?   Yes (X)   (?)   No (Y)

(152)   Do you stop yourself from being lazy?   Yes (Y)   (?)   No (X)

(153)   Are you too fair at work in your actions?   Yes (X)   (?)   No (Y)

(154)   Do you grind your teeth frequently?   Yes (Y)   (?)   No (X)

(155)   Do you sometimes question your own actions?   Yes (X)   (?)   No (Y)

(156)   If you are right, do you argue?   Yes (Y)   (?)   No (X)

(157)   Does your sympathy lie with the underdog?   Yes (X)   (?)   No (Y)

(158)   Do you sometimes cry?   Yes (X)   (?)   No (Y)

(159)   Are you regarded as too good natured?   Yes (X)   (?)   No (Y)

(160)   Do you like violent scenes at the cinema or on television?   Yes (Y)   (?)   No (X)

(161)   Do you like strong debates?   Yes (Y)   (?)   No (X)

(162)   Did you avoid fighting when you were young?   Yes (X)   (?)   No (Y)

(163)   Are you a relentless worker?   Yes (Y)   (?)   No (X)

(164)   Are you sarcastic?   Yes (Y)   (?)   No (X)

(165)   Do you like shooting galleries?   Yes (Y)   (?)   No (X)

(166)   Do you relax on holiday and forget about work?   Yes (X)   (?)   No (Y)

(167) Do you enjoy horror videos?   Yes (Y)   (?)   No (X)

(168) In an argument, do you think you are firm and
       forthright?   Yes (Y)   (?)   No (X)

(169) Are you mechanically minded?   Yes (Y)   (?)   No (X)

(170) Do you readily change your mind?   Yes (X)   (?)   No (Y)

(171) Do you dislike vulgar jokes?   Yes (X)   (?)   No (Y)

(172) Are you a patient person?   Yes (X)   (?)   No (Y)

(173) Do you get closely involved with other
       people?   Yes (X)   (?)   No (Y)

(174) Are you even tempered?   Yes (X)   (?)   No (Y)

(175) Do you think it would be beneficial if we all
       shared the same ideas and opinions?   Yes (Y)   (?)   No (X)

(176) Do you like war stories?   Yes (Y)   (?)   No (X)

(177) Do you sometimes go through the day without
       achieving anything?   Yes (X)   (?)   No (Y)

(178) Do you watch fighting scenes on television?   Yes (Y)   (?)   No (X)

(179) Are you good at bluffing?   Yes (Y)   (?)   No (X)

(180) Are you forgiving to people who have
       wronged you?   Yes (X)   (?)   No (Y)

(181) Do you always stick to your decision?   Yes (Y)   (?)   No (X)

(182) Are you happy with our Government?   Yes (X)   (?)   No (Y)

(183) Do you wish to 'better yourself'?   Yes (Y)   (?)   No (X)

(184) Do you consider that a good teacher is one
       who makes you think, rather than one who
       only teaches?   Yes (X)   (?)   No (Y)

(185) Do you enjoy watching rough sports?   Yes (Y)   (?)   No (X)

(186) Do you find that your way of tackling
       problems is better than other people's?   Yes (Y)   (?)   No (X)

(187) Do you complain to the management in
       restaurants if the service is bad?   Yes (X)   (?)   No (Y)

(188) Do you study other people's viewpoints?   Yes (Y)   (?)   No (X)

(189) Do you like to read autobiographies? Yes (Y) (?) No (X)

(190) Do you put your interests first? Yes (Y) (?) No (X)

(191) Would you hesitate to shoot a burglar? Yes (X) (?) No (Y)

(192) Do you make friends of people because they can help you? Yes (Y) (?) No (X)

(193) Do you believe there is a little truth in everybody's views? Yes (Y) (?) No (X)

(194) Do you like bustle about you? Yes (Y) (?) No (X)

(195) Do you wish you were more assertive? Yes (X) (?) No (Y)

(196) Are you sometimes irritable? Yes (X) (?) No (Y)

(197) Did you like quiet paintings, rather than vivid paintings? Yes (X) (?) No (Y)

(198) Do you lose your temper less than the average person? Yes (X) (?) No (Y)

(199) Do you agree rather than argue? Yes (X) (?) No (Y)

(200) When you are angry, do you stamp your feet? Yes (Y) (?) No (X)

(201) Do underwater sports interest you? Yes (Y) (?) No (X)

(202) Do you repeat yourself? Yes (Y) (?) No (X)

(203) Do you like helping other people? Yes (X) (?) No (Y)

(204) Would you like to try parachute jumping? Yes (Y) (?) No (X)

(205) Are you belligerent? Yes (Y) (?) No (X)

(206) Would you take part in any orgy? Yes (Y) (?) No (X)

(207) Do you mix with people of other religions? Yes (X) (?) No (Y)

(208) Do you stand up for yourself? Yes (Y) (?) No (X)

(209) Do you like to sing in a choir? Yes (X) (?) No (Y)

(210) Do you get pushed around? Yes (X) (?) No (Y)

Now count the Ys, the ?s and the Xs you have ringed.

Total score: Y . . . ., ? . . . ., X . . . .

Finished? Have you ringed one of the bracketed letters or the query for each question OK? Now turn to p. 185 for the interpretation and a chance to know thyself a little better. Remember that tests have shown that the underlying character traits disclosed here are largely inborn and so are something you can only allow for but not change much. But knowing how you vary from average, if you do (and most do not) will help you to make the best of the character your genes have instructed you to have. Intelligence can and does allow people to overcome character problems. But you have to know what they are.

PERSONALITY FACTORS

The first tests in this book correlate highly with general intelligence. It is obviously good to have an idea of this, but we have to recognize that there are many other important ways in which personality can be classified. Perhaps I should make it clear what I mean by personality. Everyone has different behaviour patterns and these vary from time to time with mood changes, fits of temper, laughter, fear or joy. Behind this changing emotional pattern we are aware of deeper patterns and more permanent sets or tendencies which make it possible for us to classify people in a number of other ways.

Once the possibility of measuring things so intangible had been explored and found to be workable as regards intelligence, psychometricians began to look at many other personality factors to try to find out to what extent they would yield to the same rigorous statistical techniques. A whole world of expressions had grown up to describe human differences of this kind. Phlegmatic, cowardly, lazy, tough-minded, melancholic; hundreds of such terms exist. The psychometricians were confronted with a mass of different variables, all apparently widely understood and representing some real differences which (though difficult to define) seemed to have genuine predictive value.

In the hope of simplifying matters, which is always the job of a scientist, they worked on the assumption that there may be a relatively few independent parameters or dimensions of difference and that all the others derived from these. To check this they used their armoury of statistical techniques to find out to what extent these factors related one to another. If there was a strong relation then it was assumed that there must be some common factor operating underneath. They found that they could be fitted into clusters or clumps which were interrelated.

In this part of the book I have chosen only four exemplary parameters of personality measurement. These factors are independent of intelligence. The first two factors concerned are extroversion–introversion (Personality Factor 1), and emotional stability (Personality Factor 2).

Personality Factor 1:   Extroversion

The extrovert and the introvert represent the extremes and most people are somewhere in between. People vary from time to time and will be more extroverted on some occasions and less on others. But usually they tend to remain about the same, with, over a long term, a slight trend towards extroversion.

The extrovert is the outward-looking, socially friendly and uninhibited type of person. He enjoys company, feels at ease in a large circle and tends to form a large number of relatively shallow relationships. Confident, assertive and friendly, we can represent this extreme type as a boisterous, talkative and friendly commercial traveller who is very much at home in a bar or at the club. The extreme introvert might perhaps be a professor or accountant, one who is much more at home in his study or taking long solitary walks with a pipe, a stick and a dog. Introverts tend to form one or a few profound attachments, enjoy books, chess and thought. They are the type who like to keep themselves to themselves and slightly disapprove of neighbours who are always in and out of one another's houses. Neither type of personality is good or bad, although it is probably preferable to be somewhere in between. Those who are extremely extroverted, according to Eysenck, have a higher probability of being criminals if they also lack emotional stability; of course, many people with very high extroversion scores and low scores on emotional stability are perfectly honest and respectable. Again, I speak only of a tendency and not of an invariable relation.

The more As you got the more introverted you are. 15 or so would make you definitely introverted, and 20 very much so. 15 Bs make you an extrovert, and 20, a bouncing extrovert like me (and jolly good luck to you too).

Your introversion/extroversion, judged by your results on the Personality Factor Test 1

No. of As	Character	No. of As	Character
20	Extremely introverted	7/8	A shade extroverted
19	Very introverted	5/6	Slightly extroverted
18	Quite introverted	3/4	Somewhat extroverted
16/17	Somewhat introverted	2	Quite extroverted
14/15	Slightly introverted	1	Very extroverted
12/13	A shade introverted	0	Extremely extroverted
9/10/11	Average		

Personality Factor 2:   Emotional stability

The answers you give decide whether you are emotionally sensitive or impervious. *Those with 20 or so Bs are very imperturbable,* people who never seem to get upset, who are equable and balanced and who probably go through life without the ups and downs of the more sensitive type of person. *If you have a score of more than 20 As you are emotional and suggestible,* and probably feel the mental strains of life more than most, needing plenty of rest and the sort of work, friendships and hobbies that can make a stable background for you. On the other hand, those with 22 or so Bs might ask themselves whether they are not a bit too phlegmatic and might try to arrange life so as to present some challenge to their placidity or even unresponsiveness.

Your stability, judged by your results on the Personality Factor Test 2

No. of Bs	Character
30/29	Unshakeable
28/27	Imperturbable
26/25	Unflappable
24/23	Calm
22/21	Balanced
20/19/18	Steady
17/16/15/14	Average
13/12/11	Sympathetic
10/9	Suggestible
8/7	Emotional
6/5	Sensitive
4/3	Oversensitive
2/1	Nervous
0	Neurotic

Professor Eysenck shows how these last two factors neatly account for the full range of Aristotle's character types. Choleric is extroverted and unstable, melancholic is introverted and unstable, phlegmatic is introverted and stable, and sanguine is extroverted and stable.

As with most personality factors but emphatically not with intelligence, it is the intermediate scores which seem to be the best.

Both tendencies have advantages in certain social roles. We might not want our lover to be too phlegmatic and insensitive. We might prefer our lawyer not to be so indecisive and anxious as to burst into tears at a harsh word from the opposing counsel.

Personality Factor 3

Personality Factor 3 is a rather doubtful one. It is Creativity or inventiveness. This will be explained later.

Instructions for marking Creativity Test

Now comes the difficult part. Take one mark for each recognizable drawing, provided it does not fall into the same category as any other drawing on the same sheet. For instance, only one human face is allowed, and a second one gets no marks unless it is a detail in the drawing and not the whole subject. *You gain marks for the variety* (of ideas, scenes or things, depicted) and *you are penalized for using the same idea twice*. If you are 'creative' you will tend to variety naturally, even if you are not instructed.

There is no *right* answer to a creativity test; there is an infinite number of possible answers and they are all equally right provided they are novel and not copied, and provided they take into account all the features of the problem situation. In these problems you are asked to utilize the whole of the diagrams given. If any part of the diagram is not accommodated into your drawing, then you must go without the mark. It is, of course, best to get a friend to mark you, after getting him to read the instructions carefully.

Your creativity, judged by your results on the 5-minute Creativity Test

Number of complete, original, unrepetitive drawings	
1	Uncreative
2	
3	
4	
5	
6	
7/8	Average
9	
10	
11	
12	
13	
14	
15	Very creative

Creativity

If the concept 'Intelligence' as a human personality factor is disputed, then the concept 'Creativity' hardly exists at all. Creativity has a relatively thin background scientifically, but a suspiciously great fuss has been made about a surprisingly little body of actual experimental work. One feels the covert influence of the egalitarian environmentalists, the Procrustean Educational Levellers. Creativity is one of those compensatory ideas which flourish in this atmosphere. 'Dim, yes,' one hears the Procrusteans say, 'but so creative!'

I shall try to consider creativity apart from its political undertones and overtones. Going by evidence which is most convincing to me and least convincing to others – that is, personal experience – I feel that it *is* possible to separate people into classes by some criterion which could be reasonably called creativity. Some people are more adept at combining and recombining mental material into original forms. The difference appears to be in the field of hypothesis-making. If, as I believe, the process of solving problems is often a matter of trial and error, of adjusting and modifying conceptual frameworks until one with a relatively good fit is found, then 'creatives' seem to me to be those who are more prolific at generating hypotheses. Their ability to judge the hypotheses when formed and to reject the inadequate would, in my intuitive view, be associated with pure intelligence. But their actual power and fruitfulness in producing sheer quantity of theories to be tested, though associated with intelligence, is not so closely associated.

The first studies in creativity were by Guilford and his associates in the USA in the early 1950s and there are plenty of references to work on creativity over 30 years. Like other psychometric tests, creativity tests must be judged by whether they can be validated statistically.

There is still a good deal of argument about creativity tests and some people feel they are simply intelligence tests in disguise. R. W. Marsh in *A Statistical Re-Analysis of Getzels' and Jackson's Data,* February, 1964, said this: 'rather than being almost independent of the general factor of intelligence, this (creativity) factor is the most constant and conspicuous ingredient . . . a conventional IQ is still the best single criterion for "creative" potential. This may be improved on by the use of other tests as well.'

The 'compensationist' fallacy

I have mentioned the kindly but mistaken tendency to believe in some law of compensation by which nature makes up to us in one way for our defects in another. There is, for instance, a well-established and widespread archetype of 'brainy' people as being thin, puny, bespectacled and unattractive. The facts, as Professor Lewis Terman has shown, do not fit. On the whole, intelligent people are healthier, stronger and better at sport than the average. It just is not fair!

I am afraid that I believe that compensationism played a part in the enormous surge of interest when J. W. Getzels and P. W. Jackson wrote *Creativity and Intelligence* (1962), a book which tended to show that there was another quality allied to intelligence but not coincident with it, which they called creativity. The meaning of the word was vague, but it is thought of as the ability to throw up original ideas and possible solutions to problems.

Creativity and problem solving

Solving a problem has three stages. First, you encounter the problem, some obstacle in the automatic response to a situation. Having reviewed the problem, the next step is to generate the lines of possible solution, to throw up options.

That is the divergent stage. The third step is to close in on the only or best solution, eliminating the others. That is the convergent stage.

On the whole intelligence testers, for very good technical reasons, concentrate on the convergent stage. So the divergent stage is eliminated. The solver is set a number of optional solutions and has only the job of choosing between them. The reason for this is purely technical. It is difficult and requires highly skilled personnel to mark tests where there is a large number of possibly right answers. The only practical solution was the limited option or closed-ended tests as they call them, those with a single 'correct' answer. Here the subject ticks a box and a clerk or computer can mark the result. The other type, the open-ended test (with many possible correct answers) does exist but requires individual administration by highly trained psychologists. Such tests are, therefore, too costly for practical purposes in schools, offices and many places.

This technical method, however, has made it possible for those seeking a cop-out to avoid the harshness of the IQ classification. So some people set out to develop tests of 'creativity'. These were said to measure the power to generate options.

To mark most of these tests one simply adds up all the different options offered by the candidate, no matter how wild they are. (The rationale is that, occasionally, what seems at first like a silly option turns out to be a good one. This is true, but very rarely so.)

Creativity tests seem to put all the emphasis on the primary 'divergent' stage in the problem-solving process. They ignore the quality of the 'solutions' offered and award creativity marks only for the number of them. They tend to classify thinkers themselves rather than the thinking process into the two stages divergent and convergent.

Some brilliant, inventive people are 'divergent' creative thinkers who are good at 'lateral' thinking. Other poor plodders are dull drabs or 'convergent' thinkers who are concerned only with eliminating errors and narrowing down to the correct or best solution.

'Never mind who got it right and made it work', is the cry, 'Mr Lateral Creativity produced scores of highly imaginative answers.'

I do believe that some creativity tests may measure a real human quality even if it is only difference between people in their tolerance for being laughed at for putting up over-imaginative solutions. It is certainly true that important and valuable innovations do in fact arise from this sort of 'lateral thinking'. When solutions are not rational but serendipitous (lucky chances) a richness of options is good.

So in spite of my sad thought that the immediate success of the concept 'creativity' arose from the compensatory compassion I have described, that 'creativity' is a comforting consolation prize for losers at 'intelligence', I include an illustrative creativity test among those in this set of personality tests.

What Getzels and Jackson discovered was this. Taking the top quarter of children on an IQ test they picked out those who were in the bottom three-quarters in tests of creativity. Calling that set the 'bright and uncreative', they then compared them with another group which we might (unfairly) call the 'creative unintelligent'. This group consisted of those in the top quarter for creativity, and below that top quarter for intelligence.

What they found was that their scholastic achievement scores were about equal. They concluded that 'creativity' was of equal importance with intelligence. There is of course a high correlation between creativity and intelligence, around 0.5.

Getzels and Jackson's book was followed by a whole spate of work in the same vein and very soon there were a large number of people who were making their reputation out of the attempt to find a rigorous way of measuring creativity. Parents, disappointed to find average IQ in their children, were given another chance and could learn with delight how 'creative' they might be.

So there are many differing so-called measures of 'creativity'. In the Marland Report to US Congress, mentioned elsewhere, it was shown that the various measures of creativity had mutual correlations which were lower in every case than the correlation of each of these measures with measures of intelligence.

Whatever was being measured, it was different in each case. The concept was obviously most imprecise. IQ tests on the other hand all correlate very highly one with another. We are fairly sure in this case that they are measuring something which is useful and predictive because at least it is common.

Measures of creativity do not appear to have this virtue.

It is possible that the future will produce new discoveries in this region and that this idea will be resuscitated, but I have a strong feeling that interest and acceptance of the creativity concept is on the decline as more research work reveals little solid to get hold of.

Personality Factor 4: Strong-mindedness

Marking the Personality Factor 4 Test

Marking is again simple. Go through the questions looking at what you have ringed. Count up the number of (Y)s you have ringed and the number of (?)s you have ringed. Count two marks for each ringed (Y) and one mark for each ringed (?). Do not bother with the ringed (X)s. Take your total and refer to the following Table. I show a continuum on Factor 4 showing scores from 400 down to zero. You can count these as points on a scale where a high score means strong-minded. High scores point to emphatic, assertive, tough-talking, manipulative, dogmatic, stimulus-hungry, adventurous traits. Low scores indicate the opposite tendency towards weak-mindedness or sub-missiveness. At the very low scores people will be weak-willed, suggestible, pacific, unambitious and unadventurous. Somewhere in between seems best and that is where most people are. Both winners and losers will tend to come from the high score end (because high Factor 4 people are risk takers), but in peaceable times survivors will tend to be low scorers. We know the 'Win or bust' attitude and the 'Don't get involved' attitude. The first would have high scores, the second low ones on this scale.

Scores

Over 400	Very aggressive, inflexible, bossy
350 – 400	Strong-willed, confrontational
300 – 350	Determined and dogmatic
250 – 300	Assertive, managerial
200 – 250	A balanced personality
150 – 200	Rather unassertive but warm-hearted
100 – 150	Sympathetic, caring, but no 'push'
50 – 100	Unambitious and placatory
Below 50	Very timid and suggestible

Personality Factor 4

Personality Factor 4 is the measure of a general attitude towards life and other people. It could be called the competitive versus co-operative factor or the strong-minded versus caring factor.

Social life involves a nice balance between competition and co-operation. A sense of competition between people induces effort, keenness and innovative adventurousness. This produces choices and options from which we can select improvements. On the other hand without mutual care, consideration and co-operation social combinations cannot survive successfully. Both are essential. In excess both are damaging.

A no-rules, dog-eat-dog society where competition reigns supreme is not a society at all. It would fall apart in anarchy and confusion or be taken over by the strongest and most ruthless. These would soon split and quarrel and life for all would be nasty, brutish and short.

On the other hand, a society which called for selfless care and unrewarded altruistic service from every citizen would go so much against the genetic hunter-gatherer nature in us all that it would break down because so many would not observe such a demanding code. Motivation would be low. No one would risk innovation and many would exploit the system to the utmost. The idea is a noble one but whenever it has been tried we have had the same result. Under a single inspired leader with a careful selection of followers, a few of such communities survive somehow for a time. But always, when the leader dies or goes they break up into factions and gradually revert to the normal human pattern.

Until at least one example of a lasting and really successful uncompetitive society emerges, it seems safest to assume that the same balance between competition and co-operation under the law is the best that this particular species can do at present.

So what we are dealing with here is variations in these two essential elements in human nature. Thus those who are very high in Factor 4 are likely to be bossy, tough-minded, competitive people who believe in self-help and are relatively unsympathetic with failure. They will want to be respected or even feared more than they will want to be loved. It sounds bad but remember, such people exist and we cannot do well without them.

Those who score lower are likely to be compassionate, caring, impressionable and even suggestible. They may prefer subordinate roles and prefer to be loved rather than feared. Such qualities too are essential to the general well-being.

There are many sincere idealists who hope that one day a perfect society based on altruism and love of one's fellows will arise and our best wishes are with them. But though some optimists like me feel we are moving slowly in the right direction, we need to be realistic while we wait for that millenium. We have to ask what can we do with the people we have.

Professor Hans Eysenck called the factor we are concerned with, 4th Personality Factor, the tough-mindedness factor and it is a good description.

The statistical distribution on the scores on this factor is instructive. Seeing how many score highly we might be discouraged about the chances of that ideal, fully co-operative, altruistic, uncompetitive society some of us dream of.

This test is based on and summates several tests, each of which measures factors which relate to general robustness of attitude. Very high scorers will be revengeful and even aggressive. High scorers will be assertive, have a strong personality, be ambitious, energetic, calculating, self-interested and concerned to raise their status. They will tend to be dogmatic, rigid, inflexible and unyielding in opinion and policy. They will have what is called 'stimulus hunger', they will like and enjoy challenge, adventure and risk taking. Lastly, this must be said even if it is unpopular with some ladies. It is unlikely that the highest scoring group on this test will contain as many women as men. This is not 'stereotyping', it is simple fact. Women span the whole range on this factor but they tend to score less than men on average.

How about low scorers? They sound so much nicer. The few *very* low scorers will be timid, humble, and low on initiative. They will be uncompetitive and unambitious, pleasant and self-effacing. They will be trusting, unselfish, caring, good-hearted and, at the extreme, suggestive even gullible. At medium low scores they will be flexible and co-operative. Unlike high scorers, they will be ready for accommodation and compromise.

A tenable view is, as I have said, that society needs some people with the full range of scores on all these personality factors and though it may be bad for the extremes it may be good for a society that some are so. Some cultures (and some times in any culture) might suit one type and other (and other times) cultures suit others. It takes all sorts. We have to note the fact that the full range of differences are there and have survived in all peoples. The differences have not been eliminated by natural selection. They seem to have been preserved by it.

6

Measuring Human Quality

Now that you have checked yourself, your children or others for intelligence and the other qualities, you might like to know more. You might ask how the *idea* that human qualities could be measured arose and whether it is valid and legitimate. You might want to hear about the controversies that rage in this area. You might want to know something of the techniques of composing and validating this kind of test.

To give the full story involves a diversion. I have to point to a development in the world which has occurred very recently on any long perspective of the human race. It is a development which has, as it were, crept up on us. Its full implications have not yet seeped into our traditional ways of thinking. It has not been accommodated into our morality and our normal thought patterns. I refer to the spread through the world of a relatively unified science-based World Culture.

No previous civilization has spread so widely around the world and all previous ones seem to have been based on a single race and culture. This World Culture is new, and the multi-racial and multi-cultural philosophy of science which underlies it is also new.

The scientific World Culture needs to be defended here because the idea of using scientific tests to measure human qualities, that is to say, differences in human qualities, jars with some traditional ideas of what is just and fair.

Tradition says that each of us should be judged on our character and performance, not on predictions or estimates of them. Tradition gives us a right to privacy which may include the right to keep to ourselves knowledge about our personal qualities.

But scientific ethics say that we are entitled to make use of any knowledge we can gain from the skilful and intelligent probing of the world.

We concede that we may be judged on our performance but suppose the

195

act of judging performance and character can be improved. Suppose it can be made more accurate and less biased. Suppose it can be reliably made earlier and with less time and trouble. Granted these things, are we morally right, or wise to say 'No! Let us stick to the slower, less sure, less fair, more biased methods we know?' Is it right to forbid experiments to improve, aid and refine human judgements?

No scientist can fairly say, 'I *can* know but I do not want to know'. His ethics call on him to find out. It is then for the people to decide what use, if any, is made of the knowledge.

(In this book I deal only in self-knowledge and knowledge of your own children and consenting associates so no question of privacy is involved here.)

HOW SCIENCE LED TO A WORLD CULTURE

Systematic science is barely 300 years old. A new set of strict disciplines which probably started with Francis Bacon seems to have led to the present, ubiquitous World Civilization supported by the World Culture. The World Culture is a selection, supported by a worldwide tacit consensus of enlightened elements in each of the patchwork of contending cultures that mankind has evolved around the world. People everywhere who are literate, intelligent and who have access to foreign ideas and one of the world languages have chosen a set of writers, artists and thinkers, systems of commerce and technology of law, science and philosophy, that they accept, in common, as good. This is the supervening culture which the intelligentsia* everywhere share in over-lapping membership each with their own local cultures. The interactions and cross-fertilization of this eclectic World Culture has brought together the best minds worldwide. The present World Civilization is the plainly seen result of that synthesis.

Today our planet Earth supports more people in good health and prosperity than it has ever done before. Art, Science, Trade, Industry flourish as never before. How did this happen?

During the last few centuries the increasing communication between the different human cultures, the convergence and combination of the arts, sciences, techniques that had developed separately, were the beginnings of our present World Culture.

This was the biggest and most important amplification of human intelligence and its effect upon our society has been almost miraculous. The important scientific discoveries of the last two centuries brought us to the point when,

---

* I use the word 'intelligentsia' in its old true sense as that body of the intelligent and educated people everywhere.

after an agricultural and then an industrial revolution, mankind could be free of the burden of manual toil and released into a world of comfort, health and wealth which would have seemed like Utopia to our ancestors.

Much of the world is already reaping this rich harvest arising from the trick of amplifying our best intelligences. If we keep our heads there is promise that we can spread these benefits further as time goes by. The changes have been very, very fast by all previous standards. We must not be impatient and ruin it all. And, of course, we must seek to avoid the great dangers that threaten us due to this risky experiment.

To produce this great cornucopia of plenty, mankind has somehow built up a vast, complex, interrelated, interacting commercial industrial society. This has made *greater and greater demands upon human ability*.

As the increasing value of intelligence to society was seen more clearly it was inevitable that a certain idea should come up. Might it be possible to be more systematic and precise in observing the variability in human thinking and problem-solving power?

HOW THE IDEA OF MEASURING HUMAN QUALITIES AROSE

Measuring

The great successes of modern science began when techniques for *exact measurement* developed. When the predictions from a scientific theory were tested *numerically,* the truth of the theory could be checked and subsequently verified or disproven. That is why mathematics plays such a large part in modern science. But as exact measurement and mathematical methods were used, a new truth emerged. It was found that there was *no such thing* as exactness. Scientists could create a theory, be totally convinced of its truth, and then discover that the predictions arising from the theory tallied only approximately with the experimental results. Scientists had to be content with this. They also learned something else – to be very suspicious of *consistent* errors. Many important advances in science arose from the refusal of scientists to ignore consistent errors. Inconsistent errors, random errors – those that showed no signs of a trend or tendency – could be accepted and ignored. They were held to be meaningless. But repetitive, consistent errors often concealed errors in theory. Scientists began to develop a theory of errors, a set of mathematical rules that helped them to know what type and degree of error could be considered reasonably compatible with a theory and what sort of error would oblige them to abandon the theory. A later name for the theory of errors was *probability theory*. The new approach developed into an academic discipline known as *statistics*.

We should look upon statistics as the *measurement* of uncertainty – an attempt to assess in numerical terms *how* sure or unsure we are of something.

To give a practical example, we conduct our lives and plan our actions on the basis of certain expectations, beliefs, or *truths*. When we say it is *true* that the sun rises every morning, we base our belief on the fact that it has been found to do so regularly. But the truth of the statement 'the sun rises every morning' is valid only for some latitudes. At the North Pole or the South Pole the truth would be that the sun rises every year. For regions between the North and South Pole, the statement 'the sun rises every morning' would be only partly true. There are periods at midsummer and midwinter when it either fails to rise or fails to set. All these differences in the *truth* of the statement at different geographical locations lead, finally, to a much more exact and predictive theory by which sunrise and sunset at any place on the earth can be predicted with a great deal of accuracy.

In its simple way, this example shows the difference between prescientific truth and postscientific, or numerical truth. On the one hand, there is a flat simple statement: 'The sun rises every day'; on the other, there is a large number of seasonal sunrise and sunset tables for as many different intervals of latitude.

However, even these tables are not absolutely accurate, and the exact moment of sunrise will be found to depend on other, more local, factors, such as the relative height above sea level of the observer and the hills at his horizon. Nonetheless, the tables are accurate enough for all practical purposes, and that, it turns out, is the most that we can usefully achieve in any science or art.

Very often, when the purposes change, we need more accuracy so that as science develops, further theories are required.

You may be getting restless, asking what all this has to do with the science of mental measurement. Patience. It is vital that your understanding of this point is perfectly clear. Science shows us that we cannot expect to know all the facts. We are limited to making the best and most practical guesses.

Science and accuracy

There are many definitions and conceptions of the purpose of that vast and expensive array of activities that come under the general heading *science*. A view that is sensible, if not orthodox, is that science is the pool of international organized knowledge about the world, nature, and ourselves that is available to mankind. It is, surprisingly, sometimes overlooked that the advantage of having such knowledge is that it gives us guidance in our behaviour, tells us what to do, and enables us to see what will happen as a result of our actions. Science is good because it is predictive. Furthermore, many scientists believe that only insofar as it is predictive is science worth doing.

The sciences vary considerably in the reliability and the accuracy of their predictions. Astronomy, the science that enables us to predict tides and sunrise, is generally very accurate and reliable in its predictions. On the other hand, meteorology is primarily informed guesswork about the weather. The predictions are not always accurate or totally reliable. Nonetheless, we are distinctly better off *with* meteorologists than we would be *without* them. Their guesses are better than ours. We make fewer mistakes with them than we would unaided. All sciences lie on a continuum of accuracy and reliability, with the more numerical and predictive sciences, such as astronomy and chemistry, at one extreme and the less reliable, less predictive, less accurate ones, such as sociology, psychology, and economics, at the other.

The sciences have been arbitrarily divided into two categories: exact and inexact: the so-called 'hard' sciences and the 'soft' sciences. Many exact scientists deny the status of true science to practitioners of inexact sciences. The science with which we are concerned – psychology – is admittedly one of the less exact. However, it remains preferable to be scientific rather than unscientific, so until we find something better, we must guide our behaviour, as it concerns the working of our own minds, by what we learn from psychology.

The specific branch of psychology with which we are concerned is *psychometry,* the science of mental measurement. Some people believe that it was only when Sir Francis Galton introduced the concept of exact measurement into the field of psychology that it disengaged itself from its place as a branch of philosophy and became a science.

But if any branch of psychology has a legitimate right to claim the status of science, it is psychometry. Though intelligence tests are 'debunked' with great regularity by physicists, chemists, astronomers, sociologists, and some ideological extremists, they remain an essential tool of educators, of clinical, counseling, and school psychologists, and especially of those who work with people who are mentally retarded. Despite the fact (which is frequently rediscovered with dramatic emphasis and publicity) that they are neither completely accurate nor completely reliable (like all other scientific knowledge), they continue to be an important source of information that can help psychologists and teachers and employers to solve people's problems.

When compared to chemistry and physics, psychometry is not as reliable or accurate. But compared to other branches of psychology, psychometry is an excellent wellspring of usable data. If the choice is between psychometric measurement of intelligence and personality and subjective guesses with no measurement at all, then psychometry is more reliable, more predictive, and consequently, fairer. It is is assuredly less ambiguous or uncertain than other methods.

How do we measure uncertainty?

There are two kinds of uncertainty: the uncertainty of a prediction which is called *probability,* and the uncertainty of a relationship, which is called *correlation.* A correlation coefficient is a measure of the relationship between variables.

What are the variables? The finite human brain, in its attempts to understand reality, is forced to simplify. Every single event and entity in the universe is unique, but it is convenient for us to think about each one as being in a *class.* A class is the name of the mental net in which we catch a large number of entities or events that are unique but similar to each other. For example, the class *human beings* embraces all the members of the human race. While each person is unique and individual, we can make a number of very useful, predictive laws and generalizations about people as a class. True, we falsify nature as soon as we classify, but the mind has a corrective technique. Having accepted that an entity is a member of a class *man,* we can then determine how he differs from other members of that class – taller or shorter, brown hair or white hair, fatter or thinner. Each of these ways of differing within a class is a variable, and of course there are a vast number of variables within the class *man.* A 'variable' is simply a way of being different.

Many useful predictive laws or generalizations of science have arisen from the discovery that one variable changes in unison with another. For example, heat given off by a wire varies in direct relation to the amount of electricity that passes through it. The relationship is very exact. In another case, however, the way in which one variable changes with another may be less exact. Two variables in human beings, lung cancer and cigarette smoking, are related. However, not everybody with lung cancer smokes, and not everybody who smokes gets lung cancer; yet there is a definite relation between the two. This is an example of a much weaker relation or correlation. It is a measure of how much one variable tells us about the other one.

Correlations are measured by a number called a *coefficient,* on a scale from 0, which means there is no relationship, to either + 1.0, which means there is an unchanging positive relation between the two variables, or −1.0, which means that they are completely related but that their relationship is reversed. As one variable increases, the other variable always decreases. It does not matter what the actual value of the variables are; it is the *strength* of the relation between them that is measured by the correlation coefficient.

The concept of a correlation coefficient, which has proven extremely useful in many other sciences as well, was first developed in connection with intelligence testing by Sir Francis Galton in the 1880s and advanced by Professor C. E. Spearman in the early 1900s.

Galton pioneered the broader discipline, anthropometry (the measurement and statistical treatment of differences in physical qualities in mankind). Height, weight, head size and shape, these and many other measurements obviously differ between people. They can be measured and the resulting data treated statistically. It is very useful for doctors, clothing manufacturers, aeroplane designers and a thousand other trades and professions to know the average and the variability of these measures. Modern industry could not manage without anthropometric data. This book is a small adventure in one field of anthropometry, called psychometry.

Measurement, precise measurement, as a technique had, as I have said, been incredibly and wonderfully productive in many other fields. So, despite obvious difficulties, certain pioneers began to explore the scientific measurement of differences in potential and ability itself.

After the pioneer work by Francis Galton in anthropometry and his very important book on genius, the Frenchman Binet in Paris devised the first intelligence test.

The theory behind intelligence testing is that among the many thousands of variables between people, there is a very important one that concerns the general ability to deal with information and to solve cognitive problems. Measuring this variable by use of the correlation coefficient scale is a useful and sensible way of differentiating between people. Evaluating human differences on a scale where the congenital idiot lies at one extreme and the genius at the other is helpful to the educator, manager, or parent. From your own experience, you are aware of these differences. You refer to one person as being intelligent, clever, perceptive, crafty, and wise and to another person as being dull, thick, and unintelligent. The adjectives may change but the measuring is always clear. However, there are scientists who seriously deny intelligence as a real factor in the human personality at all. They claim that this particular variable is unpredictive and therefore not worth bothering with, believing the evaluations to be useless. However, in the absence of an equally workable alternative, psychometry remains the only systematic method available to us.

There are many definitions of intelligence, and there is little agreement among scientists about them. It was the British scientist Sir Francis Galton who, as I said, first conceived of the idea of *measuring* differences in intelligence. Before his time the word *intelligence* had been normally used to mean *information*. For instance, the intelligence corps in the army is that part of the army concerned with getting information. But Galton used the word intelligence interchangeably with *general ability*. It was only gradually that the word came to be used in its modern sense. We do *not* use the word intelligence for abilities that are actually *skills* by which we use our bodies well and direct our movements accurately and precisely. We use the word intelligence in connection with the ability to store and deal with information. We do not mean simply good memory; rather, we are concerned with the way the material in our memory is used.

Intelligence is about information, and information is always encoded. We say that a person is intelligent if he has a good information store (memory); is good at integrating new information with the information already in store; is good at simplifying, condensing, and assimilating information to use it more efficiently; and is good at manipulating and dealing with information so as to produce solutions to problems. Here I give a more technical definition of intelligence. 'Intelligence is the capacity in any entity (living thing or artifact) to *detect, encode, store, sort, and process signals generated in the universe and transduce them into an optimal output pattern of instructions.'* Optimal means giving the most advantageous results for the individual or group for which the intelligence is operating. More simply, intelligence is the process of using information for the advantage of individuals or systems.

This is one definition of intelligence. There are many others. None is generally agreed. But all languages have many terms which are used for this complex overall quality in human beings. One of the most frequent, obvious and unwise attacks upon intelligence tests is the dear old 'How do you define it?' ploy. This is based on the peculiar view that nothing is real that cannot be defined. As H. G. Wells pointed out, you can have fun abolishing many classes or concepts by defying people to define them. 'Give me', he said, 'any definition of a chair or "chairishness" you please and I will undertake with the aid of a good carpenter to defeat it.' A horse, a clan, a face, happiness, pain, intelligence: we cannot define them so they don't exist, runs the argument.

THE NORMAL DISTRIBUTION OF INTELLIGENCE

The intelligence variable is an uninterrupted continuum; it spans evenly from the congenital idiot at one end to the genius at the other with the successive levels merging imperceptibly into each other. There are no sharp dividing lines.

Before the nineteenth century began, an important mathematical discovery concerning variability between members of a class was made by the mathematician Karl Friedrich Gauss. He found there was an extraordinary but typical way in which some things, especially living things, varied from the average. You can take variables such as height and weight and measure these for any large sample of people, and the results will show a definite relation between the number of people with any size or weight and the difference of that weight or size from the average. This is so well established that we can tell quite precisely how many people of any given height or weight there are in any population once we have taken measurements of an adequate sample. To illustrate this in terms of human intelligence, first imagine that we select at random 1,000 children from the population. Then we test all their intelligence quotients (IQs) and assign each of them a mark – 50 to one, 122 to another, 171 to a third, and so on.

Next we take them all to a field, select one child of each IQ score, and line them up side by side along one side of the field so that the child with the lowest IQ is to the left. The first child may have an IQ of 60. A child with an IQ of 61 is next, one with an IQ of 62 is next to the child with 61, and so on. At the extreme right will be that very bright child with an IQ perhaps as high as 175.

The remaining children are then asked to line up behind the child with the same score as their own so that you have a line of children with an IQ of 60, and then another line of children with an IQ of 61, then one with an IQ of 62, and so on. What Gauss' law tells us is that if we look down on the field from above, when all the children have been arranged in lines according to the numerical designation of their various IQs, we will see that the shape of the crowd is that of the Gaussian or bell curve as illustrated in the graph on the next page. The lines will be the longest around an IQ of 100, which can be considered the average. As we look at the lines of children to the left and to the right of 100, we see fewer and fewer children in each line. As you get nearer to the extreme left or extreme right, the curve tails off until there is only an odd scattering of children in each line. There are very few extremely clever or extremely retarded children a long way from the average.

We would see exactly the same pattern, though with different children in each column, whether we measure height, weight, or any other similar variable. Gauss' discovery enables us to deal with a vast range of variables among large numbers of human beings.

One generally accepted theory of intelligence is that it is the external sign of an important underlying variable of the human personality that affects the ability or competence of a person to perform many different tasks. A very large number of trials on many different populations in all parts of the world have always led to a single, invariable result: there is a persistent correlation between different abilities in the same set of children. There is a clear tendency for children who do well at one task involving handling information to do well at all such tasks. If we divide any class of children into two groups according to their ability at arithmetic, and then do the same for English, geometry, history, drawing, algebra, physics, and chemistry, we shall find that the group that scores the highest in one subject will also be above average in every other subject.

It was the unexpected and unwelcome discovery that ability did not occur on a 'fair share' basis that forced the pioneer of intelligence testing, Professor C. E. Spearman, to formulate the concept of *general ability*, an all-round mental competence or efficiency that affects the ability of the person in any field to which he applies himself. General ability is the most important of human aptitudes. The ability to store and retrieve information, to form concepts, to see relationships and to make deductions from those relationships, and to assimilate material and formulate new combinations is what distinguishes humanity from the rest of animal life. It is to this general ability, this intelligence, that man owes his present pre-eminent position as master of the earth.

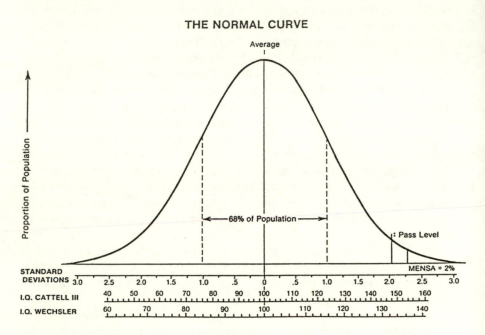

THE NORMAL CURVE

HOW INTELLIGENCE TESTING STARTED

Just after the turn of the last century as public education began to be established in Paris, the authorities had perceived a problem. They were worried about retarded children who were unable to keep up with the standard of the newly established state schools. It was thought that they might benefit by separate special remedial education.

This led to the problem of sorting them out, so as not to waste their time with education at the wrong standard.

Binet

In 1904, Alfred Binet was appointed a member of a commission convened by the Ministry of Public Instruction in Paris to study the problem of these subnormal children. He gradually evolved a series of 50 tests, later increased to 75, which were of increasing difficulty and were chosen so as to separate the children into classes.

Since children's mental ability varies with age, he had to make allowance for this. By grading the tasks in difficulty he had established the principle behind all intelligence tests ever since.

Intelligence tests are designed to stop everybody somewhere and to judge you by the point you reach on a scale. Binet created the concept of the 'mental age'. Ask the child a list of questions of increasing difficulty. Somewhere the child begins to falter.

If the child fails at a point where the *average* child of 8 years old is found statistically to fail, then, said Binet, that child has a *mental age* of 8.

The whole form of intelligence testing ever since was determined by the way in which he next proceeded in order to allow for the differences in age.

There are many ways in which he could have worked, but the method he chose was to divide the mental age by the actual age, which was called the 'chronological age'. This, of course, results in a decimal number which might be somewhere between 0 and 3 or so. He called this ratio the 'mental ratio'.

If a child of 10 years could only reach the point along the scale that the average 8-year-old could reach, then he would have a mental ratio of 0.8.

$$\text{i.e. mental ratio} = \frac{\text{mental age}}{\text{chronological age}} = \frac{8}{10} = 0.8$$

A child of 8, on the other hand, who could reach the point on the scale that the average 16-year-old child could reach, would have a mental ratio of $16/8 = 2$. By a later amendment (introduced by Prof. Lewis Terman) this inconvenient fraction was multiplied by 100, and the absolute value taken so that the mental ratio of 0.8 became an Intelligence Quotient or IQ of 80. Ever since then the practice has been to speak of the IQ. If a child's mental age is the same as its chronological age, its IQ is 100, it is of average intelligence.

Why did Binet seek out this approach? Why the concept IQ? Why not just an Intelligence Scale for all ages? This is the answer.

Binet made two very important discoveries. The first is that IQ *tends to be constant*. I *do* mean 'tends to be' not 'is'. The IQ on the average tends to remain the same as a child grows older. If it can tackle a 12-year-old's problems at 8, it can tackle a 15-year-old's problems at 10.

Later, more exact research showed exceptions to this general rule, but it still remains a good rough guide. There was a constant, quantifiable figure that can be ascribed to intelligence allowing for age.

It is not difficult to criticize this way of going about the problem. Intelligence does increase with age in children, but the assumption behind such a scheme is that intelligence *continues* to increase with age.

Then we come to Binet's second important discovery. It very soon became apparent that intelligence does *not* continue to increase with age. It is surprising to many people when they first hear it, and it was surprising to the pioneers of intelligence testing to discover that, measured in this way, on a scale of difficulty on unfamiliar intellectual tasks, intelligence does *not* appear to increase after puberty. What the experimenters found and what has been confirmed in every experiment ever since is that mental age comes to a halt at an age between 14 and 18 depending on how intelligent the subject is. The brighter you are, the later your intelligence stops increasing. But at 18 or 20 you are as bright as you will ever be. After that – it was discovered much later – it is all downhill. Once it has reached its peak at puberty there is a slow decline in brain power over the decades, a very gradual falling off with a sharper dip in the curve which falls away rather more quickly after the age of 70. Knowledge, experience, skill, effectiveness, go on increasing through life but these are only masking an underlying decline in sheer thinking power.

As the knowledge of Binet's pioneering work spread and the art of intelligence testing developed the defects of Binet's conceptual paradigm became more apparent. The mental age – chronological age system had serious flaws. I feel that the psychologists who followed Binet may be fairly condemned for their lack of creativity in not proposing a better conceptual framework. We need a new breed of psychometricians and a Kuhnian paradigm shift.

Binet's scheme broke down almost before it started. If you apply the same rule to an adult it would have the effect that the intelligence quotient falls rapidly as one gets older. There is a ceiling or cut-off at the age of 18 in mental age but, alas, 'chronological' age goes grimly on. Even if I got the maximum score at my age, I would have the proud distinction, despite the fact that I am the President of Mensa, the high IQ society, of having an IQ far below the level of those unfortunate retardates who are abandoned as untestable by the psychometricians – my IQ would be 25. The reader will have seen that the average IQ is 100, so a score of 25 for the President of a society of our pretensions, would raise questions.

Binet and the founders of this art overcame this gaping hole in their original methodology by the simple but arbitrary process of awarding every adult eternal youth. It was good of them. The concept of chronological age was modified. As far as intelligence testers are concerned humans are not allowed to become older than 18. Be my mental age what it may, my dear reader, I am a mere stripling as to chronological age – a septuagenarian teenager.

Even accepting this, the pioneer testers were still not out of trouble. Mental age is established by taking the *average* performance of many people of that age. Since mental age stops advancing between 14 and 18 the highest mental age is around 16.

At a blow the whole concept of mental excellence (and Mensa) is destroyed. An adult can at best reach the top score, a mental age of 16. Divide that by his highest permissible chronological age 18. IQ = 89. All adults are retardates!

While this might delight the egalitarians, it still had its limitations as a predictive theory which would enable us to think effectively about intelligence. So the weary Binet dragged in yet a further *ad hoc* modification to his original algorithm. He *extrapolated* mental ages. While we were all confined to 18 'chronologically' we could grow older 'mentally'. He introduced a series of more difficult tasks by which mental ages up to 30 could be extrapolated from the original scale. We do not know how he did this — a valid way to do it would have been to wait until the children who had scored IQ 170 when they were young, had reached the age of 30 and then construct fresh items so that they could reach but not pass at that level.

It seems very, very doubtful that this is what he did, so there must have been a good deal of rough and ready bodging in those early, happy, hectic, pioneer days.

Dr David Wechsler, in the United States, saw this problem fairly early on. His major contribution to psychology (apart from his well-known and well-used intelligence tests) was the concept of a deviation IQ. Wechsler, himself born in Europe, began in 1934 to develop the series of intelligence scales which carry his name. He saw the need for the measurement of adult intelligence in a more efficient way than Binet had been able to evolve. Starting in 1939, Wechsler published a series of papers on measuring individuals as they grew older, without using the Binet concept. Wechsler's abandonment of the entire mental age concept (except for the use of clinicians in certain instances), led him to the 'deviation IQ.' Wechsler tested individuals in every age group, up to and beyond 75, and substituted this 'deviation IQ,' for a mental age. Briefly, this means that an individual is measured by his standing in his own age group. Since IQs do have a tendency to remain constant, this means that a 75-year-old in the top 2% most likely was also in the top 2% of 30-year-olds when he was 30. This means of handling adult IQs, a term Wechsler did not drop, was so successful that in 1960 the Stanford-Binet was revised to use such 'deviation IQs' in its tables. The method of deriving the 'deviation I.Q.'' is slightly different, but the Stanford-Binet now uses the deviation method and not the MA/CA method for computing IQ scores. While the lay reader has no need to go into the rather abstruse statistical concepts, it is comforting to know that we need not fear taking a standard intelligence test just because we are older. The results will be as accurate as they were when we were younger.

When I first became interested in the subject as I began to take on responsibilities in Mensa, I discovered that the concept 'intelligence quotient' is highly unsatisfactory. I also discovered the better way which had been suggested by Galton but not widely adopted. The answer is to use another measure for this wonderful but elusive quality, intelligence, to use a conceptual system. But first let us turn to Spearman.

Spearman and Burt

That was the state of the art as Binet's thinking left it. The next new thinking which elaborated and improved the early notions came from the Englishman Professor Charles Spearman, who worked closely with Professor Sir Cyril Burt.

Spearman spotted the cultural effect in Binet's general knowledge questions, which unfairly advantaged middle class children, for instance. He tried to devise tests which measured general intellectual ability, but which had not this cultural bias.

This led him to a fundamental and crucial discovery, a discovery that has been the basis of almost all theory since. What he discovered was, as I described earlier, the single, general underlying measurable factor *behind* differences in ability at *all* tasks. This factor could fairly be described as the 'general intelligence' or g factor of the subject.

General ability and special abilities

It arose in this way. He did a thorough study to pin down the various elements of scholastic and other abilities. He found, as I have described, that no matter what test you used and no matter what type of mental ability you tried to test there was a correlation, a relationship between the different abilities in any largish group. He found that abilities *cluster* in people.

He would test a large sample of children of matched age for, say, arithmetic, and jigsaw puzzle solving and English comprehension and general knowledge and diagram insight. What he would always find was that, I repeat, the children who did well at any one of these tests, *tended* to do very well at *all* the others. This is true of every subject where conceptual comprehension seemed to be involved. Cognitive abilities are *not*, it seems, fully independent variables.

Spearman discovered a correlation between ability scores. In fact, he created the human thought-tool, the correlation coefficient to order our thinking about this. It has been enormously useful in many fields ever since.

This led him to elaborate a new conceptual approach. There were, he posited, for each child, special ability factors and a general ability factor. He accounted for the variation of each pupil from the norm by saying that they had different proportions of special abilities on various subjects but that there was a general factor which affected their score on every subject. These 'factors' are not put forward as real things in nature, they are human thought-tools, ways of thinking which make it possible to make sensible predictions about children and to understand how they vary in intelligence and ability.

There do appear to be in this general factor, when looked at much more closely later, subgroups of a less important type. One group of people with what is called a high g (or general ability) score will be found to be somewhat more able in verbal tests while another group are slightly superior at pattern recognition and design tests, those which test the comprehension of space relationships.

But the strength and unity of the original Spearman concept of a single general ability factor g with modifying special ability factors s has been a helpful and fruitful simplification of understanding in the world of psychiatry and psychology. It has been very useful in education (as the most predictive indication of academic achievement). It has been of significant help in industry (as a means of getting round, square and polygonal pegs into the appropriate holes with the least waste of human talent, time, patience and money).

One period of dissent from the central Spearman doctrine occurred while Professor L. L. Thurstone, working with a sample of graduates, came to the conclusion that there was *not* a single general factor but a number of quite separate factors each of which was independent of the others.

The argument raged for some time until Thurstone became convinced of his error and became a convert to the school of Spearman. The argument was a very complex one but it could be summed up in the following way.

In dealing with a group of graduates Thurstone had reduced to negligible proportions the variation of general ability in his sample; in these circumstances the other differences, the differences in special ability on many different subtests assumed an importance which they would not have had in a random sample of the whole population.

Today, among psychometric psychologists the idea that there is a single unitary general underlying factor which can be helpful and predictive and for which the label 'general ability' is appropriate is very widely accepted.

In Great Britain, one test publisher publishes ¾ million group tests per annum. In America, 150 million standardized tests were administered to school and college students during one recent year when a count was taken. Mensa tests hundreds of thousands of people a year all over the world.

Mental measurement was the newest of the sciences whose practitioners wanted it to be an exact science. Uncertainty was manifestly high, and its pioneers Spearman and Burt turned eagerly to this newly developing mental tool.

I have briefly traced the idea of that important human variable intelligence from its beginnings. I have tried to show how the idea, without any precise definition, has been divided, changed and adapted until it has become a useful and predictive thought tool which helps us in the vital human task of understanding each other and working effectively together with each other. I believe that as we advance into the future, learn more about the brain and its operation, as we develop artificial intelligence we shall improve even more this concept and its usefulness to our species in its life on earth.

7

How IQ Tests are Composed and Tested

What the intelligence examiner is trying to measure is *general* ability, which cannot be measured by a test that applies only to one particular ability. We have to employ a number of different tests, each of which is directed to examine a special aspect of general ability, or use one test that investigates several abilities. There will be tests of the ability to manipulate numbers (arithmetical tests); verbal tests, which will be concerned with the ability to use words accurately and well; tests that will inquire into the ability to understand problems concerning shapes and forms; and tests that will measure the ability to make rational decisions based on deductions from given facts. The collection is called a *battery* of tests.

The whole battery of tests consists of a number of individual questions within each category. The final result is a summary that measures or indicates the subject's all-round ability across the entire range of tests. The tests are normally arranged in a rising order of difficulty, the most difficult questions coming last. The object of a timed IQ test is to discriminate; so the most difficult questions should be such that no one can do them in the time allowed. If, for instance, the most intelligent 10% of children could do the most difficult questions, then the test would not be discriminating among the top 10%. No one should, therefore, be surprised if the child fails to finish the course. The child is either very careless or extraordinarily bright if he does – or there is something wrong with the test. Some of the tests in this book are timed, others are untimed. On these, the child may take as long as he wants. All subjects should find these tests too difficult at some point.

OPEN- AND CLOSED-ENDED TESTS

There are two types of tests: open-ended and closed-ended. The open-ended test asks questions to which there can be a number of correct answers, for example, 'Name a mammal that lives in the sea'. 'Whale' or 'porpoise' are both good answers. Closed-ended tests have multiple choice questions that give a limited number of alternatives to select from, for example, 'Which of the following animals is a mammal and also lives only in the sea – walrus, porpoise, shark, or herring'. In this case, the only answer is 'porpoise', as the others either are not mammals or spend some of the time out of the sea. The closed-ended question with a limited choice has an administrative advantage. It can be unambiguously marked by anyone with modest clerical skill. The marker does not need to understand the questions as they are marked from a key. Open-ended questions require interpretation and much more skill and intelligence in the marker. They also allow subjective judgement to affect the answer. Closed-ended questions are more objective, provided they are properly composed and the accuracy of the answers has been thoroughly checked.

A distinct disadvantage of open-ended questions is that they create significant problems statistically. It is more difficult to measure the probability of, and therefore the implication of, a correct answer.

There is always a chance in a closed-ended test that the person will arrive at the correct answer by accident. In the example of a closed-ended question given above, there are four possible answers, so there is a one-in-four chance (a probability of 0.25) that the person may get the answer right by having selected it at random, arbitrarily. You have to accept the fact that an element of chance enters into any measurement of this type of test.

However, the probability that anyone would achieve a high score in a whole battery of closed-ended tests by chance is very low. The rule is simple. The probability of getting one item right by chance, if there are four alternatives, is one in four; the probability of getting two items right is one in 16; the probability of getting three items right is one in 64. The mathematical equation for calculating this probability is

$$p = (1/a)^n$$

where a = the number of alternative answers and *n* = the number of questions. The rule is 'multiply' the probabilities. A test of 25 items with four alternatives each leaves a negligible probability (nearly 10^{16} to one) of a correct solution of all items by chance. However, there is a distinct and measurable possibility of getting a noticeably *better* score by chance, especially if the person follows the optimum strategy of guessing when the answer is not known. In most IQ tests there is no penalty for wrong answers.

Experience has shown that even when a person thinks he is making a wild guess, the answer is more affected by his intelligence than he realizes.

While the odds against succeeding by luck can be easily calculated with closed-ended tests, they cannot be so easily calculated with the open-ended ones. Obviously, when the test results are used to assess IQ an allowance is made for the chance or luck effect since this qualification cannot be eliminated.

What other uncertainties are there in intelligence testing? Each test is applied to a sample (as large as possible) of the population in order to establish both the average score and the way in which groups of people deviate from the average. This is referred to as the *standard deviation* or *spread* of the distribution. It is a sign of a good intelligence test if this spread follows the pattern of the normal distribution curve. If the test is badly constructed, it will have a distorted curve, and the psychologists will know that something is wrong.

THE TEST POPULATION

The next question of validity arises from the actual population that is used as a sample. Ideally, a random sample of the whole of humanity should be used to check the validity of a test. The psychologist has to do the best he can to obtain a widespread, random sample of people to establish an approximate average so that anyone tested can be placed with respect to it.

The psychologist is usually forced to work with one language group in one country, so what he is actually determining is the average for that subdivision of humanity and the way that group deviates from the average. But there is very good reason to suspect that different groups within one country, even though they may speak the same language, are exposed to different ideas and concepts and therefore do not perform in the same way on any test. Sociologists and anthropologists speak of these different groups as classes, cultures, subcultures, or socioeconomic groups. Sometimes these different groups have the same average score and spread of scores as others, but more frequently there are differences between one group and another. While there is not so much difference in the spread of scores, usually the average score is different.

There are two views about these differences held by sociologists and psychologists, and there is a great deal of controversy on the subject. The issue is that it is usually those groups that have less money and fewer privileges that, generally speaking, score low on these tests. The upper and middle classes tend to have a higher average score, though they still have a wide spread just as the other socioeconomic groups do. Skilled workers seem to have a medium score, while unskilled workers and underprivileged minorities are found to score, on the average, at a lower level. The difference in averages creates a controversy primarily because of its political implications.

One point of view, put forward by a group of psychologists, believes that the differences in the average score of the various groups reflect, or may reflect real differences of average mental ability between various human groupings.

Mongolians such as Eskimos, Chinese, and Japanese, they say, have the highest average score. Caucasian whites, especially northern ones, come next on the scale. Mexicans and southern Europeans generally come slightly lower, and black people lower still.

Looking at social classes, they find that working class people in skilled occupations average higher scores than those who follow manual occupations, and clerical and professional workers come successively higher.

They believe that these scores may reflect significant innate differences. Those who hold these views do not speak of the entire class or group as being higher or lower but say that the group average is higher or lower. They point out that the spread of intelligence from the brightest to the dimmest in each group is still very great.

The opposite point of view is that there is no evidence to support the belief that there are any differences between the average intelligence of different ethnic and socioeconomic groups and that it is inadmissible to investigate the question because any test of intelligence must of necessity be biased against particular groups.*

I have explained the understandable but fumbling and unsatisfactory way the pioneers developed the concept of Intelligence Quotient. In my view, it would do not great harm if the expressions mental age, chronological age and IQ were replaced with a set of concepts that were better thought out. These old expressions are part of the lore and mystery of psychometry, which, since they take a bit of understanding, help to preserve it as the realm of experts. They add little enlightenment and much confusion.

Fortunately, there is, as I have said, a much better way of doing the job that this set of concepts was set up to do. The base material of a completed, normed, and standardized IQ test is the raw scores of a random population of various age groups. From this data, we can calculate the average and the spread (standard deviation) in raw score for every age group, and from this information, we can calculate for every age group a simple figure called the percentile rating of any score for any age. The percentile rating can easily be

---

* The principle upon which my own test and Dr Langer's test have been constructed is to use items that have no content in language, because the language patterns of different groups are appreciably different and also because the test may be used in many countries.

In choosing items not associated with language (non-verbal items), we have had to make a small sacrifice of accuracy since verbal tests seem to be a better aid in determining intelligence than other types of tests. The factor *general ability* seems to have more effect on success in verbal than in non-verbal tests. Therefore, a person who is good with words may be somewhat penalized. Those whose intelligence seems to favour their understanding of shapes and forms or reasoning will be somewhat advantaged. You can make some allowance for this in assessing the results. Professor Raymond Cattell, however, feels that these 'culture fair' tests are much better at detecting innate or genetic 'fluid ability'. He feels that verbal tests measure 'crystallized ability', which is partly environmental.

illustrated in a table, and this table will explain, in a simple and comprehensible way, the only thing that an intelligence test can tell us – where an individual stands in relation to the rest of the population tested.

If you were told that your IQ was 160, you would have to acquire a good deal of experience to know exactly what that means, and you would also need to know the standard deviation of the test. But if you were told that your intelligence was such that you were in the top 10% or the top 60% of the population, you could appreciate the significance of the remark immediately. That is the way a percentile rating works.

If a child falls just within the top 5%, we say he 'falls on the 95th percentile'. If he is just in the top 10%, he 'falls on the 90th percentile'. The idea is simple; the population is divided into one hundred parts, and the scores that would create such separations are calculated statistically from the known characteristics of the normal curve.

The percentile rating is a much simpler and more comprehensible system of expressing the classification of people by intelligence than the confusing and largely historical expressions explained above. The millile works in the same way but the population is divided into a thousand parts.

SOME QUESTIONS ABOUT MENTAL TESTING

Practice effect

Can children be trained to do better at intelligence tests? Yes, but only to a limited extent if the test is well constructed. (Most tests are done on children.)

Professor Vernon, who investigated this question, finds practice will improve the score gradually up to 6 or 7 IQ points, but after that it levels off and no further improvement occurs.

The entire principle upon which intelligence tests are based is that every child should be confronting unfamiliar material for the first time. Each should be given exactly and precisely the same instructions so that everybody starts at the same level. Each time the test is given, an effort must be made to reproduce exactly the same standard conditions of testing, as far as these can be achieved. But, of course, many children do not get second tests.

A solution proposed by Professor Eysenck to the above problem is that all children should be given a certain amount of practice so that the practice effect can be absorbed and disposed of. However, if the original tests were standardized on an unpractised population, as they usually are, then the standardization will be thrown out by this procedure, and all children will achieve slightly better scores than they should.

Nonetheless, within the normal accuracy of intelligence testing, I do not think this effect is of much importance.

Are tests much affected by the subject's state of health?

A good deal of research has been done on this subject, and in a considerable number of experiments it has been shown that minor disabilities, such as headaches, coughs and colds, make very little significant difference in the test score despite the fact that the subjects often feel they have not performed at their best level.

In the tests in this book you are recommended to choose a time when your subjects are in good health. You are likely to have a better choice in timing than teachers or psychologists have, especially when they have to test large numbers within a short time.

Does a child's IQ change as it grows older?

The underlying hypothesis of intelligence testing is that IQ tends to remain the same relative to their age group as children grow older. While this is generally true, there are exceptions.

The correlation between IQ at 2 years and at 18 years is less than 0.4, while between 8 and 18 years, it is above 0.8. After the age of 10, it reaches the limits imposed by the reliability of the test itself and is about 0.9. These correlation coefficients cover changes, which may be as high as 30 points or more, over the school years in individual children. Such large changes are very uncommon. In fact, fewer than 10% of the children will change by as much as this. However, changes of 1–10 points are commonplace, and around 70% of the children tested will come within this range. Part of this fluctuation is accounted for by test error, though some of it is due to actual spurts and delays in the development of the children. Children from educationally advanced environments show a statistical bias toward a gain in IQ, as do children from backgrounds where they started off with a higher IQ. Boys appear to gain in IQ more frequently than girls, and, in fact, an advance in IQ is noticeably more prevalent in aggressive middle class males. Girls start off higher than boys and tend to lose their advantage with time.

And what if the children are not trying?

It goes without saying that any test of a competitive nature is only applicable, valid, and reliable if the people being tested are really trying. A perfectly legitimate argument against tests under standardized conditions at school or at a clinic is that some children are not motivated to do their best either through individual inattention or because of preconditioned environmental factors.

If you suspect that your child is not trying, wait for a better occasion to administer the test, or the results may be meaningless. Parents know their children pretty well, certainly much better than teachers or psychologists do, so you will know when they are trying and when they are not. The kind of spirit to encourage is the competitive spirit of a game. They should not take the test too seriously and become worried or anxious about it. Nonetheless, they should certainly go at it energetically, with enthusiasm and excitement at the prospect of pushing themselves to their own limits. We believe that one of the advantages of parental testing will be in just this area. Most children will trust their parents and do more for them than they will do for teachers or strangers, however skilled and well trained.

Regression to the mean

One way of checking the reliability of intelligence tests is to give the same tests to the same group after an interval sufficiently long to ensure that the subjects have forgotten the answers. Most people on retesting score within a few points of their initial score on a well-constructed test. Responsible test constructors will not accept a test as being valid unless the test–retest reliability, as it is called, is fairly high. However, looking at the results of these retests statistically, a trend emerges that ought to be mentioned. There is a persistent tendency for the low scorers to get slightly better scores on retesting and for the higher scorers to get slightly worse ones, while those around the average have no specific tendency, some going higher and some going lower. This is called the regression to the mean.

There is an element of chance in all results. Test constructors try to control it and keep it as low as possible, but it is always there.

The more a score deviates from the average, the greater the probability that chance has contributed to the deviation – that is, if you take a group of very high scorers, you are likely to get more people whom chance favoured rather than opposed. Similarly, with very low scorers, there will be more who were unlucky than who were lucky. Given a second chance, you cannot expect the luck or bad luck to be repeated in every case, so there will be a slight tendency for all scores to cluster closer toward the average next time. The more they do, the more part chance played in the result, but since the effect is not major, we can assume that chance played only a small part.

Is there a ceiling to intelligence?

A series of experiments with mice has shown that there appears to be a biological ceiling for the development of intelligence. Two groups of mice were bred apart as regards their ability to learn to run mazes; the quickest learners were bred together and so were the slowest. In a relatively small number of generations the two populations were so different that the slowest of the fast-learners group learned faster than the fastest of the slow learners.

But further selection from the brightest of the bright produced *no* improvements as it soon became evident that in a given stock of mice there was a natural limit to further genetic development.

My guess is that there is a similar ceiling to human intelligence. The analogy is a poker game. You shuffle your cards and everyone gets a hand; your particular hand is a matter of chance, and the probability of getting four aces is fairly low but it is predictable. By manipulating the pack and taking out some cards, you can increase the chances of a high hand but you cannot get anything higher than four aces. The more complex a species gets the less likely an improving combination is. So we may have to wait some time for a superman. Meanwhile we could, if we wanted to, arrange that more people get high hands in the genetic poker game, or we could reduce the number of low hands. But that is a new and highly controversial subject which I will have the wisdom to leave at this point, otherwise someone will say 'Hitler' or 'Eugenics' or some other swear word and all rational thought will cease.

Speed: the tester tested

Another chestnut of the antitesters is the false paradox: 'How does the tester deal with people more intelligent than he is?' The answer is a question of speed. The brighter you are the faster you solve problems, even simple ones. That is why most intelligence tests are 'speeded'. That is to say, they are deliberately designed not to give the subject sufficient time. Many of those who complain because they cannot pass the Mensa tests say, 'I didn't have enough time'. Of course they didn't. Any test which gave *everyone* sufficient time would do a poor job of discrimination. However, there is some argument about this among psychometricians, and there are other types of tests called 'power' in which what is tested is the ability to solve difficult problems: people are divided into categories according to their ability to solve them at all. It is much more difficult to devise this kind of test; they have to be much more carefully graded for difficulty and sorted into order of difficulty in the test. I agree from many years' experience in developing Mensa that there is something in this. But it may be difficult to produce a really convincing experiment to demonstrate the fact, if fact it is.

Are intelligence tests unfair to minority cultures?

To varying degrees intelligence tests, and there are many of them, have a 'cultural loading' to use the jargon. It is obvious that a test composed in Gujurati or Urdu would produce poor scores from French or Finnish children. You cannot test if you cannot communicate. But communication is not an all or none business. There are degrees of it, so as the comprehension and understanding become less so does the value of the test.

This results in unfairness only if unwarranted conclusions are drawn. If tests are used on people for whom they are unsuitable because of lowered comprehension, then they will be unpredictive.

However, the degree of the cultural loading in various tests is different. If the test is composed entirely of simple pictures and designs and there are no items involving words in any particular language, then the cultural limitations will be less and people from any culture who are familiar with such designs will be on a relatively even footing. (But primitive tribesmen, unfamiliar with diagrams will just scratch their heads.)

However, as I have said, this increased applicability of the test is bought at a price. The 'g' or general ability 'loading' of the verbal tests is very high and if verbal items are left out, then an important component of general ability is neglected. The resultant scores would have a bias in favour of those who had better comprehension of space relationships and diagrams.

There are tests for which it is claimed that they are 'culture free' or 'culture fair'. In these the above disadvantage has been accepted so as to extend the range of usefulness of the test. This seems to be sensible.

In some countries, in Northern Europe and in USA, the art of intelligence testing has developed much more than in others. As the art spreads from those countries to others it is quite useful to have some tests where the cultural effect is minimized so as to help with the problem of cultural transfer.

It must not be assumed that IQ tests always disfavour ethnic or cultural groups different from those they were standardized on. People of mongolian ethnic origin such as Chinese, Japanese and even Eskimoes do better than Caucasians (white people) *even on Western world tests*. Hopi Indians on reservations have outscored average Americans on American tests. Other ethnic and cultural groups do worse in cross-cultural tests.

Cultural bias in tests

The IQ test was originally seen as an instrument of social justice. Culturally biased though it may be, the IQ test is *less so* than any other type of test or examination which may be used in the search for mental ability. To abandon the IQ test because it disfavours certain minorities is to throw away a lifebelt because it is not a boat. It still remains the best way to find the able but disadvantaged child, who may otherwise lose all chance of getting an education to bring out his full ability. What is needed, certainly, is better and fairer tests for minorities. What will do no good at all is to scrap those we have and leave no means of detecting brilliance or retardation in minority groups at all. A great deal of work remains to be done. We depend far too much on the out-of-date work pioneers.

DEVISING AND VALIDATING TESTS

You may be interested in the actual procedure for elaborating an IQ test and checking on its discrimination, validity and predictability.

The essential process in establishing any respectable intelligence test is, as I have said, that it should have been taken by a sufficiently large sample of the random population which it intends to serve, that the statistical characteristics of that population shall become clear. The psychologist must be able to say what proportion of the target population at a given level of age would score at a given level. It is obviously no light job to make sure that the sample is a random one.

When the psychologist has the data from the tests he can construct a hysterogram which will give him both the average score and the spread of scores around this average.

To do the job properly takes about 5 years and many hundreds of thousands of pounds.

This is the procedure. A large number, some thousands of people, usually children of various ages, are tested on a trial test consisting of many items (questions). Their raw score, age, and other details are recorded. The resulting data is analysed by age and from the average and the spread of figures around it for each age group a first indication of the mental age scale can be evolved.

Test validation

In a series of stages the test items are searched and examined for unsuitable or inconsistent questions or those where some subjects see a relationship unperceived by the setters.

This often comes out when the items (questions) are re-arranged in order of difficulty on the basis of the number who get each of them right. A question that seems to be in the wrong rank has to be looked at again.

Item analysis

When the sifting and rejection process is complete the test goes through an item analysis. This is a very lengthy process by which each item is examined individually. The researchers are not interested only in how many subjects got each item right but also in how many got each possible answer. Every item has its correlation with the rest of the test calculated and checked for consistency. If the correlation coefficient is found to be low or negative the item is thrown out.

Refinement

Then the whole process has to be started again and the revised form of the test with its approximate norms is given to another comparable population so that the process of refinement can continue.

Gradually the refinement proceeds until a satisfactory test is produced. It will be such as to produce the right number of subjects in each percentile slot. The scores of the subjects will correlate well with the results for the same subjects on previously standardized tests. The score distribution will be normal or Gaussian, the test–retest variation will be within the normal range.

Subjective validation

The final stage is the subjective evaluation of the test. It is this stage which gives the lie to the ritual chant, 'IQ tests only measure the ability to pass IQ tests'. They predict and are confirmed by human judgement as well.

The age adjusted scores for all the subjects are checked and accepted only if they have a high correlation with skilled judgements which are, of course, subjective assessments of intelligence made by the testers, teachers, and other skilled experienced professionals.

When all this has been done we have a test which will sort some particular mix of people from some set of language, cultural or socioeconomic groups into IQ ranks. If the samples were well chosen and the work well done, it has been found, the tests are useful and predictable over large areas.

These methods are the best we have. When we use them we must remember that their usefulness is greater and they do a better job on those subjects nearest to the average. As we get away from the medium scorers we lose accuracy and predictability. What may be needed now are more tests such as those devised by Professor Heim, which are devised for and discriminate among the upper levels of mental ability.

The tests in this book have not been through these elaborate and expensive validation procedures. They could not be published if they had because that in itself would invalidate them and waste all the expensive checking. The method used here is different. It is that of composing tests parallel to a range of existing tests and then approximately standardizing the result by keying across on subjects whose IQ is known. Some of them are based on average populations but the advanced ones were devised for and keyed to a highly intelligent population. They are valid only for adults who are well above average intelligence. They have *not* been standardized on a random sample of the general population but on Mensa applicants. Using this sample and noting the differences in their raw scores and IQs we have been able by a projection to make what, for a first-approximation test of this kind, is an adequate extrapolation so that some assessment can be given to any person tested who is somewhat above average intelligence (IQ over 100). Within this group and the more so towards the upper levels of it, this test will give you a reasonably good first guess at your IQ.

THE FINAL VALIDATION

There are some people who, everyone agrees, are very bright. When a new test is finished, if the work is good, we find these people among the high scorers. We find that skilled judgement is largely confirmed respecting low scorers also.

We find that those who score well do well at school and have good academic achievement, and those that score poorly, very rarely do so. We find that those who score well have a much better chance of moving into the professions where it is generally supposed that high intelligence is required, and those who score poorly have a small chance of it. We find all these things match up and we begin to have more and more confidence in our test.

WHAT TESTS PROVE

What I have been saying relates to *trends* and tendencies. There is nothing we can say *definitely* about any person as a result of knowing their IQ score.

The most positive statement we can make is that if anyone from the right cultural group has tried really hard and done badly on an IQ test it is very unlikely that they will be equal to any great intellectual tasks. Only unlikely, not certain.

We can also say with some certainty: anyone who does very well on the test, if they are energetic and motivated, has a good chance of doing well academically, getting to a university, taking a degree and doing fairly well in his/her career. We are *sure* of nothing but when we know the test score we are less *unsure* than we were. We are dealing with probability, not certainty. There are exceptions, but the trend is *definite* and *positive*. More, unfortunately, in a field such as this we cannot yet say.

In a vast and complex life such as we live there are probably a very large number of things which make a difference to how well we do at school and in our jobs. Innate intelligence is one of those factors, a very important one, but sometimes not the predominant one.

STANINES, PERCENTILES AND MILLILES

Stanines

To elaborate further on what I outlined earlier about the unsuitability of the usual *scale* upon which we measure intelligence, IQ, just as we can measure the same distance in yards or metres so we can find many ways to express scalar differences in intelligence or any other human trait.

The collection of statistical data involved in producing an intelligence test can be used in various ways. We could, for instance, go to the table of Normal Distribution which arises from the Gaussian (bell) curve and get an estimate of the proportion of people in the population who would score at any given level. We could divide the population into ten equal, ranked slots and tell people which slot they fall into. Such slots are called stanines, someone in the ninth stanine is in the top 10% of the general population. Someone in the seventh stanine is in the top 30%.

Percentiles

Similarly, as I have done here in places, we can divide the population into a hundred equal groups in our mind. We can then use our test scores to find the lowest hundredth, then the 2nd group, the next hundredth up and eventually up to those in the 99th or top hundredth. These divisions are called percentiles. And if you are in the 99th percentile then only one in 100 people would equal or exceed your score.

If your IQ puts you at the 50th percentile, your score is dead-on average. About 50% of the population would do worse, and 50% better than you on the test.

Anyone who scores on the 20th percentile would find 80% of people would do better. Someone on the 95th percentile would have a score equal to or better than 95% of the population.

A further argument supporting a better way of expressing differences in intelligence is this. Theoretically all IQ tests, and there are now many of them, should have about the same standard deviation (spread of variation). In practice, tests have different standard deviations so the 'IQ' score on one test will represent a different level of intelligence (or percentile rating) from that on another. 'What is your IQ?' is a question that should be followed by the counter question 'On which test?'. On the Cattell Scale III test for instance, an IQ of 148 is equivalent only to 132 on the Wechsler scales (see p. 204). It is quite unnecessarily confusing. On both tests the percentile rating is, of course, the same.

Mensa selects at the 98th percentile, the level which I found many years ago was the real level at which we were selecting in Mensa as it was being built up.

When, as a layman, I understood the ideas which I have just elaborated, I saw that we were not selecting at the level the founder Berrill thought. It was at the level of 1% that we were supposedly selecting. However, nearly all the selection until then had been performed by unsupervised home tests. So I checked up with the help of Dr Robert Green, then a lecturer in psychology at London University. We discovered that it was the top 2% that had qualified and I made the decision that there was no good reason to change that practice.

Ever since then, selection for Mensa has been on the arbitrary level of the 98th percentile on any generally accepted test of intelligence, properly supervised.

Milliles

The principle with milliles is the same as that in stanines and percentiles. Those in the top millile score better than 999 in 1000. Those in the 998th millile can lick 998 in the average 1000 folk in tests.

Milliles are suspect as giving bogus accuracy to a very rough estimate so that they should be looked on with caution. Measuring intelligence in milliles is like measuring your height in millimetres, breathe in and your estimate is wrong.

In summary, I have described briefly the procedure for composing an intelligence test, and suggested a change in the way we designate differences in intelligence.

8

Are IQ Tests Immoral? Have they been Debunked?

If IQ tests have been successfully debunked and are generally acknowledged to be of no value, then it logically follows that they cannot be really immoral since they would be ignored.

Over the past many years, I have paid very special attention to the subject of IQ and IQ testing as it has been reported in all the communications media. Mental testing is 'debunked' with monotonous regularity every few years. However, the basis for this persistent attack does not seem to arise from new research in the subject area. Writers are usually content to express and re-emphasize doubts that were raised by the pioneers of psychometric testing themselves. Much is made of the argument concerning cultural bias, the critics claiming that this argument not only reduces the validity of the tests but also makes them 'completely meaningless'. The critics are rarely psychologists; often the attacks come from sociologists or political scientists.

This is understandable. Sociological methodology is based on the concept of the individual human being as the unit, the 'atom', as it were, of a predictable system. Sociological truths are laws concerning the relationships of people and groups, as the laws of chemistry concern the relation of atoms and molecules. Every science must simplify, even oversimplify, before it can begin to deal with the complexity of the world, and the sociological over-simplification is equivalence of all people. Psychometry and psychology, on the other hand, emphasize individual differences – an approach that is inconvenient to sociological theory.

Since sociological theory tends to explain the behaviour of groups in relation to their socioeconomic class and environmental circumstances, it also tends to explain the measurable differences in mental ability as being due to environmental differences often based on socioeconomic status.

Psychometric evidence concedes that this is at least partly true, so some sociologists find it easy to believe that environmental causes are the principal sources of manifest mental differences. They also argue, with some truth, that environmental differences are the ones we can easily do something about and so are most worthy of attention.

There are people, as I have mentioned, of strong political persuasions who claim that since groups from the more privileged socioeconomic classes have a higher average score on tests in general, these tests are used to justify and therefore to perpetuate and exaggerate class privileges. They go on to claim that the identification (or classification) of ability is therefore wrong and should not be allowed at all.

The facts are very different. In reality, people who score well on intelligence tests come from all social and economic backgrounds, and the majority of the gifted individuals in any generation always come from less privileged economic groups in that generation. The more privileged groups, however, do contribute a higher *proportion* to the gifted ranks.

Nonetheless, many outspoken professionals believe that any test or procedure that reveals or predicts the underlying differences in human ability is divisive, causing friction between man and his fellow man. However, there is no recent substantive evidence that this is so or that intelligence testing has been used to justify and perpetuate class and racial differences.

The fiercest divisions do not appear to be those between ability groups but those between formally organized power and pressure groups. There seems to be no special quarrel between the scholars and the dunces in any school, nor any public friction between the middle and working classes. Rather, our age is dominated by a struggle between organized groups, each of which is led by a cadre of tough, intelligent, and able leaders all of whom would undoubtedly do very well on intelligence tests themselves. When the mentally able students get into a conflict, it is not with the less able but with their peers or with even more able professors and lecturers, the so-called 'academic establishments', which many of them are destined to replace.

An important underlying principle of Western society is the idea of the best man for the job. Only a few rash extremists believe that jobs should be allocated at random, without respect to ability, experience, or competence. Defenders of IQ tests claim that they are the fairest methods of assessing one of these qualities, mental ability, that they are the fairest to all social classes, and that they reflect, less than any other method, the social background of the candidate.

A criticism of IQ tests that *is* justified is the argument 'Intelligence is not everything.' The debunkers point out, quite truthfully, that intelligence is not the only quality required by leaders, experts, administrators, technicians, or specialists. They are not so unwise as to say that intelligence is not required for these jobs, but they simply emphasize that other qualities such as humanity, patience, diligence, honesty, and ambition are also important. This appears to be an area of common ground. Few defenders of IQ tests will claim that intelligence is the only quality required, although some, with justification, contend that the probability is slightly higher that the other qualities required will be available in highly intelligent people.

Opponents of IQ testing also emphasize creativity as a very important quality that is not discovered by IQ tests. Critics of IQ testing, as I said, set up creative ability against intelligence, as though there were some kind of competition between the two that creativity is going to win.

EQUALITY

Those people who declare that IQ tests are immoral say that by setting up a measurement relating to mental ability, the tester has committed an act of discrimination and has emphasized individual differences by assigning a rank and number to them.

Have you ever heard of an underground war between athletes and cripples, fast and slow runners, the short and the tall, the skinny and the fat, or, indeed, between the blonds and the brunettes in any street, club, or school? It simply does not seem to be true that revealing such differences between people necessarily creates strife.

Even if we refuse to measure differences in mental ability, they will still be spotted and recognized, because nothing will stop people from observing and judging one another. What will be lost, however, is any accuracy and impartiality in these assessments. We shall also fail to recognize potential that is not always shown in early performance.

Perhaps we should look at the idea of equality again. The word is not always used in the same way. Political equality can be used to describe affairs where the political influence, rights, and opportunities available to every citizen are equal. Equality can also be extended to suggest that people's income and privileges should be equal. It can be yet further extended to suggest (and this is the extremist position) that all people are in fact equal in every way, or that any differences between them are unimportant and can be ignored.

Politicians and moralists who favour these various increasing extensions of equality always argue that acceptance of their ideas will reduce conflict. Their arguments, however, seem to be based on assumptions, not actual experience.

Social animals that live in herds, flocks, or cooperating groups have the problem of avoiding all-out competition and mutual destruction among the various members. Prominent, of course, among these social animals is man himself.

What is observed in every type of social animal, from invertebrates up to man, is that a simple social mechanism is set up – a ranking system or pecking order – by which every animal has an accepted position in the hierarchy of the social group.

Professor Wynne-Edwards observed a fact concerning the life of animals in the wild that was so obvious that it had been invisible to previous observers. He perceived that animals living in the wild without human interference were usually healthy, sleek, and well fed despite the fact that their food supply was limited. According to Thomas Robert Malthus, the 19th century British economist, a population will expand until the food supply is inadequate. Therefore, we should expect the natural state of a wild population of animals to be semistarvation. But apparently there are built-in behaviour patterns, like territoriality, pecking order, and mock fighting, which act as a kind of self-regulating system. Instead of semistarvation for the entire species, a pattern arises that means an adequate amount is provided for a limited number and the remainder are naturally eliminated. It works like this: after a series of trial, and relatively harmless, scuffles that consist of display and mock attacks, the animals sort themselves out into a rank order that is well understood and accepted by all of them. The higher ranks have first access to the food and the females of the species, a fact of life conceded by all the lower ranks. The effect of the system is to enable animals to live together in cooperating groups without excessive and damaging fighting, which would undermine the survival of the whole group.

If a social group comes upon hard times, such as food shortages, there are alternatives. The members of the group can fight among themselves until they are debilitated and make easy prey for their enemies. Alternatively, they can have an equal sharing system, which might mean having a subsistence ration for half the winter and none for the rest. The last alternative is a behaviour pattern that ensures that some still will be fully fed and retain their capacity for flight and fight. The unfortunate lower status animals perish, but the tribe or herd survives as a whole.

The lesson to be learned from this is simple: because of seasonal ups and downs and the accidents of life, it seems that, in their natural surroundings, animals that live in herds and groups find that it is *equality* that is divisive and *inequality* that makes social life possible.

A herd dedicated to the principle of total equality among its members is fighting to maintain an unstable situation. It will pay the price with a certain, though perhaps acceptable, increase in internal conflict. There is certainly no sign of reduced conflict in the increasingly egalitarian and affluent human societies of the West. Most disputes between men and management are about *differentials* – that is, about adjustments in the pecking order. The moral and emotional force behind status-preserving conflict is the strongest we encounter.

The moral values of our society – liberty, equality, and fraternity – are good and desirable, but we maintain them only by constant struggle against the biological pressure to return to a stable state of inequality. This morally desirable, unstable state, however, will only be maintained by ethical and moral traditions less available to other animals.

We men and women take it for granted that the adults, the strong and able in each generation, must support, lead, maintain, and nurture the young, whose abilities have not fully developed, and the old, whose abilities are in decay. We often do not see clearly that the ablest among the adults must make more than their fair contribution for the good of all. And we also sometimes fail to see that those who can do so much for all are worth the special attention of our educators.

It is, perhaps, the tacit realization of the inherent instability of equality as a social principle that gives force to some of the unreasoning attacks upon intelligence testing.

In his book *IQ in the Meritocracy*, R. J. Herrnstein recounts how he published an article about the history of intelligence testing and summarized the main facts that have accumulated in the technical literature for several generations about the inheritance of IQ and the social class differences involved. After the publication of his article, Herrnstein was subjected to a widespread campaign of academic vilification. His opponents seemed not to have troubled to read what he had actually written. Almost all the remarks published that were attributed to him were misquotations. He was accused of racism, though he had not touched upon the subject of race at all. The campaign was led by a small group of activists, and a number of Herrnstein's lectures, which were in no way connected with IQ testing, were packed with protesters and had to be abandoned. A more recent example has been the character assassination of Sir Cyril Burt.

As shocking as this extreme behaviour may seem, it happened, and it serves as an example of the conflict that has boiled around the use of IQ tests and the release of their results.

As you can now readily see, the arguments against intelligence tests are not consistent, nor do the critics present a cohesive, logical, or objective argument. Rather, they constitute a number of disjointed, sporadic, and often mutually contradictory attacks. The theory on which intelligence testing is based takes into consideration these divergent points of view, assimilates their intrinsic value or importance, and logically evaluates before analysing results.

To summarize the arguments that are brought forward and that do not add up:

(1)   Intelligence tests are supposed to measure intelligence, and *intelligence* is undefined.

(2)   The definitions of the quality *intelligence* are contradictory.

(3)   Intelligence tests only measure the subject's ability to do intelligence tests.

(4)   Intelligence tests measure nothing at all. (The quality they are supposed to measure, intelligence, does not exist.)

(5)   The quality intelligence tests are supposed to measure, intelligence, is not important.

(6)   Creativity is more important than intelligence.

(7)   Lateral thinking is more important than intelligence.

(8)   Other things are important as well as intelligence.

(9)   Intelligence tests are used to perpetuate racist and class privilege.

(10) The statistical background of intelligence tests is faulty and they are discredited.

(11) Intelligence tests are unreliable.

(12) Intelligence tests are unfair to underprivileged groups.

(13) Intelligence tests have no predictive value at all.

(14) Intelligence tests are self-fulfilling predictions.

(15) Intelligence tests measure only the effect of social background.

(16) Intelligence tests are of no value and can be disregarded.

(17) Intelligence tests are used to label children.

(18) Intelligence tests are used to prepare children for an unjust society.

When we see these arguments lined up, we begin to see a degree of overkill that makes us suspicious of the whole thing. For smallpox there is one simple preventive remedy, vaccination. For the common cold, which we cannot cure, there are a thousand remedies. Intelligence testing survives the ceaseless assaults of its critics, and we might suspect that the long continual virulence and persistence of the attack is a partial proof of that very attack's failure.

Opponents of IQ testing object that the tests label children. The idea is that by revealing the potential ability in some children, you unavoidably show up the lower potential ability in others. They are labelled as potential failures, and this becomes a self-fulfilling prophesy. The child's teacher lowers his expectations for low scorers and this in itself results in different academic achievements, even in different subsequent IQ scores.

There is a very much publicized finding by Rosenthal and Jacobsen, who claim that experiments reveal what they call a 'Pygmalion effect'. Teachers were given deceptive information leading them to have a false expectation that certain children were 'spurters' with high IQs and that they would do well later. The children were tested several times over a 2-year teaching period. It was claimed that the result of this experiment was that the children tended to fulfil the expectations based on the misinformation and that those labelled 'spurters' did improve in their IQ scores. From this it was deduced that teachers' expectations have a considerable effect on IQ scores, and as a result children get into self-confining ruts based on a teacher's classification.

The soundness of this experiment has been severely questioned by many experts, but it would seem that doing away with IQ testing can only make matters worse. If the children's performance is based on the teacher's expectations and we refuse to give the teacher any objective information, then he or she will be forced to rely upon his or her own subjective judgement; this has been shown often to be even less reliable than the relatively objective IQ test. The experiments do, however, present a very good argument against giving teachers misinformation about children.

Nonetheless, whether we accept the Pygmalion effect or not, the results of this experiment clearly demonstrate the need for *correct* assessment and frequent rechecking. They certainly do not bring down the large edifice of work on the assessment of intelligence and ability built up over three-quarters of a century by many psychologists.

Perhaps we should look more closely at the idea of labelling – what it implies and why it is objected to.

In any education system, there are more pupils than teachers. Each teacher has to deal with between a dozen and fifty children and must use appropriate methods. It is impossible for the teacher to establish the same kind of relationship with every child that the parent has. The teacher can try to treat each child exactly alike and work on the assumption of uniformity, or he can try as best he can to take account of the individual differences between the children as far as he can perceive and understand them. If any testing or assessment instruments, such as IQ and personality tests, are available, he can make use of this information.

In practice, every teacher has to assume a position between these two extremes. In different eras, educators have tended to go one way or the other. The 'treat them all alike' school has favoured strict discipline, stern punishment, and the concept of the child as an empty vessel that has to be filled with knowledge by the all-knowing teacher. The modern educators in the Western world tend toward the other extreme and place a great emphasis on the individual differences of children and the need to understand these children as unique persons who require individual assessment and treatment.

The paradox of modern education is as I have said, that the teacher is trying to work with two contradictory notions – the notion of equality, which says that all children are of equal potential and value, and the philosophy that each child is unique and entirely different from every other child and requires a completely individual approach. They have determined to try to understand each child as an individual, but their love of equality forces them to try to believe that all children are indistinguishable in that particular human quality that is most important in education – intelligence, or educability. The teachers have available to them evidence that is at least objective, though admittedly not infallible, concerning this most important individual difference between children.

Teachers must use this information in ways that will prove most beneficial to your children, for if it is used in a positive framework, knowledge of intelligence abilities can serve as an effective means of encouragement for the bright child and the underachiever as well.

THE CATCH QUESTIONS AND SOME OTHERS

Now I try to deal with some of the catch questions about mental testing that always come up, which are always given a perfectly satisfactory answer which never stops them coming up again – and again – and again. I try to answer other questions too.

I have dealt with most of these matters earlier in the book but this summary of questions might be useful.

My absolute favourite among these catch questions is the hoary old one always asked with a confident 'and this is the killer' smile, one which I have answered literally thousands of times on various media. It goes like this:

Interviewer (with a carefully composed, friendly, mischievous grin): 'But, Mr Serebriakoff, surely it is well known that all an intelligence test tells you is how good you are at doing IQ tests?'

Answer: 'It certainly tells you that, but once you know it you know something else as well, something quite important about a person, how good they are at the most important human skill – problem solving.'

Next one: 'Surely if you keep practising you can improve your score – so how can the test tell you anything about your underlying mental ability?'

Practice effect

There *is* a good argument against intelligence tests in this area. Is it true that the more you practise doing intelligence tests the better you will be at it. Does this invalidate the test as an instrument?

The muddled answer is yes and no. The technical jargon term is 'test sophistication' and, yes, it does exist. Repeated practice with IQ tests will raise the score a little, an average of about 5–7 IQ points is what most psychologists, e.g. Professor Vernon, who have worked in this field, find.

Embarrassing. Yes, but there is not much we can do about it.

The principle, originally, for a long time strictly observed by psychologists, was to try to avoid test sophistication by keeping the tests under strict control, having them administered only by psychologists and not letting the public get hold of any copies with which they could practise.

However, with the growth of Mensa and the gradual dissemination of information about IQ testing among the lay public, things changed. It was, I suppose, inevitable that someone would finally break the line and present tests of this type to the public for them to use themselves.

In my own book *IQ – A Mensa Analysis and History,* there was a DIY test which enabled people interested to check their general level of intelligence. Later, as I have said, there came a book from Professor Hans Eysenck *Know Your Own IQ* which presented intelligence test type questions and gave a rough assessment.

The walls of the bastion were blown by this book which had enormous sales in the Penguin series in UK and is still marketed today.

Eysenck has always been a courageous and effective popularizer in the field of psychology. Seeing that the problem of test sophistication had become a sort of poison working within the educational system he set out to do something about it. I have mentioned this earlier.

What had happened was this. Despite the determination of the psychological profession to keep this instrument pure and unsullied, teachers began to get hold of tests. Trying to do the best for the children under their tuition they knew that the IQ test was the way to open doors to higher education. They did what was best for the children *in front of them,* by giving them *training* in IQ tests. This was against all the professional tenets. It gave those children who were trained an unfair advantage over those who were not trained. Those teachers who kept the party line and observed the rules, disadvantaged the children they taught. Under these circumstances there was no hope that the taboo against test practice would hold and, increasingly, teachers began to break the rules and train children in tests. This was an unwise business educationally, a waste of time and a distortion of the system.

When he published his book, Eysenck pointed out that since that had happened the only fair thing to do was to make tests more widely available so as to dispose of that source of variation.

There was a price that had to be paid. Obviously the intelligence scores in a sophisticated population would be different from those in an unsophisticated population without any genetic difference in the population itself. Norms, means and standard deviations derived from unsophisticated populations no longer apply with sophisticated populations, so past and future data would not any longer be comparable.

The overall effect might be to disguise a general drift lower in IQ ratings or to give a false impression of raised IQ ratings. Recently Professor Lynn has found a sharp increase in mean IQ.

Thinking on these lines has led me to reflect that it might be possible to devise tests in which the order of difficulty arises from the insights of information theory and not from pragmatic tests. This way, everyone might be given a different but equivalent version of each item.

And the next question:

Are tests equally good all across the range from very bright (IQ 200) to very retarded (IQ 60)?

It is true that the higher or the lower that your IQ is, the less accurately it can be measured.

A test relies for its validity on a large statistical sample. Since scores have a strong tendency to cluster towards the centre in the normal distribution there are plentiful samples in this region which give a high reliability and validity to the test in the middle range.

However, on the upper and lower tails of the normal curve, people scoring at that level are very few. The cells are small and the statistical reliability less.

So the IQ measurement is fairly solid and reliable in the middle of the range, but becomes vaguer and less predictive towards both ends.

A lot of criticism of IQ tests has been made on the grounds of the uncertainties that are produced in this way. Working, often with that very convenient population of university students and graduates (all clustering at the upper tail of the intelligence distribution curve), it is to be expected that anomalies will arise. This sort of anomaly is then projected as an uncertainty which applies across the whole population.

What are needed are tests for very superior adults which can be tested on samples large enough to assure validity. Mensa presents a unique population for this purpose and would be available, in my opinion, to be used if the various national committees were approached.

Do those with high IQ scores do better in life?

The correlation of IQ scores with professional attainment is high, which is an important confirmation of the value of the tests. Every attempt to measure the IQ level of people who are successful in various professions has led to a similar result. The tables taken from Professor Cattell's test show how IQ was distributed among various educational groups in England in 1935.

Professor Lewis Terman did the most significant work in this field. He

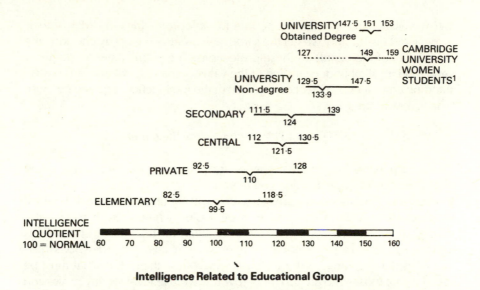

Intelligence Related to Educational Group

The length of line represents the inter-quartile range — *i.e.,* half the cases fall between the limits. The means is given by the central figure at ‿ below each line. (The limits of the dotted line for Cambridge University women students represent the extreme cases.)
Results from "Intelligence Levels in Schools of the South-west," by R. B. Cattell (*The Forum,* vol. viii, November 1930).

[1] From "The Use of Mental Tests with University Women Students," by A. Barbara Dale (*British Journal of Educational Psychology,* vol. v, 1935).

followed the careers of 1000 Californian children selected for high IQ in childhood. He compared their lives over many years with those of another similar sample who were random for IQ. The results were unequivocal. On every accepted measure of those elusive things 'success' or 'excellence' the gifted group did markedly better over a 45-year period. They wrote more books, earned more money, produced more inventions, lived better, had better jobs and excelled over the unselected control group in every way examined. They were even taller, more athletic, less delinquent and had less marital problems.

High intelligence does not ensure success, but it certainly seems to increase the chances of it significantly.

Even more significantly, we can look at it the other way and check up on the IQ of various professions.

The rank order of professions in respect of the level of intelligence of the people who follow them is very much the same as the rank order that is chosen by popular understanding.

If we ask a large number of people to rank professions in order of their respect and desirability we get the same rank order as we get by checking the average IQ of the people in those professions. The public have, evidently, a very good implicit understanding of the value of the professions. This understanding embraces a correct assessment of the intelligence required by those who follow them.

'When I know my IQ should I let it change my life pattern?'

To young persons I say that to know your IQ may save you heartache, if you allow your knowledge to guide you in your aspirations. There are exceptions to every rule, but generally speaking you will be unwise to attach yourself emotionally to a desire to serve in a profession where there is too great a discrepancy between your IQ and that required for the job. Most problems can be overcome by persistence and energy and in all of the professions there is a considerable range of IQ in those who follow them. But what must be faced is that those who are too far below the average level for any profession will have to work harder, be more persistent, take a longer time to reach their goal and do less well.

So long as this is understood we must wish good luck to the challenger who bucks the odds. However, it would be sad and wrong for people to waste time and face the risk of failure through tackling the wrong obstacle out of ignorance. Know your IQ. Challenge the figure if you must, but do so in the light of knowledge. Please do *not* say, 'I do not wish to know'.

To the under-ambitious and the under-achiever, I say it is sad when your talents are under used. Society should not be deprived of your service in the most demanding role in which you can be most effective. People in the British tradition are usually too modest, so it is more likely that they at any rate will be encouraged in their ambition by knowing their IQ. There is a chance that those who test themselves will raise their sights and tackle more difficult goals. I did this myself many years ago, when I learned, with some astonishment, from an IQ test given by the British Army that I was much brighter than I had ever imagined.

(My own subsequent career has been transformed by that discovery and I am certain in my mind that if I had never come accidentally upon that piece of knowledge, I would have been a much less happy and less satisfied man today and would have had a much less satisfactory life and career. At the age of 75, with no academic qualifications at all, and with only a scattered and insufficient schooling as my family moved from place to place, I can assert that the accidental discovery that I am bright has opened doors to me which led me to a life of achievement which I would never have thought possible, not even in my wildest dreams before I joined the British Army and was tested.

I am a successful inventor, although I am not an engineer. I am a successful author, although I have not a single qualification in English. I was the Managing Director of a successful company marketing advanced technology despite starting as a manual worker.

My experience is echoed all over Mensa. All the probes show that Mensa members, despite the wide disparity of their origins, have a strong tendency to find themselves where normal judgement would say that they are 'successful'. Sometimes their own judgement is different.)

The fact is that the IQ measures something quite definite and positive about people which relates to their ability to succeed in life, if they want to.

The 'if they want to' is vital. Motivation, perseverance, honesty, charm, likeability, even beauty, all these are important too, but intelligence is one of the things that count and it is very, very important. Lack of it can be overcome but it is the most difficult thing to overcome. Having it will compensate for big gaps in other areas. Certainly I must admit it does in my own case.

The following figure from Pirie and Butler's *Test Your IQ* shows how the IQ measurements of people in various occupations fit in closely with the expected pattern. The various hatchings show how the frequency of the IQ shades off, for each class as one moves away from its mean.

The following table from my own book *IQ – A Mensa Analysis and History* shows not only the spread of IQ across various professional groups but also the tendency of a regression to the mean in their children which I mentioned earlier.

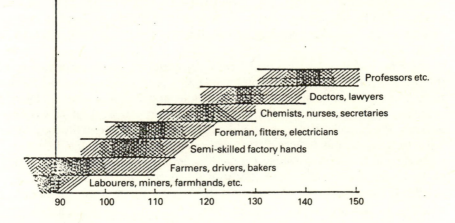

IQs of groups in eight different social strata and of their children

Professional group	Mean IQ Parents	Children
(1) Higher professional and administrative	153	120
(2) Lower professional; technical and executive	132	115
(3) Highly skilled; clerical	117	110
(4) Skilled	109	105
(5) Semi-skilled	98	97
(6) Unskilled	87	92
(7) Casual	82	89
(8) Institutional	57	67

PROCRUSTES WAS THE FIRST EGALITARIAN

Since I have been interviewed on all the media hundreds of times on this subject I have become familiar with all the questions listed in the preceding paragraphs which reporters and interviewers never tire of asking. The questions are always the same ones for a good reason.

They nearly all come from the same limited source, namely from those Egalitarian Dogmatists, the Procrusteans. The Procrusteans are a generation primarily of academics who have made their names as disciples of Procrustes. You will remember the legendary Greek bandit was such a firm believer in Equality that he insisted that everyone he captured should fit a certain bed. The tall were docked somewhere up the shin, the short were stretched on a rack.

The Procrustean academics over-emphasize equality. They have picked up the nursery principle of exact 'one for you, one for you' equality, and they have elevated it into an overriding principle and the first tenet of their morality. And it has got beyond sharing out a common stock of sweets or goodies. We have to share our individuality and personality equally too. We have to give up the delightful richness of human diversity and join the Workers Of The World People Clone. The Procrusteans attract the (often gullible) attention of the media because the public are not averse to the humbling of the superior. Also the idea that mental ability is something of a capitalist racket has a certain attraction too.

I am sure that the Procrusteans are sincere and that they truly believe that those who explore the magic variety of human nature and try to record and understand it have unworthy motives and are serving the interests of an exploiting ruling class.

We have, all of us, to come to our own conclusion on this important matter. I have come to mine and my views are obvious. I am not convinced by the Procrusteans and I am not attracted by their vision of the perfect world. If there has to be a levelling process I am afraid that the only way we can level humanity is down, there is no hope of levelling us up. So I do not care for undue levelling. The model is a sail. If you want to get the boom (the bottom) off the deck you have to lift the whole sail from the top. Then you can get the boat under way. If we lift the boom and the sail to half way all would be equal but we should not get anywhere.

9

What to do about the Gifted Child

The shape of the bell curve makes it reasonable to predict that most parents who read this book and test their children will find that their children are reassuringly average. But *some* parents will discover that these tests reveal a very high IQ or percentile rating. The probability is that these parents have a gifted child in their family – a problem, a joy, and a great responsibility. Any percentile rating over the 95th should alert parents to this possibility.

In the report *Education of the Gifted and Talented* submitted by the United States commissioner of education, S. P. Marland, Jr., to the US Congress in March 1972, Marland says:

'We know that gifted children can be identified as early as the pre-school grades and that these children in later life often make outstanding contributions to our society in the arts, politics, business and the sciences. But, disturbingly, research has confirmed that many talented children perform far below their intellectual potential. We are increasingly being stripped of the comfortable notion that a bright mind will make its own way. Intellectual and creative talent cannot survive educational neglect and apathy.'

The Marland report goes on to say, 'This loss is particularly evident in the minority groups who have, in both social and educational environments, every configuration calculated to stifle potential talent.' Under the heading 'Summary and major findings', the report continues:

'There can be few, if any, exceptions to the observations threading through this study, that the gifted and talented youth are a unique population, differing markedly from their age peers in abilities, talent, interests, and psychological maturity. The most versatile and complex of all human groups, they suffer the neglect that is typical of all groups with special educational needs. Their sensitivity to others and insight into existing school conditions, make them especially vulnerable; they frequently conceal their giftedness in standardized surroundings. The resultant waste in human terms and national resources is tragic.

The relatively few gifted students who have had the advantage of special programmes, have shown remarkable improvements in self-understanding and in ability to relate to others, as well as in improved academic and creative performance.'

But many such young people go unnoticed. In the United Kingdom, the Department of Education and Science Pamphlet, Summer 1975, points out in the introduction that

'the education of gifted children is becoming a greater focus of concern among teachers and parents. There is an increasing awareness that these children have special educational needs, and disquiet as to whether the present provisions meet them appropriately.

At school the proportion of gifted pupils who remain unrecognized is unknown, but the evidence indicates that it is probably considerable, particularly among children coming from poor families, and immigrants; environmental deprivation has its most adverse effect on the scholastic performance of the brightest children, not the average or dull. Better techniques of identification and their use by teachers (who should be on the alert for these children) are necessary.'

Most European countries have elite secondary schools where the more able children, about 20%, can obtain entrance at the ages between 10 and 12. The highly gifted child is very likely to go to these schools and is gradually selected by clearing successive hurdles as he goes through the system of school and university. However, some countries in northern Europe are in the process of transforming their system of secondary education into a comprehensive one (i.e. one type of school for all children regardless of ability); thus, they are coming up against the problem of the gifted child in such a system.

In Sweden, they do not differentiate the gifted at any early age but split the children into broad bands of ability during the seventh, eighth, and ninth years, directing the appropriate streams toward university education.

In France, children are differentiated by type of course, and the lycées are selected by the middle class parents whom they serve. So although the French are moving toward a more comprehensive system, they have not yet created a serious problem concerning their gifted children. (They have had however, a severe problem in trying to work an undiscriminating university system.)

In Russia, all children go to a neighbourhood eight year school, but there are special arrangements for the very gifted. There are four special schools that are really university boarding schools. They are in Novosibirsk, Kiev,

Moscow, and Leningrad. These schools cater to gifted children from rural areas only. Recruitment in Russia is by competitive examination where mathematics and physics are the deciding subjects.

Although each country has its own approach to the problem, they all share the common dilemma of a very special problem that has been created by the drive toward educational egalitarianism.

It is, undoubtedly, the increasing problem concerning gifted children that has motivated the setting up of the gifted children's movements in many countries.

This formation has a strange echo back to the movement towards general education which started in some European countries towards the end of the Dark Ages. Public schools were set up at which poor, bright children could be taught to read and write and become clerks, clerics and doctors. This led to present day public education which has now been somewhat corrupted. We seem to be starting again from the beginning.

The first gifted children's movements began in the United States and were well established by the early 1960s. In Britain the National Association for Gifted Children was set up in March 1966. A World Council for the Gifted was established after the World Congress on Gifted Children held in London in September 1975. There have been several more World Congresses in various countries since then. Today, Gifted Children's Associations have been set up with the object of finding some way to deal with the problem of the very able child who, in unsuitable classes without the guidance of really competent specialist teachers, is lost, bored, disillusioned and finally, alas, very often wasted.

I have taken an interest in the growth of the gifted children's movement in America and the UK and helped to trigger one in England, France and other places.

I believe that these movements have an important function and I would like to see them take their courage in their hands and tackle their problems more aggressively than they do at the moment.

There is, I believe, a contribution that Mensa could make. I report below a very preliminary attempt to make use of the Mensa pool to help with the problem of understanding what can be done for gifted children.

Mensa is a worldwide sample of grown-up gifted children, an example of the results achieved by past attempts to educate bright children. The successes and the failures of the educationalists of a past generation in making the best use of the talented pupils can be seen by looking at any Mensa sample. Mensa is not, of course, a random sample of the intelligent, but it is an easily accessible sample from which we can learn what actually happened to at least some exceptionally intelligent children in a variety of different educational systems.

One thing that emerges is that the intelligent people in our sample bear out the findings of Professor Terman in California. The intelligent have a strong tendency to be more successful in life. A survey in America conducted by Professor Powell (then Mensa's Research Officer) shows that if you are smart you are, if not rich, at least of very much above average in prosperity, no matter what your social origins.

The result was surprising to me because I had a subjective impression that Mensa is more attractive to people who have not, in their own judgement, succeeded as well as they think they might have done.

A paper by Professor Powell (who happens to be a black man from a Chicago slum) was based on a survey conducted on a sample of 1300 members of Mensa in the USA. One of the most alarming results of this survey was that developments in modern education this century have been decidedly unfavourable to the gifted, if we are to judge by their own reports.

The older members of Mensa, those who were educated under a previous system, show a very much more positive attitude towards their education and report that the more formal, disciplined and systematic educational methods found earlier in the century in the USA were much preferred. The earlier methods produced more positive attitudes and they correlate more highly with a valuable social contribution than the informal, 'progressive', 'child-centred' educational methods which became more widespread later.

In this sample of able people, the teacher was reported both as the most positive influence in the development of the mind and also as the most negative influence. The second most positive influence was reading and the second most negative influence was boredom, evidently most gifted children were not given sufficient challenge.

The most striking differences were noted between the younger and the older members. The younger gifted, those educated under modern educational systems, rated themselves as making a lower social contribution. They tended to want to change schools, they were rated as using their intelligence negatively, they found their teachers less intelligent and reported that they worked in classes of mixed ability.

The older Mensa members, those educated under the earlier tradition, tended to feel they make a greater social contribution. They wanted schools to remain as they had known them. They tended to use their intelligence positively. They also tended to have worked in classes of homogeneous ability.

Professor Powell's conclusions were that the earlier educational systems, those we must remember, associated with enormous industrial technological advances in America, were those in which gifted children found themselves in small classes with other gifted children, where they studied a much narrower curriculum under teachers who were intelligent. However, expectedly, Professor Powell showed that gifted women, even of the older generation, suffered a good deal of frustration and were not as satisfied with the educational system as were the men.

The message is that to get the most from each new generation of the gifted we should look at the modern educational system and consider the possibility of a return to some aspects of former methods. But we should correct the unfairness of all former systems to women.

Parents may ask why a movement to deal with and make the best social use of very intelligent children should have been called the 'Gifted Children's Movement'. I want to elaborate here what I have already mentioned. The term *gifted* as a description for very bright children has been adopted rather than *intelligent* or *able* because the definition of the term is intended to have a broader range and thus include children with talents other than those clearly associated with intelligence (which is seen as problem-solving ability and the ability to see and understand relationships). However, the meaning attached to the word *gifted* does not really include *all* the gifted or exceptionally able. Usually, for instance, athletic skills are not included in the meaning. The principal types of giftedness that *are* included, other than those specifically associated with intelligence itself, are artistic and musical talents. All authorities seem to be dissatisfied with the vagueness of the definition of giftedness, and there is considerable disagreement.

More precision could be brought to the definition of giftedness if it were more clearly seen that there are essentially three ways in which children can excel – ways in which their performance can be termed excellent, or exceptionally able.

The three apparently independent directions of ability are:

(1)   Those associated with skilful, co-ordinated use of the body, as in sports and mechanical skills;

(2)   Those associated with an urge to create – innovate, draw, paint, make music;

(3)   Those associated with intellectual functions – the ability to think, to reason, to see relationships, to draw conclusions, and to classify information correctly.

This last direction – cognitive or intellectual ability – might almost be called data processing ability.

Considerable experimentation has shown that there is some correlation between these various abilities, but this correlation is difficult to establish because for psychomotor ability and artistic ability there exist no standardized methods of measurement. In addition, most authorities agree that the development of psychomotor skills, which occurs very early in life, is a separate process not closely bound up with the development of intelligence itself. On psychomotor tests, baby monkeys can beat human babies quite easily.

The Marland report states that performance tests designed to measure general intelligence have been the most widely used criteria of giftedness both in research and selection. This has occurred because these tests are so widely available.

With regard to the level of selection, there is a tendency to accept the criterion established by Terman in his original study on gifted Californian children. This method determines giftedness at the IQ level 140. In other words, about four children per thousand are in this group and are considered to be the most highly gifted school children. However, other authorities place the lower limit of giftedness at the 98th percentile (the Mensa level).

It is preferable to choose the lower level simply because the normal standard intelligence test is quite good at identifying the top 5% or the top 2% of high ability children, but it becomes far less certain when we attempt to discriminate above that level. It would be better to use a number of different tests. For very high levels of intelligence, tests such as those developed by Professor Alice Heim in England are preferable because they are designed to discriminate at a high level. Unfortunately, these are only applicable to older children.

Perhaps one of the best definitions of giftedness is the legal definition employed in Illinois.

'Gifted children are those children whose mental development is accelerated beyond the average to the extent that they need and can profit from specially planned educational services.'

The problem of identifying the gifted is not easy. The Marland report points out that some young people with potential mask their abilities in order to adapt to the group they are working in. Others cannot find an outlet in school for their particular talents.

To help you in your determination of your child's abilities, there is the following checklist of 20 points to watch for in your children. If your children are gifted, they may:

(1)   Possess superior powers of reasoning, of dealing with abstractions, of generalizing from specific facts, of understanding meanings, and of seeing into relationships;

(2)   Have great intellectual curiosity;

(3)   Learn easily and readily;

(4)   Have a wide range of interests;

(5)   Have a broad attention span that enables them to concentrate and persevere in solving problems and pursuing interests;

(6)   Be superior in the quantity and quality of vocabulary as compared with other children of their own age;

(7)   Have ability to do effective work independently;

(8)   Have learned to read early (often well before school age);

(9)   Exhibit keen powers of observation;

(10)   Show initiative and originality in intellectual work;

(11)   Show alertness and quick response to new ideas;

(12)   Be able to memorize quickly;

(13)   Have great interest in the nature of man and the universe (problems of origins and destiny, and so on);

(14)   Possess unusual imagination;

(15)   Follow complex directions easily;

(16)   Be rapid readers;

(17)   Have several hobbies;

(18)   Have reading interests that cover a wide range of subjects;

(19)   Make frequent and effective use of the library;

(20)   Be superior in mathematics, particularly in problem solving.

Can teachers spot gifted children? Marland quotes from several surveys where teachers did not, on the average, appear to be very good at identifying children with the ability to score well. Only one-fifth of the superior boys and two-fifths of the superior girls were described as precocious or mentally quick. Yet these children were at the one-in-a-thousand level on the mental ability test. Some of these very bright children were even classed as dull or mentally sluggish.

Ignoring teachers' impressions, scientific personality tests were applied to all the children, and the conclusions were very obvious indeed. The exceptionally bright children stood out from the children with lower scores, on the average, in every respect and were rated to have a significantly 'superior' personality from the point of view of the experimenters. The characteristic that stood out most was adventurousness. A substantially higher proportion of the very gifted group were said to be adventurous – more than twice as many as those who scored in the top 10%. The bright children were classed as being ambitious, dependable, energetic, friendly, happy, honest, and investigative. They were leaders; they liked jokes; they were original; they were polite and tidy. Obviously, these characteristics did not apply to all the high scoring children. These were the comments that were most frequently made about that group in comparison with the lower scoring children.

The evidence from a number of studies is perhaps the strongest ground for the view that the group of children that is potentially of most value to the next generation is the very highly gifted.

One speaker at the World Congress for Gifted Children spoke of children being 'severely gifted' and felt that they ought to be looked at as an especially disadvantaged group for whom special treatment would be both wise and appropriate. Just as we treat the mentally or physically handicapped with special educational facilities, so too should we provide the gifted with special educational opportunities. It is clearly to our advantage to exploit this most precious of resources available to us.

It is our duty to foster the development of exceptional talents for the benefit of the next generation. Parents who are fortunate enough to have a child in the highly gifted range on these tests should seek the attention of those responsible for the child's education and get in touch with their local gifted children's association.

One of the tragic facts to emerge from Project Talent, a survey conducted on 450,000 secondary students throughout the United States, was that parents are not at all good at spotting talents in their own children. Only 17% of the parents of highly gifted children desired a higher level of education for the children. Even worse, 18% of the parents, as a whole, set their ambitions for the education of their children at very low levels or had no ambition for them at all.

The failure of parents to stimulate gifted children leads to an enormous waste of talent. The critical importance of early stimulation for children was pointed out by Sir John Eccles in *Facing Reality*. He showed that the actual development of the nervous system is physically inhibited by lack of stimulation. He experimented with a group of mice, covering one eye and leaving one eye with normal sight on each mouse. The number of synaptic knobs on the nerve dendrites in the normal visual cortex of mice 24 and 48 days old respectively was extremely depleted in each case in areas associated with the blind eye. Those associated with the effective eye were very much richer in dendritic spines, which, in turn, are associated with mental action. A similar phenomenon has been noticed with animals brought up in the dark. The evidence indicates that those dendrite buds that do not develop properly because of lack of stimulation cannot later be developed if stimulation happens after the latency period in very early life.

Marland said that the majority of the gifted were underachievers. Their attainments, although much higher than those of the rest of the school population, were very much below their potential. These underachievers suffered greatly from a lack of stimulation. Those that did appear to be achieving their potential were examined for any factors that might be relevant. The factor that emerged most strongly was that 74% of the high achieving group of gifted children had some person, described as a mentor, who took a special interest in the child. These mentors were often parents but sometimes teachers, sometimes favourite uncles, and sometimes casual friends. The mentors appeared to be people of intelligence and discernment who had spotted the talent in the child and were doing their best to foster it.

Obviously, the best person to be a mentor to a child is a parent. The idea of calling on someone from outside might be distasteful to many, but sensible parents who recognize their own limitations will want to use such outside help. No parent should object to consulting a doctor or psychiatrist when he recognizes that his own medical and psychological skills are not enough. Parents who feel that they do not have the time, knowledge, ability, or interest to develop the educational and intellectual interest of their outstandingly bright children can find others who have all these qualities and who are very willing to help. I must emphasize, however, that selecting a mentor is a delicate process. The bringing together of gifted children and suitable mentors is a matter requiring the skill of a qualified professional.

Let me give more detail here about the work of Professor Lewis Terman. In California between 1925 and 1968, Terman and Oden selected a group of 10-year-old children and another group of 15 year olds on the basis of a score at the level of 140 IQ. There were 1470 subjects selected from a population of one million.

25 years later, 71% of this group were in professional, semiprofessional, or managerial occupations, compared with 13.7% of the Californian population as a whole. Their average income was higher than that of the typical college graduate.

In another aspect of this study, the most successful and the least successful 20% of the gifted group were compared. Ratings by parents, spouses and the subjects themselves showed that what was lacking in the unsuccessful group was perseverance and integration toward goals. In addition, they tended to suffer from inferiority feelings.

The evidence accumulated by Terman and Oden can be summed up as follows: most of the gifted do become successful according to the usual criteria, but the 20% of the gifted who do not succeed do not feel themselves to be failures. They have often deliberately shunned the pursuit of occupational success. The successful group tended to come from stable, middle class homes where books were available and where parents emphasized the importance of education and had high expectations for their children. In such homes, children developed strong intellectual interests and strong drives for achievement. However about half of the gifted women in the sample had remained in the home.

These general conclusions were noted by the British Department of Education:

(1) There is a strong tendency for children to fulfil early promise; their performance in later years reflects early performance indications.

(2) The best indication of how a child will develop at school is given by intelligence tests. They are better than personality tests or other types of assessment.

(3) High IQ alone does not guarantee success. The child needs ambition to do well – the drive and determination to succeed.

(4) Family background and environment are vital. They are the most important factor in how well a bright child realizes his promise.

(5) Very bright children may be of equal intellectual ability but they are extraordinarily different in personality, interests, and achievement.

In the modern world, which is so devoted to the idea of equality, there is a very real problem for the parents and educators of gifted children. Ideas of justice and social equality have created a drive toward homogeneous mixed ability classes in comprehensive schools to which all children must go. The educational system in some countries is being pushed into this mould at a rate many people think is dangerously fast. Bright students are now likely to be submerged in these schools, where the opportunities to receive the special teaching and stimulation they require are likely to be significantly reduced.

This tendency places a special extra responsibility on parents. It means they should try to produce the needed extra stimulus and challenge outside the school environment. Responsible associations for gifted children strongly recommend that bright children be brought together into classes outside school hours where they can benefit from mutual stimulus and challenge and where they can be taught by teachers who can become skilled in the special problems of the gifted.

Whatever the moral arguments are against segregating gifted children, there can be little doubt about the success of the system introduced many generations ago, which produced highly educated and able scholars and administrators – an intellectual cadre that has been of inestimable value to society. It is important that we do not dry up the supply altogether by ignoring the able and gifted students. We need an improvement, not a reduction, in the quality of education and the supply of highly educated people to do the complicated work of a complex society. The work of Terman finally dispelled the myth that the highly intelligent are somehow odd, puny, or unhealthy. Neither are they necessarily from the upper class economically. An examination of 45,000 children, in over 455 schools and 310 communities, carried out by the Co-ordinated Studies in Education Incorporated showed that the popular opinion that the most superior children came from upper class homes was far from the truth. All the very superior children, at levels up to one in a thousand, were rated as to the social and economic background of the parents, the father's occupation, the possession of middle-class implements (telephone, car, radio, and amount of living space occupied).

The results were unequivocal. The children who, on objective selection tests, turned out to be the most gifted group of all, came from parents from the full range of social and occupational classes. The possible home background class ratings ranged from 0 to 18, and the gifted group spanned the range from 2 to 15. The same point is raised by Eysenck in his book *The Inequality of Man,* where he states that all social and occupational classes contribute to the pool of the gifted.

Terman's analysis of the life history of the 150 most successful and 150 least successful among the very gifted adult males he studied since childhood is very interesting. The group with the better social and emotional adjustment was overwhelmingly the most successful group. This raises the question of the effect of putting a brilliant child into a class of normal children. The sharp contrast between the child and its peers may represent a handicap that holds the child back in its future development and thus denies to society as a whole the full fruit of its talents.

One should ask whether enough is done for the gifted. Considering that gifted children are those who can contribute greatly to the prosperity and stability of the world in the next generation and who should have a disproportionately high role in solving the serious problems that confront humanity, we might reasonably expect that all possible aid be given to these exceptional children to help them fulfil their potential. If one looks at the amount of money spent as an indication of the effort made, then certainly society has no such view. The Marland report notes that in 27 school districts in the US that have programmes for gifted children, the expenditure per pupil on the intellectually gifted was $92. Compare this expenditure with the approximately $721 spent on each mentally retarded pupil and $1729 for each physically handicapped pupil.

Frequently, teachers have to rely on their unaided judgement, and experience shows that teachers are able to identify about half the gifted. But teachers do less well when it comes to identifying the *highly* gifted, and in one study, it was shown that 25% of the most gifted were missed altogether.

In a programme conducted by Dr Bridges known as the Brentwood experiment, a group of gifted children were withdrawn from their own schools for one afternoon a week for 30 weeks each year. The level chosen was an IQ of 140 and over, and a pilot group and two other groups were experimented with over a number of years.

The problem that immediately emerged was that it was difficult to find teachers for these gifted children. Some teachers were astounded and alarmed by the speed with which some children answered questions. The teachers felt they would not have the quickness of mind to deal with such children.

It became very clear that being educated among normal children, the gifted became accustomed to a lower level of expectation by teachers and parents, so that the gifted students' demands upon themselves were very low. The effect of mixing them in with other gifted children was to raise their own aspirations and make them more self-critical. Another thing revealed by their being taught with normal children was the tendency to impatience. The gifted children quickly mastered what the teacher was trying to put over, got tired, and became bored. Dr Bridges felt that this situation might lead to the development of a 'butterfly mind' – one that has trouble concentrating – unless the child could be given sufficient challenge and stimulation.

In his experiments on the gifted children who had been selected, Dr Bridges found that, although most of them were moderately popular in their own schools, some were almost completely isolated from the other children. In this respect, the findings concur with the Marland report because after a period away at the new school, isolated gifted children began integrating much better with their peers in their own school, and, contrary to what might be expected, the other children in the school did not show any signs of resentment toward those who had been chosen for the gifted children's experiment. The teachers confirmed this finding.

The saddest thing that Dr Bridges discovered was that gifted children often incurred the resentment and jealousy of their *parents* and of their *teachers*. One family whose child had an IQ of 170 was not pleased at having a bright child but upset, bewildered, and annoyed by his quickness of thought, which they could not match. Much worse was the case of one bright child selected for Dr Bridges's experiments who was often scolded by the teacher at his normal school until he dissolved into tears. His behaviour at the classes with other gifted children was exemplary.

The most serious problem was summed up by Dr Bridges:

'Our finding has been that underachievement can occur when a bright child has powers much in excess of what he is called on to use in school: such a child may be first in his class and still, from the viewpoint of his intellectual gifts, be underachieving. In such cases the measure of under-achievement is obscured by the general satisfaction of a relatively good achievement. Underachievement, therefore, may go unrecognized, so that a child coasts along quite satisfactorily but with little use of his powers.'

Dr Bridges referred to what he called the 'stint', or given level of achievement that gifted children often set up for themselves, which was often far below the level of their potential achievement.

Being accustomed to easy success among normal children, the gifted students at Dr Bridges's school had to learn that mistakes and failures were not all-important. The gifted children had to be *taught* to set their sights higher. However, Bridges pointed out that the level of difficulty must not be raised too high or the child pushed too fast. It was essential that the child had a certain level of success all the time; otherwise, he or she would become discouraged. There was the rarer, but still existent, problem of overchallenging the gifted child so that it got discouraged by too long a succession of failures.

Dr Bridges was very firm on one point. He said that the gifted child needed more teaching, not less teaching, than the normal child and that the idea that the gifted child would make its own way and manage on its own was completely fallacious.

In *How to Raise a Brighter Child,* Joan Beck points out that the best time for many kinds of learning and, more important, for stimulating the basic learning abilities, is already passed by the time the child reaches 5 years of age and enters school. Unavoidably, every parent has the important responsibility of setting the stage in these early years for the child's performance during the rest of its life.

All studies concur in their findings that these early formative years are of the utmost importance. This means that the child's future ability and effectiveness is very much affected by his pre-school home environment. Very bright children can be taught to read and deal with numbers from as early as 3–4 years old, and there is no evidence supporting those who would claim that this can be harmful. On the contrary, those who are given an early opportunity to learn seem to benefit from this all their lives.

Joan Beck's views, as a result of her experience with bright young children, is that most people greatly underestimate what children under 5 can and should be learning. She feels that these children's intelligence, enthusiasm, and happiness can be greatly improved by more intensive methods of early education.

Young children, and especially intelligent young children, need stimulation and excitement. The urge to explore, experiment, examine, probe, be into everything, and, yes, take everything to pieces, is as right and natural as hunger and thirst. It is necessary to the development of the child that it be given plentiful opportunities to explore everything around it and to keep its mind occupied with a constant succession of fresh images and opportunities.

In addition, child care theories that discourage parents from 'overstimulating' the child are quite likely to do more harm than good. The old fear against putting pressure on children is gradually fading as the results of this policy become clear. There is a return to the idea that there can be no harm in a child's curiosity and eagerness for learning.

The lesson for parents is very clear. Your child needs plenty of stimulation and interest to feed its curiosity. If you have reason to believe it is a gifted child, it is even more important for it to gain early experience and knowledge. Your child can begin to learn its letters and numbers as soon as you like. It needs pictures, books, travel and experience as much as it needs food and medical care.

The Gifted Children's Movement, like Mensa, started because of a return to a respect for and a proper valuation of mental excellence. We must ask more of the people who devote their time to it. We have a long way to go to return to the virtues of our fathers in respect of preference for that mental excellence.

Tomorrow's most important human problem is that of finding, motivating and suitably educating the next generation of talented and able children so that they can solve the many daunting problems which have to be solved, if our present world civilization is to last much into the next century.

10

What to do about the Retarded Child

Mental deficiency, mental defect, retardation, mental handicap, feeble-mindedness – these are some of the many labels given to a clearly definable condition noticed in a small proportion of children. If the evidence of testing gives you even a slight suspicion that your child falls into this class, seek expert guidance immediately.

The first person to see is your doctor. Some experts believe that the condition results only from some disturbance or abnormality – a defect in the organization of the brain that may either be due to brain damage or be inborn. The other view is that the condition is usually due to the normal variability of human intelligence and simply represents the lower tail of the normal distribution curve. Most experts seem to think that both views are valid and that they are not mutually exclusive. There can be pathological and familial reasons in different cases, or in many cases, there can be a combination of both reasons. There is also an argument on the effect of upbringing on a child and the extent to which mental defects can be attributed to it, and there is evidence that brain damaged children who have been institutionalized do visibly worse than those who have had individual care in good families.

The genetic contribution to retardedness is well established. Despite some correlation between low intelligence in the parent and retardedness in the children, retardedness is found in varying proportions in children from parents of all levels of intelligence and from all sections of the community.

The classification of the condition must be arbitrary because one class of feeblemindedness merges into the next. The usual classification is on the basis of IQ.

255

IQ	Description
70–90	Low
50–70	Mild Retardation
20–50	Moderate Retardation
0–20	Severe Retardation

At the lower end of this unhappy scale are the untestables, those whose responses are not adequate to an IQ test. There is not a great deal that can probably be done for children who are unfortunate enough to be born with moderate or severe retardation, and generally speaking we can say that the closer to normal the IQ score, the greater the possibility of remedial action. However, some remarkable results have been achieved recently with very severely retarded children, but the relative expenditure of time, money and skill required is often, unfortunately, at a very high level.

Despite the intensive criticism of IQ tests as a measure of mental excellence, there is little dispute about their value as a diagnostic tool in dealing with problems of mental retardation. No one in the field of psychiatry seems to be able to propose a better way of distinguishing between the various levels of retardation. Obviously, the administration of an intelligence test becomes progressively more difficult as we approach *either* extreme, and it is perhaps more so when we approach the extreme of mental defects. Therefore, we do not recommend amateur attempts to test IQ at any level much below IQ 80, the borderline of retardation. If, as a result of testing your child, you find the result is anywhere in that region, you must consider the possibility of faults in your procedure. However, a very poor result must not be ignored. You should seek the advice of a doctor or qualified psychologist. This can be done, as I said, by consulting the family doctor.

Mental retardation is seen by most psychiatrists as being a very distinct and separate type of mental abnormality from the neurotic or psychotic abnormalities, though of course there is some overlap, and neurotic and psychotic conditions do exist in retardates.

A fair view of the incidence of retardation is given by the following diagram. The curve shows the distribution of intelligence and retardation. On many grounds, this graph gives the most likely explanation of what is observed.

This curve is based on the work of Binet. What it indicates is that the Gaussian curve, which indicates the normal distribution of intelligence, is distorted at the lower tail by a hump that reflects the incidence of severe disability caused either by accidental damage to the brain itself or by severe

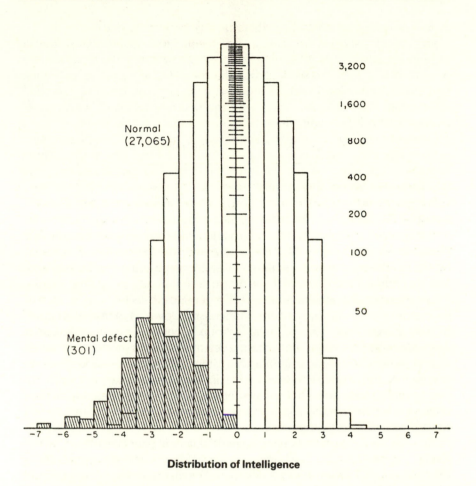

Distribution of Intelligence

genetic abnormalities. In their *Handbook of Abnormal Psychology*, A. M. and A. D. B. Clarke say: 'If the reader expected to gain clear knowledge from experimental studies of the precise nature and extent of the retardates' deficiencies and the methods by which these can be ameliorated, he will have been disappointed. In almost every area in which the methods of experimental psychology have been applied, apparently conflicting results have been reported.'

We are, unfortunately, confined once again to the strategy of the best guess. On the whole, however, the Clarkes support the concept that there are two separate kinds of mental defects: those where there is some visible organic impairment and those where there is not. There seem to be no clear behavioural differences between the two groups. They both seem to fit the general pattern at the low end of the normal distribution curve for intelligence.

The greatest success in dealing with mental retardation comes from a technique called *operant learning*. At the very low end of the range it is the only thing that seems to work at all. It has been found useful in controlling undesirable behaviour, such as head banging, window breaking, and bad toilet habits, and it works even with the severely retarded, where other training methods fail completely.

Operant learning is a straightforward system of reward and punishment, euphemistically called positive and negative reinforcement. The more immediate the response and the more it is related to the action, the more quickly and permanently the child responds.

The preferred method is to transfer the training from the actual to the symbolic. To begin with, for instance, the child is given a desirable reward for a success, accompanied by a smile and encouraging words. For a failure, it is given a mild slap or deprived of something, and with tutor frowns and scolds. Eventually the reward and the slap can be eliminated as the training proceeds and the child is found to react to the praise or scolding.

Some severe abnormalities have visible genetic effects that can be seen by an examination of the body's cells. Mongolism (Down's syndrome) is caused by a small extra chromosome in the G group. Mongoloids have 47 instead of 46 chromosomes. Mongolism, although determined at the moment of conception, does not seem to run in families but rather appears to be a kind of genetic accident. Many of these children used to die, but now the chance of survival is much better. Mongoloid children are frequently very easy to deal with and are often very much loved by their parents, who find looking after them can be a rewarding and loving experience.

Another very clearly noticeable genetic defect is phenylketonuria, which affects five per 100,000 live births. It is caused by a single gene, and 25% of the brothers and sisters of those who have the disease have it themselves. A high proportion, up to 10%, of the parents of children with phenylketonuria are first cousins. The condition has a definite effect on the body chemistry, and the results on the mentality of the child depend on nutrition. If the condition is discovered at birth and a special diet started immediately, the average IQ of those children on the special diet can be almost normal. But if the special diet is started after the 72nd month, the average IQ is only 57.

Retardates tend to be others-directed, not inner-directed as most normal children are — that is, in a problem situation, retardates look for cues and suggestions from the behaviour of other children around them, trying to see what solutions other children are using. They do this rather than trust their own judgement. This occurs, not because of the defect itself, but from a continuous experience of failure. The behaviour and learning failures of retardates thus tend to be self-reinforcing.

One wonders whether this explains the well known tractability and amiability of retardate children. Parents confronted with naughty, obstinate, and excessively self-willed (inner-directed) children may find them irritating, but they will be happy to accept this as it bodes well for the final personality and ability of the child.

The lesson for the parent of a retarded child is that the level of problem setting should be very carefully adjusted to give the child an adequate ration of success so as to encourage it to trust its judgement up to a realistic level. It should be encouraged to learn its limitations but not to exaggerate them.

Severe retardation is usually caused by birth trauma such as anoxia. Anoxia occurs when the foetal brain is deprived of oxygen for a period sufficiently long for it to suffer permanent damage. Other causes of such retardation are certain infective diseases of the mother, such as German measles (rubella), syphilis and toxoplasmosis.

It is the less severe forms of retardation which sometimes seem to have familial causes. In these cases, the near relatives of the affected child are often retarded themselves. In the investigation of such cases an incestuous relationship is often suspected. Unfortunately incest appears to be more frequent among retarded people. Since the same genes in related individuals are deficient, the children produced are likely to be severely retarded.

Another group of retardates are those where the genetic instructions are normal but where the development of the brain is prevented by other faults of the system. Cretinism, for example, is usually caused by a thyroid deficiency. If observed early enough the deficiency can be corrected by injections and the child will develop more normally.

Failures of development can be caused by encephalitis and epilepsy. Although these diseases are not in themselves associated with mental defect, they can cause brain damage because children who have frequent fits suffer brain damage from anoxia. Maternal malnutrition and deprivation of stimulus to the baby can also reduce mental development.

There are also certain poisons which can hinder full development. One of these, which is being more noticed recently, is lead poisoning.

THE AUTISTIC CHILD

One of the conditions of mental testing as pointed out, is that the child or person tested is motivated to succeed. The subject must respond, or the results are meaningless.

Among those who will be labelled untestable on the normal IQ test is a class of children who are variously called autistic or non-communicating children. Like many terms employed in psychology and psychiatry, the term *autistic* seems to have a number of differing meanings and probably covers a number of different functional conditions. Among the parents who are perplexed about their children and who turn to this book for guidance, there may be some who have an autistic child. If the description of the symptoms seems to fit their child, they should apply immediately for medical advice.

The condition was first diagnosed as a syndrome, or collection of typical symptoms, by Dr Leo Kanner, of Johns Hopkins University in Baltimore, Maryland. Dr Kanner says:

> 'Autistic children are those who show extreme aloneness from the beginning of life, and an anxiously obsessive desire for the preservation of sameness . . . The common denominator in all these patients is a disability to relate themselves in the ordinary way to people and situations from the beginning of life . . . The case histories indicate invariably the presence from the start of extreme autistic aloneness which, wherever possible, shuts out anything that comes to the child from the outside . . . They reject reality, tend to brood, and become obsessed with small repetitious activities.'

Translated into lay terms, the above quotation means that there are nine points to watch for. Almost all normal children will exhibit *some* of these characteristics *some* of the time. A parent should be concerned only if the child shows *excessive* tendencies in a number of these directions. Autistic children show:

(1) Impaired emotional relationships with people and abnormal behaviour toward them such as 'treating them like tools or objects. Long lasting difficulty in playing with other children';

(2) Unawareness of self beyond the usual age; the child may hurt itself by head banging or other types of aggression toward the self;

(3) Posturing or undue exploration and scrutiny of parts of the body;

(4) Undue and unduly prolonged attention to articles without regard to how they are used;

(5) A determined and prolonged resistance to any change in the surroundings and continued attempts to maintain or restore what they are used to – the children seem to be attracted to complete monotony;

(6) Exaggerated or diminished response to normal happenings – for example, refusing to see or listen, or being insensitive to pain and temperature; excessive and illogical anxiety beyond what would normally be expected in a child; strange fears and phobias of harmless objects;

(7) Failure to learn to talk or very much delayed talking; strange mannerisms in speech that seem to have no meaning;

(8) Strange postures and mannerisms, rocking or spinning, 'freezing' in one attitude;

(9)   Odd mixtures of apparent retardedness with occasional normal or near normal interludes.

Those who work with autistic children feel that it is not the intelligence of the child that is in doubt. They feel there is a fundamental defect that prevents the child from forming proper relationships and responding normally to what happens.

There is no advice that a layman can sensibly give a parent with an autistic child except to seek proper professional help as quickly as possible. There have been encouraging results reported as the consequence of good long-term management.

DYSLEXIA

Dyslexia, or *word blindness,* is the condition of a child who is otherwise of normal intelligence. The child has a special disability that prevents it from learning to read. However, informed opinion appears to be crystallizing around the position that this is not an entirely accurate concept.

Several careful studies in fair-sized sample populations seem to suggest that there is no real distinction between dyslexia and normal retardation or backwardness. More recent work, however, contradicts this finding and we are left in a position of considerable uncertainty. Seek medical advice if your child is apparently bright but an unduly slow reader. Much research and development is currently being undertaken in this field.

BRAIN DAMAGE

Cerebral palsy, spasticity and epilepsy are, it is generally agreed, usually due to brain damage — often brain damage that occurred during birth. Difficult births and breach births are well known to involve an increased risk.

Cerebral palsy, a disorder of movement and posture, may be associated with epilepsy, retardation and disturbances of personality and emotion. It might show itself in simple cases as clumsiness in movement — the failure to use one of the senses effectively. The child may be able to see, but it cannot recognize objects by sight though it can do so by touch. Parents should seek medical advice if they have the slightest suspicion that the description fits their child.

What are the chances that your child will be retarded? In 1951 in the United Kingdom, it was estimated that a little over 1% of the population exhibited some degree of mental subnormality. In general, the upper limit of IQ for retardates has been arbitrarily set at 70, and about 75% of children classified as retarded are usually between IQ 50 and 70, 20% are between IQ 20 and 50, and 5% are more or less untestable at IQ 20 or below.

If the score you obtain for your child gives an IQ of below 70, it would be wise, before you commit yourself to a final judgement, to wait a few weeks until the child has forgotten the test and try again under the most favourable circumstances you can contrive. If the second result confirms the first one, then you should seek professional advice. Remember that the tests you have given your child should not be regarded as definitive – but merely an approximate first indication.

REDUCING THE RISK OF HAVING A SUBNORMAL CHILD

Far too little is known about the causation of the various types of mental subnormality, and almost all authorities agree that much more research needs to be done. Nonetheless, a considerable body of information has been accumulated, and there are some precautions that can, at least to some extent, minimize the risk for any parent.

Generally speaking, the evidence points to three types of mental subnormality. In the first type, the causation is largely inborn, and this can be divided into two classes. One class involves a gross chromosomal defect, such as phenylketonuria or Down's syndrome (Mongolism), where there is some apparent and visible defect in the body of one or both parents that can be detected by examination of body cells. Particularly if there is any incidence of heritable mental abnormality in the family would it be wise for a couple to consult genetic counsellors about the risk before they are married or, at any rate, before they have children of their own. One such specific risk that is genetic is rhesus incompatibility, or the *RH factor,* in which the blood types of the mother and father are incompatible and cause the mother to be sensitized after the first birth so that later babies are at risk.

The second type of genetic defect is much more difficult to deal with; it is a defect due to the normal variations in human ability. The first type is due to one simple defect in a chromosome; the second is probably multifactorial. The particular mix of genes that the child happens to have is an unfortunate one. There seems to be little that can be done about this problem. We can only say that the risk of having a seriously subnormal child is lower for those people whose mental ability is above normal but even for them it is not eliminated. Generally speaking, each generation will tend to have children who are nearer to the average than they are, both upward and downward.

The third type of mental subnormality results from the damage that the child might sustain either while it is in the womb or at birth. Forceps deliveries sometimes cause brain damage that may lead to mental subnormality. An imperfect diet during pregnancy may cause problems, but this risk has been exaggerated and it is probably not great. A much more serious source of risk is medication, particularly self-medication. The thalidomide children represent only an extreme example of the risks associated with the taking of drugs, which may not always be realized even by the doctors who prescribe them. Self-medication is obviously more dangerous than drugs prescribed by doctors. On the whole, we may say that the fewer drugs of any kind a woman takes during pregnancy, the lower the risk of abnormalities. All the drugs taken for pleasure are included here. The legal ones, alcohol and tobacco, and all the illegal ones should be avoided by a pregnant woman. Shortage or excess of oxygen given during childbirth can cause problems, and an excess of oxygen in particular has been shown to cause a certain type of blindness. Age is another factor since it is well known that the incidence of Down's syndrome increases with the mother's age. Bearing children after 35 or so may be risky. In some cases such as hydrocephalus (water on the brain) and spina bifida, there is a very clear mixture of heredity and environmental factors.

If there seems to be a predisposition in the mother that is probably inherited, it can be reduced or increased according to her diet at the time of pregnancy. If you are aware of any of these diseases in your ancestry, you would be wise to consult a specialist.

11

Does Intelligence Run In Families?

During the development of our World Culture strange, great disputes arise. Educated and informed people suddenly polarize in opinion on some question. Two strongly opposed factions are formed. These great dividing issues are often seen, in retrospect, to be unimportant, exaggerated and even unreal. At the time they are raging, however, they develop a disproportionate head of emotional steam. The supporters of the contrasting views become so extreme that we suspect that some hidden social mechanism is at work.

On most questions there is a range of opinion from one extreme to the other with people holding every gradation of view. On the questions which at certain times and places certain cultures select for an intellectual fracas, this situation is reversed and people move out of the centre ground to one of the two, always two, different positions, both of them extreme. Both of them usually wrong.

The great capital punishment debate is one of these. You are either a believer in capital punishment or you are an abolitionist. On these questions the 'don't knows' shrink to a tiny proportion. Both sides get very heated, both sides completely ignore the arguments of the other side. Prohibition in America was such an issue. Religion is still such a one in Ireland. The dispute between the two Christian sects, Catholic and Protestant all over Europe, used to be such a division.

The interesting thing about this kind of debate is the way it ends. In the course of time the debate simply goes away. It is not resolved. Neither side proves to be 'right' or 'wrong'. Humanity turns its attention away and begins to quarrel about something else.

INTELLIGENCE? NATURE? NURTURE?

The great Nature/Nurture debate about intelligence falls into this class. The question is simple. To what extent are heredity and environment respectively responsible for manifest differences in intelligence? What you believe about this seems to depend more upon your general quasi-political views rather than upon any evidence.

I shall try to give a brief review of the different points of view and the reader must do his best to sort out what he thinks. I am not pretending to be unbiased. My own view, having studied the literature fairly carefully, is this. Differences in manifest measured intelligence are associated both with heredity, the particular ticket in the genetic lottery that the subject has drawn, and with environment, the treatment, the upbringing and the experience of the subject. Neither of the extreme views is correct. To say that heredity has no effect on intelligence is as false as to say that environment has no effect on intelligence.

The unreality of the whole dispute is exposed by the following. Actually, hardly anyone *defends* the extreme positions, yet it is these extreme positions that those of the opposite view constantly attack. Both sides are tilting at windmills of their own invention.

I cannot find anywhere in the literature a hereditarian, as we call those who emphasize the genetic component in intelligence differences, who has claimed that *all* differences are due to heredity. On the other side we get closer. There are those who say that there is no proof of a hereditary influence and that there are those as I have said, who say that 'intelligence', the concept which we are trying to measure, is unreal, unimportant or deceptive.

Take Professor Leon J. Kamin; I quote from his book *The Science and Politics of IQ.*

'The present work arrives at two conclusions. The first stems from a detailed examination of the empirical evidence which has been adduced in support of the idea of heritability, and it can be stated simply. There exists no data which should lead a prudent man to accept the hypothesis that IQ Test Scores are in any degree heritable.'

Those who claim to be scientists are usually very careful not to advance negative hypotheses because they can never be proved.

An IQ test result cannot be completely random. If you give any normal and rational test whatever to a large sample of people it is bound to sort them into some sort of mental classes. You would expect the normal people to do better than those who are retarded on any written test of any kind.

We soon see what leads this sincere and probably kindly academic to a well known and widespread dogma. For Professor Kamin goes on to say:

'The IQ test in America, and the way in which we think about it, has been fostered by men committed to a particular social view . . . the consequence has been that the IQ test has served as an instrument of oppression against the poor – dressed in the trappings of science, rather than politics.'

Opposite this introduction is Dr Kamin's dedication to two persons 'who taught different, and wonderful things'. Different, yes, wonderful, yes, I, at least, wonder at them. Let me follow Professor Kamin's statement by one of my own. 'There are no published data which would lead a prudent woman to accept the hypothesis that IQ test scores are in any way affected by the environment.'

Dr Kamin goes on to suggest that the reason why the overwhelming majority of psychologists have the view that mental differences are at least partially explained by heredity, is that they are committed to a particular political view and that they disseminate the view that they do for political reasons. This public proclamation that thousands of psychometric psychologists all over the world are dedicated to the oppression of the poor is, I must admit it, a strain upon my credulity. You may find it a strain on yours too. I've met hundreds of psychometric psychologists. Honestly, they do not seem like oppressors. Really.

Professor Kamin is certainly right in one thing, namely that the vast majority of students of the subject take a view less extreme than his own, they feel that there might be some hereditary influence on IQ. I want to propose a model which may help to clarify the reader's view.

If the genes, heredity, had *absolutely* no effect upon manifest intelligence then we ought to expect a dog, a mouse or even a worm to have the same spread of IQ scores as men and women. There exist no IQ tests for dogs or worms, they fall in the class 'untestable'. The position Kamin seems to be left in then, is really quite extraordinary. If we are to accept his view that there are no genetic differences (because we can't prove that there are) then we have to assume that intelligence, problem-solving ability, is unlike any other human variable such as weight, skin colour, eye colour and the shape of our features, length of our fingers, everything measurable about a man or woman which varies from one person to another.

All of these variations between people on different parameters (in different ways) fall onto the Gaussian curve, the normal distribution. No-one, but no-one would feel happy with the view that all these differences are due to upbringing. What Professor Kamin is asking us to believe is that in one respect only, intelligence, there is no genetic variation at all, everyone is born with exactly the same. This kind of variation is absolutely unlike any other.

Dr Kamin, of course, does not advance this view, but it is implicit in his rejection of any possibility of genetic variation. I have in fact read accounts which do accept this extraordinary view, but even they are forced to allow for exceptions; where there is a visible chromosome defect, as in Mongolism. It is a fundamental human experience that we inherit from our parents the shape of our nose, the colour of our hair, the length of our hands, our height, weight, strength, skin colour, and nearly everything else. But concerning the most important thing of all, our ability to solve problems, despite our experience in our own lives which tells us the opposite, we are told that it would be 'imprudent', as Professor Kamin puts it, 'to believe', for instance, that two very bright able parents had a better chance of having a bright able child than a pair of unfortunate retardates.

Dr Kamin seems to ignore the work of Karl Popper. I do not have to produce 'data to lead a prudent man to believe' one hypothesis, that IQ test scores are heritable. Nor do I have to produce data to support my own hypothesis that both heredity and environment affect scores. Each of these hypotheses has the same initial standing scientifically. The way modern scientists settle the matter is to try really hard to falsify both hypotheses. If we fail to do so with one of them we may provisionally accept it.

Starting with his particular preconceptions Professor Kamin would have been prudent not to have chosen to try to disprove the hypothesis of intelligence heritability, even if this hypothesis is uncongenial to him. A less ideologically attached scientist would have tried to disprove the hypothesis that the environment is wholly or mainly responsible for mental differences. If he had convincingly failed in this task how much more credible would have been his invitation to reject all thoughts of the heritability of intelligence?

I am not a qualified scientist, but let me propose a more scientific approach. Let me now advance the hypothesis that differences in manifest IQ correlate in some measure both with hereditary and also with environmental differences. What the scientist has to do is to try to falsify that, and fail. Then we may believe it. Provisionally.

Let me put this forward as the working hypothesis which it would be sensible to follow as long as it is not falsified. Karl Popper might argue that it is not a scientific statement at all, because it is not falsifiable.

But I can propose a paper experiment which would falsify it. Take two samples of babies, all born on the same day and bring them up in an environment which is kept as similar as possible. Give them all the same food, clothing and treat them alike in every respect. Let there be a matched sample of adequate size which remains with their parents and are brought up in the usual way.

(I call this a paper experiment because no one would think of making it. I want to show that the hypothesis is falsifiable. There are, in fact, many orphanages which have a uniform environment. Many children in them came there as small babies.)

If, when the children reach testable age, the institutionalized group has a negligible range or spread of IQ scores, one much lower than the other group, then we shall have failed to falsify the environmental theory. If the spread of difference in IQ score were normal and not negligible, then we should have falsified the hypothesis of a purely environmental explanation. Well we know the results for orphanages. Numerous studies at orphanages on children who have been institutionalized since shortly after birth (all obviously in a closely similar environment) do not show any perceptible reduction in the IQ range as we would be expecting on a purely environmental hypothesis.

The second paper experiment would be an attempt to falsify the absolutist hypothesis that 'all differences in IQ scores or intelligence are of genetic origin'. We should have to use multiple clone births, separate them and bring them up in a range of environments. Then check the IQ scores. If the spread of IQ scores were negligible we should have failed to falsify the hypothesis and might accept it. If the spread were completely normal we should have falsified the hypothesis and could reject it.

But we know what the result is from many studies, in many countries, by many researchers with uniovular twins separated at birth. (We can exclude those by Sir Cyril Burt.)

All the work *does* falsify the absolutist hypothesis because the spread is *not* negligible. But it *is* very much less than with unrelated children. So we may *not* reject the dual hypothesis, that both factors, heredity *and* environment, contribute to differences in IQ scores.

The above 'thought experiment' clearly illustrates the problem. In the first group, since the environment was closely similar, the differences would be largely genetic with only a small contribution from the environment due to the differences in interaction between the children. In the second experiment virtually all the variation in IQ scores on the cloned group could be confidently ascribed to environment since there would be very little genetic variation. What this establishes is that there is no magic correct figure for the contributions of heredity and environment. Many estimates based on twin studies (excluding Burt's) suggest that about 70%–80% of the variation *in the normal population* is genetic. But this depends on an actual population at some definite time and place, nothing else.

I am trying to show that it is possible to create a group of people in which all differences in intelligence are due to the genes they were born with and another group where all differences are due to what happened to them since birth, their environment. Such groups would be highly artificial and to create them would be absurd and unrealistic (not to mention harmful).

We have to deal with real populations where both factors influence the final manifest intelligence. And every population will be different. Small inbreeding communities would have one proportion, large multiracial ones another. Less developed Third World communities where many people are living at or below subsistence level are likely to have a large environmental contribution to mental differences. Developed, First World and Second World communities where no one starves and the poorest are well above subsistence level are likely to have more genetic influence.

The fierce and highly political public debate is about the *proportional* contribution to mental differences of the two factors. Now some people are locked into dogmatic ideological assumptions of clone-like natal equality. But those who look at the evidence agree that both factors count. They disagree as to the proportion and although they do not specify it they are talking about the Western developed world where the research has been done. In that world minimum standards of living are higher and therefore the genetic contribution to differences is likely to be highest. Their estimates vary between about 50% contribution from the genes to 95%. The most recent and best researched estimates are that between 75 and 80% of adult mental differences are genetic in origin.

Now the political argument suggests that in the developed countries there is a large class that is *relatively deprived*. Although they are well above minimum standards and rich compared with the poor of most of the world they are still counted as underprivileged and environmentally handicapped locally. We ought to note that what counts in *this* context is not relative poverty but actual poverty, real shortage of essentials. It seems reasonable to assume that the further from the subsistence level we get the less the environment can affect differences in intelligence. The children of the millionaire are not appreciably disadvantaged environmentally compared with those of the multi-millionaire.

Consider Kamin's second implied thesis that psychometric psychologists all round the world are engaged in an effort to maintain social inequality and are using IQ tests to oppress the poor. I have read his book to find his evidence for this rash implication of his second 'conclusion'.

He produces a number of genuine quotations which seem to support this notion. I shall quote one of the most extreme of these from a Professor who was well regarded in his day, Professor Lewis Terman.

'Only recently we have begun to recognise how serious a menace it is to the social, economic and moral welfare of the State . . . that the feeble minded continue to multiply . . . Organised charities . . . often contribute to the survival of individuals who would otherwise not be able to survive and reproduce . . .

If we would preserve our state for a class of people worthy to possess it we must prevent as far as possible, the propagation of mental degenerates, . . . curtailing the increasing spawn of degeneracy.'

This certainly sounds very strange but when was it written? It was written in 1917! It was written at a time when many nations were proudly racialist, when such strange sounding sentiments were normal in many places.

I found that the first part of Kamin's book was an assiduous collection of such writings which covered a period up to about 1925 before the Hitler war and before either racialism or anti-racialism had been widely thought of. Many nations then (as some still do) saw themselves as superior in breed and in every other way. They called it patriotism.

Kamin does not produce and in many years reading I have not seen a single *recent* pronouncement from the psychometric profession which gives the remotest support to these ideas.

The question we are forced to ask is this. Why did the good professor search for and dig up these long forgotten racialist pronouncements by psychologists? The answer seems to be that he was trying to make an ideological point. It is clear from all his writings that he believes in an egalitarian society where as many as possible of the differences between people can and should be removed.

He is entitled to this idealistic view but is it not possible that it colours his judgement? It is of this that he accuses his opponents. Their desire for continued advantage for the rich made them believe in and use unfair and ineffective tests to oppress the poor. May we not say to Professor Kamin, 'You too! Your politics have affected your beliefs.'

Here is a view from the other side, from Professor Hans Eysenck, referring to justified criticisms of Burt, 'clearly these critics (e.g. Kamin) have taken their criticism too far, and in turn committed serious errors of statistical calculation and genetic estimation as Fulker (1975) for instance has pointed out, in a very thorough re-analysis of the data criticised by Kamin (1974)'. One may not doubt that Kamin is sincere and that his motivation is honourable. He believes that what he is doing is moral and good.

In such a complex and neglected science as psychometry it is good and right that a wide range of views should be published and that criticism should have free rein.

People like Kamin have every right to want and propose that human differences should be suppressed or ignored if they truly believe that is possible. They may want all service, goods and property to be rationed out on the basis of need and desire and without any consideration of reward, motivation or contribution. It is a legitimate and honourable and even attractive desire. The opponents of this desire may be defending privilege and so may be suspected of self-interest. But that in itself does not *prove* they, the doubters, are wrong or that the desire for social equality is a practical and possible one.

The opposing argument is that, as I have already said, except in very small closed and protected communities this attractive ideal has never worked well or for long. And attempts to impose it have more often led to dreadful tyrannies than to egalitarian Utopias. Sceptics further argue that mankind is not by nature or tradition sufficiently unselfish and altruistic for egalitarianism to work on any large scale. Outside of strongly bonded, small face-to-face groups, people need to be motivated and rewarded to get them to do the work or perform the services that meet the needs and desires of their fellows. Unselfishness and group loyalty that work well in a small family or tribe seem to break down in larger associations. And modern affluence and good living depend on a great interlinking of well organized large groups. With motivating systems, incentives, there come, inevitably, differentials, inequality. Suppressing these, whenever tried, creates poverty, queues, rationing and a poor life style for all. Permitting them makes even the poor richer and the rich very much so.

Standards of living and inequality increase smoothly together. The price we have to pay for wealth and comfort is envy which is not nice but acceptable because of the benefits for all. Most of us would rather live well in envy of our neighbour who lives better than starve together in equality with him or her. That is the argument. It is natural that the poor like it less than the rich but that does not prove or disprove it. To find the truth we need evidence.

So we may disagree with the idealistic Professor and still defend his right to advance his egalitarian views.

But we may reasonably condemn his *argumentum ad hominem*. The accusations against all his colleagues who practise psychometry, that they are oppressors of the poor, are another matter, that is simple invective not science or politics. Was Professor Kamin carried away by his convictions? We all are sometimes.

CHARACTER ASSASSINATION AS A SCIENTIFIC ARGUMENT

I now have to report much sadder and less pleasant facts. The general ascription of a desire to oppress the poor to a whole profession is relatively harmless because it is so absurd. But the worldwide character assassination of the late Sir Cyril Burt is a very different matter.

Professor Sir Cyril Burt was the first World President of Mensa, a man of great talent and character, a Two-Cultures Renaissance man, a scientist, mathematician, classical scholar and an educational reformer who was widely acclaimed for his work for retarded children and also for able, under-privileged children who were disadvantaged in the pre-war British educational system. It was he that helped to transform that system in their interests. For this he was knighted at the request of the Socialist Prime Minister Harold Wilson. In 1975 Sir Cyril was shamefully and falsely traduced and subjected to a world scale character assassination.

When I first met him in 1953 Burt was the world doyen of psychometric psychologists. His acceptance of the Mensa Presidency (the post I now have the honour to hold) made my work in building up that unlikely but fascinating society much easier because his name carried so much weight.

Sir Cyril could not defend himself from the vicious attacks upon his reputation that were to be launched in October 1975 because he was dead.

It started like this. Professor A R Jensen is a follower of Burt. His researches have convinced him of a strong genetic effect on intelligence differences and as a result he himself has often been scandalously attacked by the political ideologues of the 'environmentalist' school (those who assert that there is no genetic influence at all). It was he who was the first to report mistakes and carelessness in Burt's later work on twin studies. Jensen is an honest scientist who is concerned with the truth more than with proving a preconceived case. He reported the transparent errors in a journal.

For instance, Burt published a table of 66 correlation coefficients between uniovular twins reared together and apart. He did this on different variables on three different dates as the samples grew. Jensen noticed that two of these sets of figures were exactly the same to three decimal places, a result which is statistically unlikely (but not impossible). A charitable explanation would be that Burt had made a copying error and not noticed it. But much more was made of it than that. A transparent error which would certainly have been corrected by a deceiver was used to 'prove' that Burt was a 'faker' and a 'fraud'.

It seems to have been Jensen's paper revealing Burt's imperfect work which set off work to cast doubt on the evidence, so uncongenial to many ideologues, that intelligence differences have a genetic component. They went through Burt's work with great pains searching for further slips. Finding some more errors they suggested that the whole of the work in the great man's long career must now be regarded as suspect. Burt's work had led to many other studies and all these too were branded, by association, as worthless.

There were errors in Burt's work. These were rightly condemned as bad science. But the errors were not those of a deceiver, they were transparent. The ageing Burt had been careless. He was not a swindler.

But any scandal about the eminent makes a good headline and, rather belatedly, the press got on to what would otherwise have been a minor academic disagreement.

About 2 years after the attack was published a British newspaper published an article in which Burt was accused of fraud and the deliberate falsification of evidence. The attack on Burt and psychometry generally and the suggestion that IQ testers were the oppressors of working class children seem to have been swallowed whole.

Nothing could have been less credible to those who had known Burt. Burt used intelligence tests on London slum children for exactly the opposite purpose. Traditional English *academic* selection tests favoured the children of the rich. Burt's *intelligence* tests like all such were devised especially to *eliminate* the bias and were much fairer to the poor. Burt's work with poor families and his influence on the educational system resulted in a big increase in the proportion of children from poor families at schools for brighter studious children. This is a matter of record.

After the first article it became open season for wildly sensational journalistic attacks on Burt all over the world. Burt's obvious senescent carelessness was exaggerated into deliberate deception, 'scientific chicanery' and 'fraud'. Burt was accused of 'inventing' collaborators and it was confidently assumed that the minor imperfections in his genetic twin studies invalidated many other such studies. The comfortable doctrine that we are all born equal not only in our rights but in every which way was finally 'proved' by 'disproving' Burt's opposite view. Bad science proves nothing at all but Burt's bad science was taken as proof that his conclusions were wrong. His errors conveniently 'proved' that *all* differences in adult intelligence were due to environmental deprivation, and the oppression of the poor. The cure for retardation? Egalitarian socialism. It cures such inequalities as genius too!

Rarely before has such a justly high reputation been so quickly and ruthlessly destroyed by sensation seeking, excellence-knocking, journalists around the world. Respectable academic journals steered clear, plainly scared of getting involved.

A few unheard voices were raised in protest. I had defended my late friend in the Mensa journals and in one of my books. Prof. Hans Eysenck loyally defended Burt and so did Jensen and a few others.

But times and modes change and those who contributed to the destruction of Burt's reputation in 1975, are now themselves under attack. Mensa's first President, Burt, is being vindicated.

With no little courage, Professor Ronald Fletcher who held the Chair of Sociology at Reading University, has made a thundering counter-attack. In the Spring edition, 1987 of *Social Policy and Administration* (Basil Blackwell) Fletcher, in a carefully researched paper, quietly and efficiently takes the case against Burt apart and shows how biased and wildly exaggerated it was.

In a two-page article in the Sunday Telegraph published in August 1987 he took the case further and turning on Burt's detractors exposed the bad science and ideologically biased thinking of the original academic attacks. In a carefully documented case he did much to detail the fallacies on which these attacks had been based and to turn the focus once again on the outstanding contribution Burt had made in the field of education.

WHY WE MUST CLASSIFY

In this world we have one fundamental mental tool, that of classification. Thus, despite the great variations between one man and another it is convenient to classify the whole species, as 'mankind' because any member of this class shows more difference from other mammals than he does from other men. But the dividing lines are in our minds.

Once we have classified things, because each of them is unique and because there are many differences between members of the class, we have to resort to a secondary tactic, that of describing and modifying concepts affecting the original classification concepts. Once we have the useful class, man, to help us with our thinking we can then begin to talk about 'big men', 'small men', 'old men', 'clever men', 'strong men' and so on. The properties 'age' and 'size' need not represent anything in the real world. They are convenient mental tools to help us to understand people, fit their clothes to them, provide them with strong enough chairs and make tables the right size for them.

As an advanced civilization develops and men have to live and work in larger and more complex groups, institutions and societies, we need to know more and more about these differences between them in order to make this big and complex wealth-producing machine, the industrial society, work properly.

Early mankind found out that one of the important differences between people was in their problem-solving ability, their memory, their power to understand and see relationships, their ability to understand, remember and use language and transmit ideas from one to another.

There truly are variations between one man or woman and another in these ways. Some people never learn to talk at all and are quite incapable of performing the simplest tasks. Others are extremely able, good at solving problems, able to absorb and understand very difficult concepts and ideas. They have creative imaginations, become scientists, inventors, writers, engineers, doctors, surgeons, so that they can serve their fellow man and their own interest at the same time.

Whatever the ideologues shout through the dogma bars of their thought prisons, what I describe above is plainly visible to anyone who has lived in the world for any time. Whether or not we go about it systematically and scientifically, we shall continue to have to make judgement about people on this continuum from extreme mental defect to genius. There is absolutely no way that any modern complex society could possibly get along if it really followed this neo-Marxist dogma that there really *are* no differences. Lenin and the Communists were more sensible. There are special schools for academic 'high flyer' children in Novosibirsk, Kiev and Moscow such as should drive our advocates of mixed-ability schools into a frenzy.

EARLIER VIEWS ABOUT INTELLIGENCE

Early ideas about the inheritance of human qualities are confused. Being of good *stock* or of good *blood* once clearly had the implication of genetic superiority – an idea probably taken from stock breeding. But the meaning of *good breeding* was an odd mixture of inheritence and good manners – that is, the behaviour usual in the upper classes. The idea that there was some special quality attached to royal or aristocratic *noble* families was universally accepted. This quality was a mixture of nature and nurture. There was no preciseness as to the properties involved. Characteristics such as *nobility* or *baseness* were deemed to be inheritable, but they seemed to relate more to martial qualities, courage, and aggressiveness than to intelligence.

With the major social changes that have occurred over the past 300 years, the idea that one particular social class has a monopoly of desirable human qualities has been rejected. It was a simple, observable fact that such qualities could be found in any social class. The rising middle class slowly and cautiously rejected the assumption of hereditary superiority held by their traditional rulers. The process is not yet complete, and there remains a residual respect for aristocrats, who still enjoy a reputation (or at least a *cachet*) that has little justification. The middle classes have mimicked the traditional upper class inbreeding and now have their own unstated claim to genetic superiority. But the set of ideas that underlies the policies in most countries today is opposed to the notion of genetic superiority on any level.

This idea lies behind the French and American revolutions and Western democracy. I agree with it.

The idea that there is *general* 'superior', aristocratic hereditary quality of any kind is clearly false. Heredity is Mendelian, particulate, there simply is no set of 'good' or 'bad' genes which justifies the many races or tribes and groups around the world who claim a general virtue for their breed.

Certain ethnic groups may be more viable in particular geographic or cultural environments. What is 'superior' here or in this life style may be 'inferior' there and in that life style.

The great increase in ethnic cross-breeding recently has made little difference to this. There remain many 'ethnic' or 'ethno-cultural' groups where the genetic variability within the group is less than the variability between such groups. So there are differences in ethnic group averages. But the variability within each group is such that they all merge at the extremes. Almost without exception overtly or covertly these ethnic groups show what we call 'patriotism' if we belong to them or 'racism' if we do not. That is hardly surprising since the groups have often been in conflict for space or resources for millenia. In warfare group loyalty, or patriotism is useful. Nearly all the shooting struggles and wars in the world today deeply involve ethno-cultural differences.

Anti-racism is something quite new, it is barely 40 years old. My generation of English schoolboys were taught at school to be white supremacist and racist (and sexist as well). Now a fervent anti-racist myself I have to admit that anti-racism is a modern cult which is spreading among the educated middle classes of the colour blind World Culture of which I have written earlier. Racism as an accusation is normally applied only to Caucasian whites who do not subscribe to the cult. Other ethnic groups are expected to be self-approving racially.

It is my view that the urgent, almost desperate, attacks upon any attempt to assess or measure cognitive mental ability arise from a confusion, perhaps a natural one, between the idea of aristocratic or racial 'superiority' and the simple fact that in all races and groups there are differences in intelligence as well as many other traits. There is a fear that this is an attempt to re-introduce the 'class' or 'race' superiority in a disguised form. But since psychometric research proves the precise opposite, that all 'races' and 'classes' have the full range of mental ability from genius to dullard it is a foolish and damaging fear.

TWIN STUDIES

Let us now take a brief look at the twin studies by many workers which have all been 'discredited' by a couple of improbable figures in one of them. Here is the hard evidence which makes it imprudent, as Professor Kamin would say, to work to the unproven hypothesis that all differences in mental ability are caused by the way people live.

About one in 87 births is that of twins. Twins are of two types: fraternal (from two eggs) and identical (from one egg). Fraternal twins have the same relation as two brothers or two sisters; they come from two separate ova fertilized by two separate sperm. Identical twins come from the splitting of a single ovum fertilized by a single sperm. They are, from a genetic point of view, very nearly identical.

Anyone who has met identical twins is aware how close the resemblance is. They offer us a good clue as to the amount of variation that can be expected due to environment and due to heredity. During the early years of the century, it was common to split up pairs of twins because the parents were unable economically to cope with both.

A great similarity between the intelligence assessments of identical twins had long been known, but it had always been argued by the environmentalists that if they were brought up together their environmental circumstances would also be very similar.

Sir Cyril Burt was the first to use separated twins as a means of answering this argument. Since then, completely independent studies have been done, and large numbers of separated identical twins have been discovered. The result of this mass of work in many places by many researchers has always shown the same tendency. It has shown, first, that one-egg twins reared apart resemble one another very much more in intelligence than two-egg twins reared together. They have also shown that one-egg twins brought up together show even more resemblance in intelligence quotient. Thus, it is conclusively shown that there is both a genetic and environmental influence on the manifest IQ and that the effect of heredity is more important.

Erlenmeyer-Kimling and Jarvik in 1963 summarized the evidence of 52 genetic studies from eight countries, spanning half a century of time, and employing a wide variety of tests and subjects. They found the following data:

| | Correlation coefficients | |
| | Reared apart | Reared together |
Group		
Unrelated persons	−0.01	0.23
Foster parents and their children		0.20
Parents and their children		0.5
Brothers and sisters	0.4	0.49
Fraternal twins		0.53
Identical twins	0.75	0.87

The most significant thing in this table is that completely unrelated persons reared together show a very low resemblance in intelligence (0.23), whereas twins, who have exactly the same genetic make-up reared apart show a very high resemblance in IQ (0.75).

These studies show conclusively that the genetic effect is a very strong one and that certainly the environmental influence is also important.

It should also be noted that the brother and sister, fraternal twins, and parent and child correlation coefficients are all around the 0.5 level, which would be predicted by a genetic explanation. It is very difficult to think of an explanation on environmental grounds alone which is compatible with figures like these.

One refuge for the environmentalists has been to say that similarities between twins reared apart can be accounted for by the fact that the very early environment has an extremely strong influence so that the similarity of the twins is established even before the separation. Against this, it has been shown in one study that the age of parting makes no difference. In fact, another study showed that twins separated earlier show *more* similarity instead of less.

In a series of interesting investigations with identical and fraternal twins reared together and apart, it was shown that the correlations between the pairs in educational attainment were much more closely related to their environment than was their intelligence measure.

When the IQ of one-egg twins and two-egg twins are compared, results in absolutely all cases fail to falsify the hypothesis that there is genetic contribution to mental differences. We have to scrap Burt's own data because they are suspect, but all other studies show similar results. Herman and Hogburn in 1933 found that with 65 pairs of one-egg twins and 234 pairs of two-egg twins the mean IQ difference between the twins was 9.2 in case of the one-egg twins and 17.8 in the case of the two-egg twins. The correlation coefficient between pairs of one-egg twins was 0.84 and that between pairs of two-egg twins of the same sex 0.47, which is very close to the figure expected between brothers on a genetic explanation.

THE HERITABILITY OF RETARDATION

Approximately a quarter of the children admitted to institutions as severely subnormal have visible chromosome aberrations such as Mongolism, and as many as 45% have fairly clear genetic factors – for instance, a family history of retardation, which would appear to predispose the children to their infirmity.

The evidence of mental defects in the relatives of defective children is interesting and in some ways contradictory. The most severely handicapped children, those with an IQ range from 35 to 60, have brothers and sisters who appear to be fairly normal. These severely handicapped children's disabilities seem to be serious and are probably rare genetic effects. They are very often visible, as mentioned above, as a major defect that can be seen in the body or the chromosomes. The brothers and sisters of the less severely disabled group, those from a IQ 60 upward, tend to be diagnosed as definitely retarded. Usually the IQ of this group of siblings tends to be about halfway between the average of the defective group and the average for all children. This could be accounted for if we assume that the higher grade defectives or retardates are accounted for by the normal inherited variations between individuals (they are simply on the lower tail of the distribution curve), whereas the extremely low grade defectives result from, as suggested, a more dramatic and rarer gross genetic defect, which is unlikely to affect two members of one family. A gross genetic defect cannot be passed on to the next generation because almost all those affected are, in fact, sterile. These defects can only happen by a rare unhappy genetic accident, a mutation.

Parent type and subnormal children

The families of a group of subnormal children were examined with these results:

Parents	Siblings of subject who are subnormal (%)
Both subnormal	42.1
One subnormal	19.9
Both normal, with subnormal uncles or aunts	12.9
All relatives normal	5.7

It is established beyond any reasonable doubt that the causes of high or low intelligence in children are a mixture of both environment and heredity. The consensus is that heredity plays a more important part.

Some people ask, 'If intelligence is largely genetic, is the general level of intelligence of the community rising or falling?' Some geneticists in the past have had serious fears that there may be a lowering of the general level of intelligence because of the observed trend of differential fertility of different social groups and the difference in intelligence in those groups. It was observed that the families of parents with lower intelligence test scores were on the average larger than those of parents with higher scores. A later study showed that this effect is outbalanced by a reduced fertility at the lower end of the test score spectrum. It is rare for severely retarded persons to have children or to marry at all. In addition, recently there has been a marked increase in fertility at the top end of the intelligence score scale in some countries. The answer is not known and, as the subject is controversial, there is little being done to find out.

The reader who would like to know more about the question of heredity and environment and their contribution to the variations in intelligence test scores can get a very good account from Professor Eysenck's book *The Inequality of Man*. In this book, the arguments pro and con are dealt with very carefully and systematically. Professor Eysenck points out that, whereas any conclusion in this field is open to some uncertainty, all the evidence there is is consistent with the hypothesis that about 20% of the variability in IQ scores can be accounted for by environment and about 80% must be attributed to heredity.

Professor Eysenck confirms that the nature of the problem is misunderstood. Every characteristic of an animal is both genetic and environmental in origin;

any argument can only be about the contribution of the different causes. The inborn, or genetic, characteristics will present a ceiling. The environment, or the way the child is brought up, determines how close to that ceiling the child can get. Eysenck goes on to say that in the past there has been uncertainty because it was difficult to determine the effect of the interaction between the inborn and environmental factors. Now that it is known to be both measurable and quite small, accurate estimates can be made. It turns out that the estimates of early researchers, notably Holzinger, Freeman, and Burt, were not far out despite the fact that their methods were open to, and certainly received, much subsequent criticism. Recent work with more refined methods has produced figures very similar to these first estimates.

Two points are often missed. The first is that any error or uncertainty in the reliability of the tests themselves will automatically have the effect of reducing any estimate that may be made of the inheritability of intelligence. The uncertainty from the test instrument itself would tend to reduce the high correlations found between unrelated children reared together.

Any such unreliability would tend to diminish differences shown in the correlation coefficient. Despite this, in all investigations into one-egg twins reared together and apart, fraternal twins, and brothers and sisters reared together and apart, the correlation between the test scores of children adopted at birth and their natural parents, the correlation between the scores of children brought up in the same environment – as in orphanages – but of different parentage, and the correlation between the scores of children and foster parents tend to confirm the 80% contribution by heredity to mental differences.

THE EVIDENCE FROM MENSA

There is an argument which gives assurance to the commonsense view that both nature and nurture are concerned in the inheritance of mental ability.

If the environmental view were correct we should find little evidence of people moving up and down the class structure (social mobility is the technical term). Looking at Mensa – all members are bright – we *should* find that they are largely of middle and upper class origin. Well, they are not.

In Mensa we have our own sample of extreme social mobility. According to theory there should be only a tiny proportion of Mensa members who are of lower class origin. In fact in a study with Mensa members, each of whom has scored in the top 2% on an intelligence test, it was found that only 36½% of the members' parents came from the top quarter from the point of view of social class. No fewer than 37% were of 'blue collar' origin, that is, the fathers were manual workers, and nearly 19% of the fathers were in the lower echelons of that category.

The very high upward social mobility associated with high intelligence is demonstrated by the fact that 96% of members in the study are now in the two upper occupational classes, over 76% in the highest. Blue collar workers are only 4%, with 1% in the lowest echelons.

Now, it seems to me it would be very hard to find an argument against accepting that whatever it is that makes people score well on intelligence tests also has the effect of moving them towards the upper levels of the occupational class structure. A sample of 352 people assembled because of a high score on an IQ test is examined and it is shown that, while 36% of the fathers were in the top occupational class, 76% of the sons were in that class.

To conclude, I would urge the commonsense view that differences in mental ability, between people, like any other differences are at least partly due to heredity. I think we should continue to plan and act on this traditional, sensible, intermediate hypothesis until conclusive evidence shall falsify it, if ever it does.

I feel sure that anyone, who reads the literature on both sides carefully and without preconceptions, must come to the conclusion that the hypothesis that there is a large innate influence on differences in measured intelligence has not been falsified. Any such investigator must find it risky to assume that our parentage has no effect at all on our manifest intelligence.

So we have to ask, 'Is it wise to work on Professor Kamin's apparent assumption that differences in mental ability arise from social causes and can all be "cured" by social action?'

This is not an unworthy thought but an attractive one. The motivation for it is decent. It would be good if it were true that we could, by the right social policies, make people more equal mentally, by improving the mental powers of backward people and fitting them for the mentally demanding future which I foresee.

But it would be harmful to follow such policies if the assumption were, as seems likely, untrue. It would raise false expectations and disappoint them. This would be divisive. It would misdirect money and talent into unproductive channels. It would cause frustration to teachers and bureaucrats by setting an impossible task. Much worse, it would misuse and underuse the limited stock of real talent. It would be a bad investment of talent and money which would threaten the nation concerned with lowered standards.

I concede that the debate is not over and that neither the dual causation hypothesis nor the single cause environmental hypothesis has gained full consensus. So policy making authorities are faced with a dilemma. Which hypothesis should be used as the working hypothesis? Which policy has the least error cost? Shall we work towards more equality or towards more excellence? The reader must decide.

12

Making Use of our Mental Resources

There are few who would deny that the human brain is the best instrument for data processing that we know of in the universe, and so we can claim that the most human thing about human beings is their highly developed intelligence.

In the author's opinion the advantages to humanity of the human being's very large and elaborate brain do not lie in the brain's effectiveness for the individual but in its service to the societies that humans live in. Animals with brains inferior to human brains are quite capable of a solitary life or of life in small groups. The increased size of the human brain may have evolved so that human beings could live successfully in well organized and stable groups.

It follows that smaller, simpler social groupings do not require as high a level of intelligence for their organization as do larger, more complicated ones like those that have appeared in the developed world in the last few hundred years.

Zipf and other researchers have shown that the liability to error and the complexity of an information network increase exponentially with size. We may expect, therefore, that as the separate living societies of the world coalesce into one worldwide society, if they do, the problems of communication and organization will become increasingly severe. Added to these problems are those presented by the accelerating growth of population in many lands. Few people would deny that in the next century, mankind as a whole will be faced by problems that will require the most intensive application of that most human quality – intelligence.

The demand for human ability, intelligence, and talent will be great and increasing if all these problems are to be solved. The world of tomorrow, even more than the world of today, will need to find, motivate, educate, exploit and use all the talent that is available to it in each generation.

We shall be unable to afford the enormous waste of talent that exists even in

283

the developed world, much less the waste in the vast population that is living at subsistence level in the underdeveloped nations. The people in these countries, without access to proper education, books and stimulation, spend their lives at simple tasks that could be performed well by machine. After the explosive increase in world population recently mankind is faced with two alternatives: either man will have to use his brain, collectively and individually, more effectively, or he will have to revert to an earlier, simpler style of life and reduce his numbers drastically.

If this latter road is taken, whether by choice or by incompetence and failure, the changes required are so severe and all-encompassing that the human inhabitants of this world can look forward only to several generations of calamity.

The only other viable alternative is for our societies to think of ways out of the problems our successes have created. The options are few. Our societies will have to find the right course if we are to avoid the many kinds of disaster that could overwhelm us.

Parents who want to realize a good future for their children and their children's can best do this by making sure that their children fulfil their potential so that they can be of the most service to society. The parents whose problem and privilege it is to have a gifted child have an even more urgent task and duty because it is from these children that we must recruit those who can do most for the rest of us.

When we review the enormous range in human ability and behaviour from the uncommunicating autistic child, on the one hand, to the brilliant, eagerly learning, able child on the other, it is difficult to understand how anyone can believe that benefits to the children and to society can be achieved by a monolithic undiscriminating system built on the hypothesis that all variations in humans are unimportant or largely culturally determined.

The idea that every man shall have equal rights – that all men are legally, morally, and socially equal – is an essential element of any humane society. But the extension of this idea – that all men are in reality equal, that there is a kind of international standard man to which we all conform – is one of the more extreme ideas of Rousseau. It is a comic idea, and it is comic that it is taken seriously. But the consequences of taking it seriously and of trying to formulate educational policy in its light are not comic, they are tragic. They constitute an abandonment of that essential ethic of Western society's success, the doctrine of 'the best man for the job'.

It is not the able people especially who will suffer from society's neglect; they can look after themselves in most circumstances and will, as always, do better than average under any system, no matter how much it may try to handicap them. It is the society as a whole that will be impoverished, as it is in areas of the world where nepotism, corruption, and ideological or religious conformity not ability, are the basis of selection and promotion.

The principal virtue of an open society is that it releases the talents of the people to contend in fair competition so that ability emerges where it can have the most influence. The defect of the system is that individual objectives are often merely private profit and personal advancement. What the world needs is a system that provides a viable programme of selection that would face with clear eyes the inequality of man and would make the best, compassionate, humane and effective use of human mental resources. The subject would seem to be one that is worthy of a great deal more study than it has attracted so far.

We hope that eventually a climate of opinion will emerge that will make it possible to study the demand for, the supply of, the social motivation of, and the education and training of that most precious of human resources – intelligence.

USING MENTAL RESOURCES: THE POLITICAL PROBLEM

The industrial age has brought many benefits to at least some of mankind. But before it could really spread from its first base in North Europe, there had to be a great change in the way people thought about role allocation. The wealth, power, privileges and influence of an aristocratic ruling class had to be limited and a long established traditional way of allocating roles utterly changed. In many countries (e.g. America and France) this was done in a traumatic and painful revolution.

The resulting changes brought prosperity and progress but like any revolutionary changes, they have had undesirable side-effects. The aristocrats had traditions of personal responsibility and habits of charity which, though unreliable, seemed more human and natural than the impersonal bureaucratic modern versions. Many people feel happier under the personal protection of a local overlord than they do in a society where they have to cope with the red tape and rigidity of modern local government 'carers'. This may account for the resilience and strength, even today, of the Mafia and organizations like it. These are an evil survival in a criminalized form of a more ancient tradition.

Once the idea that opportunities should be equally open to all and that systems of traditional familial and tribal privileges should be broken up, everyone was in an uncharted sea of change. It might be good to put down the powerful overlord but it is disconcerting when those we have been taught to think of as below us, rise above us rich and powerful. It is very disturbing. And the changes caused many disturbances as the last couple of centuries shows.

So in various ways reaction arose. One form the reaction took was quite ingenious. It took the form of overextending the case and 'playing the egalitarians at their own game'. 'You want equality of opportunity', was the cry. 'That is not enough, we want equality of outcome'. 'Having an equal chance is not enough, we want to really *be* equal. All must have exactly equal shares. There must be no advantage for the excellent and the industrious and no disadvantage to the idle, unsocial or feckless.'

The two errors of this extremist view are obvious.

Firstly, if there really is both freedom and equality of opportunity, then even if all start even, the differences in human qualities, in intelligence, acquisitiveness, industriousness, energy, persuasiveness, etc., will soon create new differences. It is only by giving up freedom that equality of outcome can be assured.

Secondly, the view is based on a false assumption. That is, that it is a zero-sum game, that the amount of goods and services that can be provided is fixed and limited, that we all have to share a single fixed cake. Our experience tells us different. The systems of distribution are not all equal in their power to stimulate the production and provision of goods and services. Those which allow inequality of outcome seem to cause such an enlargement of the cake that even when unequally shared, the lowest on the inequality ladder are higher than they could be under a strict equal shares system.

This zero-sum social paradigm has now spread widely in the Western world and is keeping many people in bureaucratic poverty traps.

Most of us think that extreme social inequalities should be reduced and that rich nations can afford to and should put an end to poverty among their citizens. Most of us would agree that those unfortunate children who are born with limited mental powers should receive special treatment. But the extension of this view to a policy that all children, no matter how gifted they are, should be given exactly the same treatment is dangerous and wrong. This would mean that the pace of the group will be the pace of the slowest. This is destructive of everything which our civilization, against great odds has achieved in its struggles over many centuries.

From good motives, some modern educationalists are doing a great disservice to the community. They insist that those at the lower tail of the intelligence curve should be treated as if their capabilities could be improved until they became high achievers. These devoted and compassionate efforts can only create disappointment for both teachers and their pupils. Limited resources of teaching talent and educational funds will be wasted in a battle which is predestined to failure. Dedicated self-deceivers will always produce the exceptional case to prove that their efforts are worthwhile. We are left to admire their devotion, their motivation, their love of humanity, but we can only deplore their common sense and the use to which they put the resources we make available. The best humanitarian must still keep an eye on the cost/ benefit advantage. If we concentrate all our educational effort on levelling up less able children we shall find ourselves without a cadre of trained, intelligent people to do the same for the next generation, and without the funds to do it.

The cadre of educationalists today are largely from that class which have had good fortune both in family background and in the genetic lottery and are of above average intelligence.

Having had a good education, having been given access to a cultural inheritance from generations of scholars, some of them would deny these privileges to their successors, the able and effective of the next generation. They would systematically deflate and denigrate those who should carry the torch from them. It would seem to be another example of the cobbler's children going barefoot.

There is a fundamental political error in this thinking about education. Because education was at one time available only to the children of the upper social classes it has come to be looked upon as a privilege, a contribution by the State to the children of the citizens. My view is the opposite. Education is not a privilege, it is a preparation for service, a *contribution*. Children would prefer to be playing or indulging in their hobbies. They are compelled by law or parents to attend schools so as to prepare themselves to be responsible citizens. The function of schools is vital to any advanced civilization. It is the vital job of guarding and passing on and improving the heredity of knowledge, arts, skills, techniques and know-how, that has been accumulated by past generations. This is the task.

Concern for the gifted has nothing to do with politics or social class. If the existence of Mensa has proved anything, it has proved what Terman showed, that the gifted people, the savants, of each generation come from all social and occupational classes and transcend all social environments.

Education is a time-consuming, hard-working period of unpaid or underpaid work by young people which enables them to make a better, more effective contribution to the common pool in the next generation.

Among the young people whose effort we command for these social purposes are the gifted. The work and effort we should and must demand of them can be greater than we can demand from the less able. We must ask them to work longer and harder at more difficult work. We are not giving them a privilege. I repeat it. We are asking them to make an increased contribution. 'From each according to his ability.' Let us learn that wisdom from Karl Marx. No one is wrong all the time.

13

Social Implications

There are three questions that people ask themselves about the implications for political and social policy of what we know about mental differences.

(1) What social policies will best help us to reduce the harmful social effects, if any, of manifest inequalities in intelligence and performance?

(2) In the western world, are we sure that there is not an underlying decline in the genetic aspect of general intelligence; if there is and assuming it is desirable to do so, what social policies will best correct the decline?

(3) How can societies make best use of their mental resources?

Let us look at the first question from three points of view, the extreme environmentalist, the extreme geneticist and the intermediate view.

Assuming that all mental differences have purely environmental origin, the outlook is not good – the amount of social engineering required to correct differences in mental ability would be great. Why? The experts find that the problems arise in the pre-school years where State action cannot easily operate. From the Robbins report to the British Government we hear:

'Within each ability group at age of 11+ there is no significant difference in performance between children from different classes who stay on . . . it is clear that differences of social class have ceased to be effective determinants of achievement at this level, at this age.'

The differences appear to be connected with the home and family background before the age of 5, when the children start school and this caused Professor Wiseman to say,

'the question now arises, what can we do to counteract the effect of poor environment? The prognosis is bleak, since it seems more than likely that

289

the greatest harm to the child occurs before he ever reaches school at 5 years of age, and that any efforts the school might make are rather in the nature of the shutting of the stable door after the horse has bolted. We may reasonably conclude that the mixture of causes of poor performance in school include, as very important factors, things which are outside the control of the educational system. It is unfortunately true to say that when the child arrives at school at the age of 5, his final fate is already much more determined than we should like.'

The environmentalists at this point will say, to achieve the all round equality we want, we must raise the standards in the homes of the pre-school children. What the environmentalist will undoubtedly mean by that is that we must make the people in these homes richer, give them more money, goods and services and all will come right. Well, during the course of my long life I have seen this happen. The 'lower classes' of which I was, as a child, a member, have become much more prosperous in England but there is no sign of any reduction in the range of intelligence. There has even been a marked increase in illiteracy. What I have not seen is any improvement in the proportion of children reaching school who reach higher levels of attainment. (I am *not* suggesting that the increase in the standard of living is responsible for the decline.)

Let us look at the problem unemotionally and try to decide what is the right social policy to correct mental inequalities if that is desirable.

What would be the solution that would arise if the environmentalists were right? The environmentalists start off with the assumption that the reason some people are intelligent and prosperous and others less so, is entirely and only because of inherited privilege. They deny any influence of mental inadequacy as a causative factor of poverty in some cases. They think of a 'vicious circle' in which 'deprivation', by which they mean having an income below the national average (not the world average), causes inadequacy which in turn causes deprivation. Break the circle, they argue, give people an average income, their achievement will go up and all will be well.

They thus assume that working class culture, in less advantaged families, turns out to be unfavourable to that type of conceptual intelligence which is associated with academic and career success. Environmentalists deprecate the 'bourgeois', middle-class culture. Yet paradoxically they imply that it is *favourable* to the development of logical rational thinking power and to academic and career success. These things are usually held to be important for the wealth creation in the nation.

If working class people followed the views of the extreme environmentalists, they would blame themselves, their family habits and customs and their own behaviour, for the relative failure of their children to progress.

Middle-class families would, if they accept this environmentalist view, have every reason to congratulate themselves on their way of bringing up their children. They could take credit for the fact that the children were more likely to grow up to fit in with the needs of our particular technological society.

I do not, of course, believe that this is fair or reasonable to either. I think the self-congratulation of the middle-class family would, if it happened, be unearned, because it seems a good part of the apparent advantages in intelligence shown by their children is probably genetic, giving a reason for neither pride nor shame. Similarly, according to this hypothesis the parents of working class origin would be wrong to blame themselves for what may be at least partially of genetic origin.

Regarding the second question, what happens if we cling to the position that we must base policies on the assumption that genetics play no part in mental differences? We then come to these consequences.

The administrative decisions that would follow this theory would be to cease all genetic counselling to the severely retarded. We know that the pattern sets early. So we should act on the assumption that mental defect and a low manifest intelligence are caused by the environmental family circumstances. So, assuming we think we should find remedies for the sake of the children, we should try to improve these by intervening in the families, where disabilities occur, regulating the way they bring up their children; perhaps, in extreme cases, taking the children away from them!

Proceeding on the same hypothesis schools which produce a very low level of educational success should be shut down or drastically changed. Where there are ethnic minorities which have poor achievement, every measure should be taken to help them to change the domestic environment and the way of life, which according to this hypothesis is causing the problem. We should induce them to imitate groups with better achievement. This would be the extraordinary and ridiculous set of measures which would follow from the acceptance of the extreme environmentalist view. I need hardly say that I find these policies distasteful and authoritarian – but they follow from the premise.

The sensible, intermediate hypothesis, that differences in conceptual intelligence are partly innate, partly environmental would lead to a set of policies much like the traditional practices in the more successful societies. If a nation is richer, and healthier, more stable than many others, caution would suggest that it should not be too quick to change its educational practices on the basis of any new extreme hypothesis which they are asked to accept simply on the grounds that evidence for the *opposite* extreme hypothesis can be challenged.

Until we know much more – few changes. Meanwhile, let us do what we can to help by genetic counselling to families where there is a risk of retardation and do everything to encourage all parents to provide a varied cultivated and stimulating environment for their children especially in the preschool years.

The central point is that we *have* to make decisions every day on some assumption. If we are not sure about the Nature/Nurture problem yet — if it is still in dispute — we cannot suspend all action. The intermediate hypothesis seems best while we wait for certainty.

THE INCREASING NEED FOR ABLE PEOPLE

Many people of egalitarian persuasion have pinned their hopes of a better, fairer world on achieving socialism via the working class movement. In the days before mechanization and automation, when the class of manual factory workers was very much larger and more vital, this seemed like the only hope of breaking down what were seen as the bastions of wealth and privilege that had been built up. In parts of the world this still holds good. In other parts the proletariat is now less important than the large class of farmers who get a subsistence living directly from the soil. But in the more developed countries, the proletariat has been shrinking. As automatic machines and processes have become more complex, people have been moving away from working with things and processes into the world of working with information.

In the Western world the transformation of agriculture is almost complete. Whereas it used to take, in England for instance, the work of 85% of the population as land workers, to provide the food, much of it is now provided by the work of only 2 or 3%.

More recently, the need for unskilled factory workers, labourers, and all those performing mentally undemanding tasks is now falling rapidly. The number of professionals, clerks, accountants, typists, skilled workers, computer operators, programmers, the large body of information workers has flourished and grown.

What does this signify from the point of view of the demand for mental resources?

There is a continuum of human occupations from the unskilled labourer or packer up to the engineering designer, the economist and the mathematician and along this continuum the demand for that supreme human quality, intelligence, increases as we move up the scale. This scale is not presented as my own value judgement. It is amply confirmed by opinion poll ratings and social surveys. There is no question that the industrial changes that have taken place in the developed world have been overwhelmingly in the direction of increasing the demand for those who have the power to solve problems involving conceptual intelligence and diminishing the demand for those less endowed. We shall be ill-advised if we fail to face up to this difficult problem and fudge or dodge the issue.

The industrial working classes of the future, those who are required to do the central and important work connected with providing us with food, goods and services will have to be more intelligent than those we have managed with in the past. Fair or unfair, divisive or not, distasteful or not, politically undesirable or not, regardless of what we do about it we shall have to face this fundamental, central fact. There is going to be a lot more demand for the work of our intelligent citizens and a great deal less, at least until after a period of adjustment, for those with less skill and power in the field of conceptual intelligence.

The political implications of this revolution are great, the changes that are going on right now cannot fail vastly to transform the political thinking of tomorrow. Already the shape of the new, changed political world is visible. Old political parties are changing or dying, new ones are being formed. Mankind is adjusting itself to the coming of a new age, an Age of Information. We are getting ready to adjust to Artificial Intelligence which is not very far round the corner.

Now, it seems to me, we in the West must either adjust to this changing world or we shall be superseded by those groups and societies that do. A head-in-the-sand attitude of not wanting to know about these nasty divisive differences will be no help to anyone and especially not to the 'deprived', the 'disadvantaged' and the 'underprivileged' who depend on the general success of our society for their subsistence, unsatisfactory though they may find it.

Two lectures to Mensa At Cambridge illustrate this point. In 1982, Professor Richard Lynn noted a strong eugenic trend as regards intelligence in Japan. He said that he could not believe the figures he obtained when he tested the Japanese on IQ tests – tests which were based on what was to the Japanese an alien culture, America. He did the experiment 27 times to confirm his results. Two startling things emerged. The average IQ of Japanese – on these American tests – was four points above that of Americans and Europeans. This was in the group aged 40–60 years. Then he looked at the younger age group and was bowled over to find that the mean IQ of Japanese aged 20 was 120, a 14 points increase in a generation!

Professor Lynn told me that he felt this incredibly quick rise in measured IQ might be a genetic effect. He felt that it might be that the way the Japanese as a nation have tackled birth control since the war had caused a real rise in average intelligence. But Professor Lynn has recently discovered a similar increase in average IQ in many countries and we are left wondering how big a part test sophistication may play or whether the genetic effects apply all round. The effect, for instance, of following Eysenck's suggestion and giving (for fairness) all children a chance to practise IQ tests would be to show a non-genetic jump in average IQ score of several points.

We can observe, however, that Japanese commerce and industry and especially their high technology, which calls for a highly intelligent work force, have done extremely well since World War II. It would be imprudent to draw the conclusion that this was helped by the quality, whatever it is, that made the high average IQ score possible. But, in our ignorance, it might be equally imprudent to affirm the view that the two effects are completely unconnected.

Mensa is an institution which is free of dogma, because it has no collective views. Its members are prepared to listen to unpopular or taboo subjects.

Adolph Hitler was a uniquely evil man and he did more harm to his generation than anyone before or since. One of the evil ideas he espoused was that of the master race. He was not the first to do that and he was not to be the last. The doctrine of ethnic superiority is reviled in the Caucasian Western world but it is alive and well in quite a number of contemporary ethno-cultural groups. And it remains a bad and dangerous ideal.

The reason is simple. There is no such thing as a general purpose super-person, there cannot even be superpeople for this or that culture or situation. Each life style needs a range of types of people, a good mix. And even if a super mix were found it would be wrong because there is a further need for variability. There must be a ready pool of the types who are not suitable for society and the world as it is but who may be suitable for the next phase after an unpredictable catastrophic (or even gradual) geological, meteorological, social or other change. Hitler's vision of a super race was one of military overlords dominating the serving *untermenschen*. It was evil but childishly ill-informed and unrealistic also.

But among the evil results of Hitler's amateur philosophizing was one he did not intend. He brought a kind of guilt by association to any serious thinking about human genetic policy so that the whole field of thought is now taboo. Civilized mankind has no genetic policy and refuses to consider one.

It is one thing to condemn the simplistic and frankly racist views which were normal early in the century as Darwinian theory and Mendelian genetics began to be understood. It is right to condemn a man who set out to stock-breed supermen. It is quite another to refuse even to speculate about the genetic effects that might follow from greatly changed and vastly improved practices in medicine and welfare in many large populations around the world. It could well be that our descendants may curse Hitler more for that effect on our generation than for any other.

Let me put another case that 200 multi-disciplinary Mensans heard that year. At the same meeting at Queen's College, Cambridge in 1983 we had a talk from Dr Robert Klark Graham. Speech tends to be more free than usual in its meetings. He gave it as his firm conclusion that while the Japanese are advancing in IQ we in the West are declining. His claim is that one of the long-term side-effects of welfare provision in the modern state is that unfortunate retarded people are better able to bring up families than they were in harsher times. If there *is*, in fact, *any* genetic factor at work it would be difficult to falsify his hypothesis that this might cause a decline in average intelligence.

To my mind we can draw only an unhappy conclusion. We pose the not unimportant question, 'Are people in the advanced world gaining or losing in the average genetic intelligence?' Answer: 'We have no idea.'

The reason? Only a few exceptionally courageous people like the Professors Lynn and Eysenck and, yes, Dr Graham, will touch the subject with a barge pole. No one really knows for sure or seems to want to know.

This is my own condensation of arguments put by other lecturers and in the discussion.

Whatever consistent policies or practices a social group follows must have genetic consequences. Each policy will make some difference, however slight, to the sort of mix of people who survive and breed in future generations. Further, as Haldane has shown, such differences are cumulative.

If these policies or practices change it cannot be without an effect upon the genetic mix of future generations.

It seems sensible to try to estimate what are the genetic side-effects of any social policy. No one is doing that.

There have been changes in social policy over the last hundred years in many of the advanced countries. There have also been great changes in the standard of living, work and work practice, in medical treatment for all and welfare for many in large parts of the world.

Looking at medicine first, the improvement is the most dramatic. Very many killing diseases are now curable. The average age has risen sharply and infantile mortality is now but a fraction of what it was. A very large number of people are being kept alive who would have died in societies where medical and welfare provision was not made. Some of those that have been kept alive have children. We know for sure that some of the diseases and conditions which would have caused earlier death are hereditary. Cystic fibrosis and phenylketonuria are examples. Many other causes of early death, which are now curable, may have at least a partially genetic cause. Since people vary in every possible way genetically it would be risky to deny that they will vary genetically in their susceptibility and power of resistance to these now curable diseases. And compared with the past, many are being kept alive to have children who would not have done before the advantageous changes in medical practice.

No one likes to be told what follows from that. It follows that it would be unwise to assume that the generations which follow ours will not have a greater proportion of people in them who will need medical treatment to stay healthy. It would be wise to prepare for a future in which, increasingly, it takes a greater medical and welfare effort to get the same amount of health and social provision. This is an example of the Universal Law of Damned Cussedness. By this we know that whatever you try to do, Nature tries to stop.

Let us look at this in a longer perspective. Our species and its forerunners, the hominids, have lived for nearly all the time they have been on Earth as mutually repelling hunter-gatherer groups. This way of living came to an end generally only 6000–7000 years ago and it still continues in a few spots around the world.

Relative to the great sweep of evolution, billions of years, we are talking about the last 5 minutes. Almost the entire animal population of the world are juveniles. In every species the great majority of those who are born fail to come to maturity. Ten or twelve young starlings have to be reared to produce one breeding pair, many fish produce millions of fry to do the same. Over nearly all of his career, man, who is one of the most efficient in this respect, had had to produce eight to ten children per pair to produce one breeding pair. Another way of putting this is to say that infant mortality used to be 70–80%. Obviously, from an evolutionary point of view, a severe selection was taking place at each generation.

We are in a world, whether we like it or not, of tough competition. If Christian or Socialist principles forbid some societies to do anything about the side-effect problems which come with the enormous advantages of a compassionate, caring welfare state, there will be other nations and groups with different ideas and, if there is any genetic influence, those nations and groups may supersede those that are more 'caring' but more *careless* of consequences.

Now there are those who would favour a return to the days before modern medicine existed (certain religious sects) but they are a small minority and I disagree with them. However, I remind you of what Haldane said: 'Genetic changes are cumulative.' Not much harm can have been done in the few generations since these changes but in this respect, at any rate, we seem to be on a long-term loser.

Social policy, as I have pointed out before, is going on all the time, bureaucrats, officials, doctors, politicians have to make decisions every day. They cannot await the results of long-term scientific experiments. They are forced to work, I repeat, with inadequate information. They are forced to work on the balance of probabilities.

What policies would arise from the considerations given above, if they were taken fully into account? I shall not attempt to answer the question, it is a very difficult one. There is one thing that is quite certain, however. We do not want to go back to a high infantile mortality rate. We do not want to cease to save every life we can in our hospitals and clinics. Is there not something that can be done, before it is too late, before a long-term trend sets in, to deal with the 'genetic side-effect' problem without too seriously disrupting our present habits, practices and norms?

14

The Future of Human Quality Control

Quality control is a vital part of any activity which obtains, makes or provides goods, information or services for people. It is simply the process of ensuring that what is made or done or provided is adequately suited to the purpose it is intended to serve. Without quality control no human group could thrive or even survive.

I am satisfied that enough writers are busy asserting peoples' rights in their role as consumers. My concern here is that some of the people have to have another role, that of contributor, or producer. That role involves responsibilities and duties. Perhaps these need more attention. The viability and success of all societies depends on them and the way they are met and carried out.

I define *human* quality control as the similar process of ensuring that the training and ability of people in their roles as contributors are suited to the position, role or purpose they serve in our societies. In other words, I am concerned with the efficiency of the process of allocating roles of responsibility and contribution. The phrase 'human quality control' seems strange, at first sight. I have deliberately used a term that is unusual in this context because it dramatizes something essential that we all do as naturally as we breathe and almost as unconsciously. I am talking about the business of judging, choosing (or discriminating between) our associates as to what they can do and whether they can be relied on to do it and do it well.

In this age, that of the 'ordinary man', this essential judgemental task is often performed covertly. We do it quietly and privately, whispering behind our hands and giving each other knowing looks. We do not admit that we are doing it because openly judging the character and abilities of our associates has become unfashionable in today's political climate. It is frowned on because we have a political paradigm that people are really equal (not only in their rights but in fact). Therefore all comparisons are odious, invidious and unfair.

Some trade unions, for instance, take the position that the ability and skill of every one of their members is exactly the same. They insist that all those in the same broad occupational class should be rewarded equally and that all should have equal opportunity to be selected for various jobs. The implicit assumption is that there are no qualitative differences in performance and so no need for human quality judgements at all. That is a test for another human quality. Credulity.

But all this has begun to change as I shall show.

THE SUCCESS OF THE WEST

My general case is that the success and prosperity of the Western world and the rest of the world which followed its lead is dependent on a very special skill which has been developed in them. This special skill is the art and nascent science of human quality control.

Industrialism brought many social changes and with them many traumas and troubles but it also brought great and fairly general prosperity. Not the least important principle of the industrial society, as I have said, is that of 'the best person for the job'. The skill of role allocation is the most vital in modern societies. It is for lack of it that industrialization often fails.

There are signs that this vital principle is in danger of being forgotten today in the pioneer industrial countries such as Britain. Insidiously, ancient, less successful principles of selection and role allocation are returning. This is to the general detriment.

In less developed countries, ancient tribal and familial traditions of role allocation, which were sound and good for pre-industrial life, have been continued when the life style has changed. An essential pre-condition of the commercial-industrial life style has not been installed. Jobs, roles and status are awarded in traditional, nepotic, familial ways instead of on the basis of practised judgements about ability and potential. Under these circumstances the industrial and commercial life style appears not to work very well. This is especially the case where undemocratic centralist bureaucratic regimes are in power.

In order to guess the future we are forced to look at the only information we have, that from the past.

In medieval communities which were largely rural, everyone knew everyone else from birth. They observed and gossiped about each other and had intimate knowledge, each of the other's character, skills and abilities. The leaders of such communities knew everyone too. Selection and role allocation were established by a combination of the local aristocrat's will, traditional practice and community judgement. It worked well enough and there were few disputes about it.

In the towns matters were different; there the specialist trades developed and the family work group broke down. It was replaced by the craft work group and the system of selecting and training apprentices from among strangers instead of fellow villagers and relatives. Apprentices could be dismissed or fail to qualify as a tradesman. Relatives and feudal serfs who were unsuitable for their role could not be so disposed of.

Thus the possibility of assembling work teams of strangers arose. The population from which these could be selected, sorted and refined was therefore very much larger than the tiny inward-facing rural communities of the time could provide. There was more choice and so a much better range of skills and abilities could be brought together than ever could have been done under the traditional rural system. Much more skilful and suitable work groups were now possible. Products accordingly could be more complex, and much better suited to a wider range of purposes.

The next development took a long time to start. The factory system gradually evolved. This was, in effect, a welding together of several city craft teams, into super teams where many craftworkers could combine their skills to make such products as required many rare specialist skills. Joiners, wheel makers, smiths, painters, all different guildsmen could now co-operate in a new kind of trade under one roof, that of say, a coach maker. This would be impossible in the small familiar traditional communities of the time simply because the groups that knew each other well were not large enough a base. All the required skills and abilities were unlikely to be found in them.

The vital point is that what had, perforce, to grow up was another skill, the ability-*selection* skill required to assemble and maintain such teams. Gradually the ethics and practice of selecting people on such grounds instead of the traditional ones arose.

Now I come to my main point. While it is very advantageous to choose talent from a large pool and thus find rarer more specialized skills or those capable of learning them, there are disadvantages also. Firstly the candidates in this system are likely to be strangers about whom the chooser knows little or nothing. The complete mutual knowledge of the primitive community is lost. So other methods of judging peoples' abilities than the traditional ones have to be developed. Secondly, the variety and difficulty of the skills and abilities required both become greater as the sophistication of products grows. The skill-selecting skill required is yet again more difficult.

Now I come to the present, in advanced industrial societies. The process has continued and the number, the variety of the jobs as well as the degree of ability and the amount of training required have continued to escalate. The burden upon the selectors who have to assemble these talent teams has increased exponentially because of the multiplicative effect of these two factors.

The amount and the variety of goods and services available to the average person in the advanced societies have been expanding explosively. Consequently, the number of different jobs that have to be filled to meet the increasing demand has expanded equally. Further, the difficulty and complexity of those jobs have increased. This has happened for the obvious reason that the variety and the technical complexity of products and services have greatly expanded.

The trend is further amplified by a less visible factor, the mechanization of routine work. With every decade there are many more demanding tasks and many less undemanding ones. There are signs that the widespread unemployment problem may be to some extent an unemployability problem. If this be so we are in trouble because we are not allowed, in the present political climate, to recognize the fact. This makes it less likely that we shall solve it.

So the unmistakable trend is towards making the personnel selection task (as it is strangely called) more and more difficult. More different skills, more demanding skills, more selection problems: that is the way it goes.

That is one trend we must expect to continue in the future. Those in the human selection trade will be out to find and use any system or method which would make their task easier and their judgements and predictions better. We must expect the demand for and the sophistication and quality of any kind of human ability and measurement method to increase. There will be more psychometry.

But there is a serious problem. In a historical perspective the commercial-industrial system is new and the untraditional role allocation methods it requires are not fully accepted as being fair, reasonable and advantageous. There has been a political reaction which has caused the negative attitude I described earlier. Role allocation and selection have been politicized so that the people doing it are under social and political pressures that reduce their efficiency.

Unwisely, in my view, some of the trade unions have developed the negative attitude towards any selection which I described. They have obstructed and imposed limitations on managers and selection officers which hinder their vital work. Some unions have even taken over the job allocation role themselves and, since many of them do not accept the simple fact of human differences, they do not do it well. This may be one reason why they are becoming less relevant in many countries. They are being by-passed because they work against the true needs of the system. I believe their future would be much surer if they were to do what their forebears, the medieval guilds, did.

These guilds were themselves in the business of the quality assurance of workers. An apprentice had to be passed out as competent by the guild. Employers grew to trust and prefer the guildsman.

Trade unions were formed and were relevant when there were very large numbers of people all doing the same or very similar jobs. They performed a needed function at that period. Today in the Western world many have become politicized and confrontational and so are often inimical to the interests of their members. But some are getting the message of the times and are seeking a new role. There is one waiting for them if they can be flexible enough to change quickly enough.

I predict that the unions of the future, those that survive, will be much more the agents of their members. They will see themselves as developing, quality assuring and marketing the skills of their members, helping instead of hindering with the vital and increasingly difficult task of getting the right-shaped pegs into the proper holes in tomorrow's industry. They may well take on education, training and examination and certification of the product they are trying to sell: human ability and excellence.

Whether or not the trade unions do this, it is safe to predict that the present businesses and associations connected with measuring and assessing human qualities as producers or contributors will flourish and develop. Head hunters, training companies, qualifications awarding companies and associations will flourish. We may expect that many more such institutions will arise and spread.

Together with the above developments, we are likely to see a return to serious research in the field of psychometry. The last few generations of those in this field seem to have concentrated on the criticism of the work of the pioneers. None seem to have turned their minds to the much more demanding task of improving the early work or answering the criticisms and correcting the faults they have been so eager to expose.

As the commercial-industrial complex develops and pulls more and more of the Earth's peoples into its network these problems become more difficult. In the developed world there are now so many goods and services available to so many people that the mere business of getting the right goods to the right people, the informational system needed to do this, occupies half the work force. Nearly 50% of us are now dealing only with information and not with the making or getting or moving of food or other products.

We may now expect that a similar revolution may occur in the field of role allocation.

Further we may say that, just as we have gradually discovered that fulfilling the needs via the bureaucratic machinery of a centralist state may not be the best way, the business of role allocation is one with which the state should not be concerned.

What goes wrong, in a democracy with state provision, is that the job becomes a political battle ground with all the political parties, especially those in opposition, being unable to resist the temptation to appeal to the envy of those who see themselves as the unchosen. They promise them a 'fairer' system which inevitably turns out to be a less efficient and more wasteful one. The political parties are drawn into an equalizing competition which results in an industrial decline.

As an example of this I turn again to the attitude of much of the educational establishment in a country like Britain where most education is funded by the state. The anti-excellence paradigm has been in force for half a century. The tendency has been to devalue qualifications by making sure that every student gets them almost regardless of performance.

In the past the schools and universities saw their function as that of passing on the heritage of knowledge, skills, know-how, technology, art and science. Their further function was seen to be that of certification, quality assurance, giving a trusted qualification or sign of approval to adequately graduating students. This was a great help to those who have to integrate them into society's role structure.

But when your masters are politicians you are inclined to skimp that vital job and try to make sure that there are no complaints from students to the politicians. If you were responsible to the institutions which are the *consumer* of your product, graduate students, if you as an educationalist had to answer to the firms and other institutions which take your students, you might be competing to get a better reputation for the quality of your educational work and the reliability of the quality assurance judgements and measurements you made.

It seems safe to predict that there will be improvements in this area too. Either there will be a new type of qualification-awarding body which will try to raise and keep up standards or the present educational establishment will return to its former role and do the job much better than it has done recently. The big unsolved problem here is that, almost necessarily, the education of each generation fits them for the society of the previous generation. No one can guess in advance what the next development in a rapidly changing society will be and so the match of the supply of skills and abilities with the demand is often likely to be bad.

We must expect the development of institutions for re-education, re-training and re-qualifying people in the future. The role of psychometric science in this is likely to be an expanding one.

We can be very sure of one thing. The countries and the institutions within them that ignore this problem will not do as well as those that take the trouble to tackle it. Societies and the network of role structures within them are unlikely to stop growing. These kinds of integration problems grow, according to Zipf, with the cube of the size. Let us prepare for an age when we shall be able to use more science for the most vital job of all, fitting us all, comfortably, suitably, and rewardingly into that great network. Once abject poverty is abolished the next important source of human misery is, in my estimation, the mis-allocation of human resources. Scientific method has helped us in many other fields. Let us see what science can do, if we brush aside the dogmas of the ideologues and seek its help in the vital field of role allocation.

Further Reading

Beck, J. (1970). *How to Raise a Brighter Child.* (Fontana)

Binet, A. (1896). La Psychologie Individuelle. *Aneé Psychol.*

Block, N. and Dworkin, G. (eds.) *The IQ Controversy.* Quartet Books. (Harper and Row)

Bridges, S. (1969). *Gifted Children and the Brentwood Experiment*

Cattell, R. (1957). *Personality and Motivation Structure and Movement.* (Hanah)

Clarke, A. M. and Clarke, A. D. B. *Handbook of Abnormal Psychology*

Erlenmeyer-Kimling, L. and Jarvik, L. F. (1963). Genetics and intelligence: a review. *Science*

Eysenck, H. J. (1952). *The Scientific Study of Personality.* (Routledge, Kegan Paul)

Eysenck, H. J. (1970). *The Structure of Human Personality.* (Methuen)

Eysenck, H. *Know Your Own IQ.* (Penguin)

Fletcher, R. (1987). *Social Policy and Administration.* (Basil Blackwell)

Flew, A. (1987). *Power to Parent: Reversing Educational Decline.* (Sherwood Press)

Galton, F. (1873). Hereditary Genius. *Frayers Magazine,* Jan.

Galton, F. (1893). *Enquiries into Human Faculty and Its Development.* (Macmillan)

Gauss, J. K. F. In Asimov's *Biographical Encyclopedia of Science and Technology* (1964). (Avon Books)

Getzel, J. W. and Jackson, P. W. (1962). *Creativity and Intelligence*

Guildford, J. P. (1967). *The Nature of Human Intelligence.* (McGraw-Hill)

Haldane, J. B. S. (1949). *Quantitive Measurement of Rates of Evolution*

Heim, A. (1970). *Intelligence and Personality.* (Pelican)

Herrman, L. and Hogben, L. (1932). The intellectual resemblance of twins. *Proc. R. Soc. Edin.*

Herrnstein, R. J. (1973). *IQ in the Meritocracy.* (Allen Lane)

Jensen, A. R. (1973). *Educability and Group Differences.* (Methuen)

Jensen, A. R. *Genetics and Education*

Kamin, L. J. (1974). *The Science and Politics of IQ.* (John Wiley & Sons)

Lynn, R. (1977). The Intelligence of the Japanese. *Bull. Br. Psychol.*

Malthus, T. R. (1798). *Essay on Population*

Marland, S. P. (1972). *Education of the Gifted and Talented*

Marsh, R. W. (1964). *A Statistical Re-Analysis of Getzel's and Jackson's Data*

Marx, K. *Criticism of the Gotha Program*

Oden, M. H. (1968). The fulfilment of promise: 40 year follow up of the Terman Gifted group. *Genet. Psychol. Monogr.*

Pirie and Butler (1983). *Test Your IQ.* (Pan Books)

Pope, A. *Essays on Man*

Popper, K. (1959). *The Logic of Scientific Discovery.* (Hutchinson)

Powell, P. M. Elementary education personal adjustment and personal achievement of a national sample of gifted adults. Presented at *World Congress for Gifted and Talented Children*

Rosenthal, R. and Jacobsen, L. (1968). *Pygmalion in the Classroom.* (New York: Rinebart and Winston)

Serebriakoff, V. (1965). *IQ – A Mensa Analysis and History.* (Hutchinson)

Spearman, C. E. (1923). *The Nature of Intelligence and the Principles of Cognition.* (Macmillan)

Sunday Times, October 24th, 1976

Terman, L. M. and Oden, M. N. (1959). *The Gifted Children at Mid Life.* (Stanford University Press)

Thurstone, L. L. Reported in Eysenck, H. J. (1979). *The Structure and Measurement of Intelligence.* (Springer-Verlag)

Vernon, P. E. (1963). *Personality Assessment.* (Open University)

Wilson, G. and Eysenck, H. J. (1976). *Known Your Own Personality.* (Book Club Associates)

Wiseman, S. (1972). *Readings in Human Intelligence.* (University Paperbacks)

Wynne-Edwards, V. C. (1962). *Animal Dispersion in Relation to Social Behaviour.* (Oliver Boyd)

Zipf, G. K. (1949). *Human Behaviour and the Principle of Least Effort.* (New York: Haffner)

Index